Airways of the United States

Nine years after the end of World War I, the

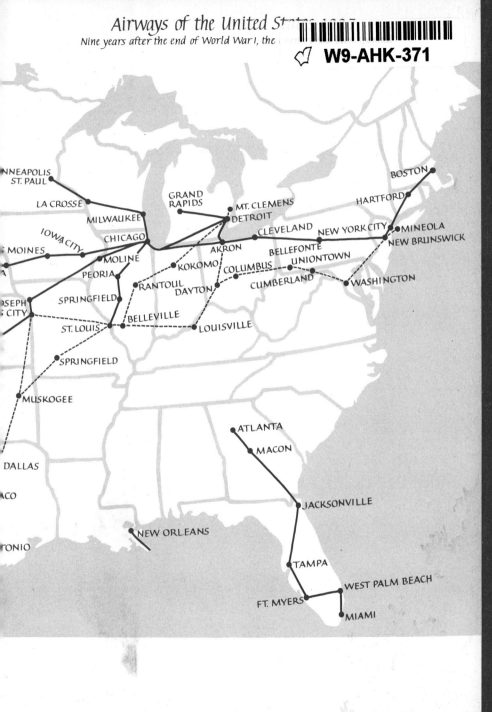

LECKEY, J.W.
MARCH '71

The Sky's the Limit

A History of the U. S. Airlines

The Sky's The Limit

◆ ◆ ◆

by Arch Whitehouse

THE MACMILLAN COMPANY, NEW YORK, NEW YORK

COLLIER-MACMILLAN LIMITED, LONDON

The Macmillan Company
866 Third Avenue, New York, N.Y. 10022
Collier-Macmillan Canada Ltd., Toronto, Ontario

Library of Congress Catalog Card Number: 71-116779

First Printing

Printed in the United States of America

CONTENTS

INTRODUCTION

On January 21, 1970, approximately sixty-six years after the Wright brothers' biplane floundered off the sand dunes at Kitty Hawk, the Boeing 747 superjet airliner made its first scheduled passenger flight from New York to London under the insignia of Pan American World Airways. It was the largest airplane ever constructed for commercial aviation, designed to carry between 350 and 500 passengers, or more than 100 tons of cargo over distances up to 6,000 miles. With the exception of Lockheed's projected C-5A military cargo plane, intended to carry 350 fully equipped soldiers on transoceanic trips, the 747 is the largest passenger-carrying plane ever constructed and flown. In its complete configuration it outweighs Columbus's *Santa Maria* more than three times.

Although tagged with the ugly name of "jumbo," the Boeing 747 is a beautiful aircraft with a luxury cabin that can accommodate an unusual load of passengers in rare comfort and safety. Seating arrangements provide two aisles and a straight wall interior, a distinct change from previous tubular format, and will permit the tallest passenger to stand upright in any window seat. In the original cabin mock-up another innovation was in the forward first-class section. A spiral staircase leads to an upper level that is equipped with special seats and lounge accommodations for the luxury trade. This compartment can also be arranged as a private lounge or a bedroom suite; a convenience it is hoped the affluent will identify with the earlier roominess of the ocean liner.

Apart from its passenger accommodations, the 747 will be seen to be a magnificiently proportioned aircraft. Its overall length is 231 feet, or approximately three-quarters the length of a football field. Its wing span stretches out more than 195 feet, while the tail assembly would block off the view from a five-story window, if such an improbable comparison could be arranged.

Fully loaded, in its standard version, the 747 weighs 710,000 pounds. Compared to this, the Super DC-8, so popular today, is a lightweight, topping only 353,000 pounds while carrying 250 passengers. Using four new Pratt & Whitney engines, each rated at 43,500 pounds of thrust—more than twice the power of the largest U.S. commercial engines on current jetliners, Boeing's superjet will cruise at 625 mph, which is only slightly faster than any previous Boeing airliner, but because of its high-lift wings and distribution of weight on the 18-wheel undercarriage, it will be able to use any present-day jet runway. Boeing claims that the new engines will run much quieter and should produce less air pollution than previous power plants from the same firm, a feature that would make the 747 most welcome at many major air terminals.

Another superjet of the seventies that must be considered in the same bracket as the Boeing is the Lockheed L-1011 TriStar passenger transport which should enter airline service in late 1971. The TriStar listed in the 600-mph classification was originated in a flexible design format and continued as such through its development. As larger versions are required for special routes by the airlines, the L-1011 will be "stretched" for added range and additional accommodations for passengers. It is powered with three Rolls-Royce high-bypass-ratio turbofan engines, each rated at 40,000 pounds of thrust. No details of predicted top or cruising speeds have been announced at this writing. Eastern Air Lines has ordered fifty L-1011s, TWA forty, and Air Holdings, Ltd, of Great Britain fifty, which are intended for resale outside the United States.

But at present it is the Boeing 747 that inspires fantastic figures and comparisons. Before its first test flight was carried out more than twenty domestic and foreign airlines had ordered 160 at an estimated price of $20,000,000 each, setting up an initial backlog of $3,560,000,000. The 747 not only will transport large lists of passengers, but will increase the demands for aircraft services, and accelerate the desire for air travel. This will advance the development of shuttle or feeder lines and intensify the requirements of airbus equipment necessary to transport from 350 to 500 passengers; vehicles that previously accommodated 50–60 passengers, flying to or from our major air terminals. Will the helicopter or the STOL (Slow Take-off and Landing) type of craft be introduced to take over added short-haul problems?

The use of such a massive aircraft, employing tremendous power, demands in turn new and lighter metals and other materials to keep the overall weight down. New and varied mass-manufacturing problems will be encountered, and the manning of such advanced airplanes will require the training of hundreds of new industrial and in-flight specialists.

The next question that arises is how our domestic, and the international, airports will accommodate these giant machines and their overwhelming loads of passengers and commercial cargo. Where foreign travel is concerned there will be the necessity for the revision of customs and immigration procedures; to say nothing of handling the baggage which already is a major problem in commercial aviation. However, in the 747 a new version of the shipping container will be introduced for quick mechanical loading and unloading of baggage. Special compartments, contoured to the configuration of the forward fuselage and made of balsa wood covered with an aluminum "skin," were originally developed by the Goodyear Aerospace Corporation for Air Force cargo handling, but have been adopted for the 747. Some time ago Goodyear announced it had contracted to deliver 708 of these compartments for the Pan Am jets. Each container stands about 5 feet high, is 7½ feet long, and contains shelving to hold well over fifty suitcases. Empty, they weigh only 250 pounds, but fully loaded will hold more than 2,500 pounds of passenger baggage.

Aircraft form the vital sinews of commercial aviation, but they would be unable to fly without the facilities of the modern airport. How long will the "modern" airport be able to accommodate these giants, landing but minutes apart and delivering 5,000–10,000 passengers a day? How long will the present runways, taxiways, and gateways be able to accept these superjets of tomorrow? It takes years to plan, purchase the land, and build a modern airport, but every year a new and more complex airplane is put into service to create more problems for the staffs of the landing fields. No one wants a busy airport in his particular vicinity, but everyone who uses air transportation wishes the terminals were more convenient to his home or the center of key cities. State politicians yearn for the income derived from a busy airport, but because they also thrive on the issues of the ballot box they must defer to every complaint about jetliner noise as voiced by their constituents.

It has not been the intent of the writer to present every technical detail of the airplanes, the horsepower or range of every engine, the day-by-day history of every airline, or to analyze wide columns of figures in order to relate the story of America's transportation system. More important are the personalities who made it possible, their heroic pathfinder flights, the heart-breaking toil, the far-reaching imagination, and some of the amazing corporate moves that were necessary to finance these billion-dollar organizations.

Space will not allow the detailed history of every airline or its success over its assigned routes, but I have selected several representative lines, each of wide interest for its particular accomplishments and contributions to the industry. I have also limited the story to American carriers, although several foreign-flag airlines have made notable contributions to the history of international commerce. Again, space does not allow for the international story. Instead, I have tried to prepare a balanced account of our country's commercial aviation industry, one that will interest the lay reader with its profiles, courageous airmen, historic flights, and the chapters of corporate adventure that mark this most modern of industries.

ARCH WHITEHOUSE
Montvale, N. J.
February, 1971

1

Why Should Man Want to Fly?

Commercial aviation the world over has flown a stormy course from its inception. It was early agreed that if man were meant to fly his creator would have provided him with wings, and stodgy scientists, looking at a Gustave Doré angel, pointed out that if the human frame was to include space for muscles to flap a pair of wings large enough to lift even a heavenly figure off the ground, the lady would have been supplied with a sternum that would protrude more than two feet. Any suggestion of aerial voyaging immediately aroused the imaginations of comedians, cartoonists, humorists, and most writers of satire. Long before the Wrights opened their bicycle shop, John Townsend Trowbridge, who had written a series of boys' adventure stories with small reward, gained world renown by penning, in 1880, *Darius Green and His Flying Machine*, a classic in which "D. Green, whose body was long and lean—just right for flying, as will be seen," convulsed the whole country. The idea that man would one day fly, or dare to attempt to fly "like the birds," was always good for a quip, a cartoon, or another shaft of derision. A popular limerick of the time ran:

> There was a young man of Park Lane
> Who constructed a new aeroplane.
> It flew, so we heard,
> Like a beautiful bird.
> His tombstone was pretty, but plain.

In 1885 an imaginative German artist produced a print showing a government official absconding with a bag of money. He is astride a flapping-wing flying machine, powdered by what appears to be a rocket engine, and is being intercepted by a police official wearing a spiked helmet, who is also mounted on a rocket-powered machine with flapping wings. The print is still to be seen in the Prussian State Library.

Great Britain's incorrigible cartoonist Heath Robinson spent most of his professional life depicting aerial cricket matches, traffic policemen who teetered on top of inflated balloons at busy skyway crossings, and petty pilferers who, with a pitchfork fastened to the fronts of their comic flying machines, swooped down on suburban backyards and made off with clotheslines of family laundry. One gentleman in deep thought went aloft in his monoplane and turned over on his back to scratch his head on the steeple of the village church. This aerial antic kept Britain in stitches for months.

It was much the same in the United States, once the Wright brothers proved man could fly if he were willing to risk his neck. In 1909 A. B. Walker, a noted American caricaturist, amused the country with his drawings of portly policemen with wings strapped to their shoulders, directing other fliers around "that cloud to your left," while in the shelter of another cloud an aerial thug, dangling from a small dirigible, is holding up a silk-hatted gentleman with the order, "Wings up!" A dashing young swain who is wearing wings intercepts a pretty girl in flight and steals a kiss, while a short distance below an aerial Nimrod, huddling in a balloon basket, suitably camouflaged with a chunk of stage-scenery cloud, is blazing away at a covey of wild ducks.

But it was the famous American artist Harry Grant Dart who presaged what was actually to happen in the new age of the air. In 1909 Dart turned out an imaginative drawing of rare skill and workmanship in which he portrayed a Transcontinental Flyer, a massive machine with a modern-day cabin, supported by what might be considered a set of swept-back delta wings. The pilot has become lost in a storm and the flying machine is shown stranded on a high peak in the Rocky Mountains. Rescue teams are making their way up the side of a precipice, using ropes and alpen-stocks, while some of the passengers have disembarked and are standing in the snow calmly awaiting rescue or show-ing aloof interest in the general operations. In this instance, Dart's cabin could be equipped with modern wings, four jet engines, and an undercarriage, and its arrival at any air-port would arouse only passing interest. No one would ques-tion its design, but some might inquire which airline was using it.

Amazingly, America—which had given birth to the Wright brothers, who in turn gave the world the first, suc-cessful heavier-than-air machine—not only ignored the Wrights' contribution to science, but for several years, in the face of reliable photographic evidence, refused to be-lieve the brothers had ever been off the ground. The idea that any such comic contraption as the general public had planted in its mind would be of practical use as a means of transportation was completely out of the question. The United States was a vast continent, and distances between coasts or major cities were reckoned in the thousands of miles. An "aeroplane," as it was patented by the Wrights, was nothing more than a novelty to be exhibited at country fairs. After all, the illustrious Professor Samuel Langley, a recognized authority who had been given $50,000 by Presi-dent McKinley to solve the law of aerodynamics, had failed to produce a machine that would fly. The evidence had been seen in every newspaper. Langley's "Aerodrome" had twice floundered off its catapult and dived to the bottom of the Potomac. The Wrights were only a couple of crackpot bicycle mechanics.

It took six years and a series of triumphant exhibitions in Europe, where frantic financiers bid small fortunes for the manufacturing rights to the Wright biplane, before an aroused America accepted the Dayton men. Then the reception machinery went into high gear. At a public ceremony held in the local ball park, Governor Judson Harmon of Ohio pinned the Gold Medal of the State of Ohio on the two brothers. The mayor of Dayton bestowed a special medal from the town, and the Medal of the United States Congress—awarded by special resolution—was presented by two unnamed military officers who represented the government of the United States. This multiple ceremony took place in May 1909, nearly six years after the Wrights had first flown on December 17, 1903. Is it any wonder that the United States was years in appreciating the commercial value of the heavier-than-air machine?

In Europe the situation was in direct contrast. There, sportsmen, scientists, manufacturers, and government officials revealed immediate and vital interest in the heavier-than-air machine, despite the lighter-than-air success of Count Ferdinand von Zeppelin of Germany. This jovial military man, who had watched the employment of kite or captive balloons in the American Civil War, had, in his retirement, devoted his mind and his small fortune to the development of the dirigible balloon. By the summer of 1900 he had made a successful controlled flight over Lake Constance, establishing a new era of navigation by airship.

Count von Zeppelin continued his experiments and by 1909, when other men had flown successfully by means of cambered wings and a propeller, he was making sensational flights between Lake Constance and Berlin. He had already formed the Zeppelin Airship Company and plans were being drawn for a network of dirigible routes over most of Europe.

The hydrogen-filled airship did not attract much interest in the United States. It was considered a cigar-shaped version of the country-fair balloon. Captain Tom Baldwin, a noted parachutist, had built in 1904 the *California Arrow*, America's first practical airship, a small example powered by a lightweight engine designed by Glenn Curtiss, who had been turning out motorcycle engines in a small factory at Hammondsport, New York. Aboard the *California Arrow*, Lincoln Beachy made a number of daring exhibitions, and Baldwin's ship was the only successful lighter-than-air craft displayed at the 1904 St. Louis Exposition. This craft, and another so-called dirigible built by Dr. August Greth of San Francisco, were the first American airships to fly with any degree of success, but they were not true dirigibles with rigid frames to support the gas cells; they were simply built to the dirigible form and held their shape under pressure of the lifting gas. The term dirigible was widely misused in those days, and any balloon that departed from the standard circular contour of the free-floating bag was called a dirigible. For instance, in 1877 a Professor Richell of Hartford, Connecticut, produced a foot-powered "dirigible" which he claimed to have flown to a height of 200 feet on June 12, 1878. In this instance the bag was simply a tubular affair with blunt ends, and when inflated carried a harness from which hung a light framework. Professor Richell had devised a pedal-to-propeller arrangement with which he powered his craft and sailed over Hartford, and then, after more than an hour, returned safely to his starting point.

The dirigible and various forms of the free balloon held the bulk of the world's attention until the outbreak of World War I. Von Zeppelin's dirigibles were real money-makers; his company was operating routes all over Germany and it was evident that the long-proclaimed Berlin-to-Baghdad connection was about to be completed—by air. Until 1914 the heavier-than-air machine was a mechanical novelty, a sportsman's toy, the feature attraction of country fairs everywhere. Its advent and progress had been long drawn out, and in the mind of the general public the aeroplane— or airplane as it has been Americanized—was nothing more than the expensive toy of a certain group of sports- men or shaggy fairground performers. Certainly it prom- ised little as an invention for financial investment; indeed far less than the noisy, smoky motorcar which had come to the fore at about the same time.

Let's face it. What was the heavier-than-air machine good for? True, the early models were fairly cheap to build and not too expensive to fly, but once the initial flush of aviating had worn off, once the pilot had flown in some aerial competition or put on a number of country-fair ex- hibitions, what was there to justify the continued hazard? One might carry a passenger or give a public official a thrilling ride, but beyond that what financial reward was promised to the early aeroplane aeronaut? If he were lucky, he might win a few money prizes, but, except in unusual situations, the rewards were slim and only a few well- heeled airmen could afford to buy a reliable aircraft and purchase the fuel necessary to participate in these profes- sional exhibitions. In most instances the planes had to be shipped from exhibition to exhibition, and reasonably skilled mechanics paid to service, repair, and accompany them from field to field.

There was little or no money in the manufacture of heavier-than-air machines. A sportsman might buy one, or an exhibition flier might order one—and hope to pay for it by his winnings in city-to-city races. There was no demand for fleets of airplanes, for there was no field of operations where great numbers might be used. There always was talk of "sports flying" for the young gentleman who had a wealthy father. Flying clubs were only in the minds of imaginative salesmen who hoped to sell airplanes in job lots and promoters who planned to get rid of stretches of waste land to be used for what were called flying fields. For some reason the word "aerodrome" was anathema to the American mind, although years later it accepted such trade names as "lubritorium" and "lumberama" without question. But no matter in what light the airplane was viewed, until the outbreak of the Great War it appeared to have an obscure future. In Europe there were a few companies engaged in the production of planes, but what were turned out, in many instances, became a glut on the market. The exhibition fliers could use only one or two at a time, and if they were damaged in accidents it was easy to make repairs with kiln-dried stock from any nearby lumberyard. Engines were little more than refined versions of any standard motorcar plant, and spare parts usually were available in any nearby town. The undercarriages used bicycle or motorcycle wheels and tires, and the spring suspension was provided by exerciser elastic cord to be found in any sporting goods shop. In a few instances damaged wings had to be replaced by spares from the company factory, but in emergencies even major repairs could be carried out by local cabinetmakers. Their wives were quite capable of cutting out and fitting linen wing-covering which, when doped in the proper manner, became sleek, taut, and suitable for immediate replacements.

Only broken propellers gave real trouble, for these laminated devices were costly and well beyond the spoke-shave skill of most carpenter-shop artisans. They had to be almost perfectly balanced, whether two-bladed or four-bladed airscrews, and had to be produced by skilled workmen using the best grade materials in shops where suitable machinery and tools were available. Before the gunstock lathe could be modified for propeller production it took six weeks to carve the blades of a propeller and allow the glue of the laminations to set perfectly.

Until 1908 heavier-than-air craft production was in the

hands of the Wright brothers, Glenn Curtiss, and a small circle of European manufacturers who had the spirit and finances to take up the development of this upstart science. At that time, too, there were but forty licensed aviators in the whole world, men who were to provide the will and energy for an aviation industry.

After a number of successful demonstrations abroad, the Wrights sold the manufacturing rights to several European combines, and came to certain contractual arrangements with their own government; in fact, for a few years they seemed to hold the full potential of the airplane in their hands. How their business hopes reached fruition and then dissolved to little more than an industrial memory makes interesting reading.

Once the Wright biplane had been accepted as the basic model of a practical flying machine a few commercial firms saw certain possibilities in the Wright patents, and a handful of American financiers considered proposals to form a manufacturing company, but none of the original plans reached a satisfactory conclusion. Later, the first American company organized to manufacture the Dayton biplane was formed by Clinton R. Peterkin, a young man only twenty-four years old. From the age of fifteen, Clinton Peterkin had worked in the office of J. P. Morgan & Company, productive years in which he made the most of his opportunities. He saw how new business enterprises were conceived and put into operation. On hearing that Wilbur Wright would be spending a few days in New York City, young Peterkin called on him at his hotel and laid out his ideas. Wilbur was kind and understanding but explained that he would prefer to deal with a company in which men of financial stature and business consequence were guiding its destinies. When Peterkin explained that he "had worked for Mr. J. P. Morgan," Wilbur smiled and told him to go ahead and see what progress could be made.

Intrigued by this Horatio Alger story, Mr. Morgan showed

immediate interest and assured Peterkin he would make a small investment and added he would induce his friend Judge Elbert H. Gary, head of the United States Steel Corporation, to consider such a project. Next, De Lancy Nichol, a distant relative of Peterkin and senior partner in a law firm, on learning what the young man was promoting, offered his assistance. In a short time an impressive list of influential men had enrolled in the proposed company. Among them were Cornelius Vanderbilt, August Belmont, Howard Gould, Theodore P. Shonts, Allan A. Ryan, Morton F. Plant, and Andrew Freedman. Realizing the efforts of young Peterkin were coming to a business head, the Wrights announced that they wished to include their friends Robert J. Collier, a publisher of *Collier's Weekly*, and Frederick M. Alger of Detroit.

By this time most of the subscribers, drawn into the venture by the magnetism of the Morgan-Gary interest, began to sense that these two powerful financiers would soon dominate the company. Both men were advised offhandedly that the Wright venture stock had been oversubscribed. Mr. Morgan suspicioned the behind-the-scenes strategy, promptly withdrew his offer, and influenced Judge Gary to follow suit.

Less than a month after Peterkin had first talked with Wilbur, the Wright Company was incorporated on November 22, 1909, with a capital stock of $200,000. The Wright brothers received stock and cash for all rights to their patents in the United States and a royalty of 10 percent on all planes sold. The Wright Company thenceforward would bear the expenses of prosecuting all suits against patent infringements.

The company first opened an administration office at 527 Fifth Avenue, New York City, but its factory was to be built in Dayton and ground was broken in January 1910. The modern plant was to be ready for operations by November where hurriedly recruited workmen would soon be producing two Wright biplanes a month. In the meantime the company rented floor space in another building.

As soon as machines and pilots were available, plans were made to attract financial returns from public exhibitions. Roy Knabenshue, a Toledo aeronaut who had been making balloon flights since his early teens, was called in to handle this outside project. Knabenshue was most adept in promotional work and soon had a number of Wright pilots performing all over the country.

By 1910 the Wrights had finally accepted the wheeled undercarriage and discarded the catapult take-off device, used since their Kitty Hawk days. Whether they themselves adopted the bicycle-wheel gear, or whether it was the influence of European manufacturers of their machines, who had used wheeled landing gears to compete with the Farmans and Blériots, has never been made clear. But by 1910 the Wrights were meeting this competition.

When the United States Army began buying early forms of the Wright biplane the designers were forced to make a dramatic change in the control system. In their 1910 models a new control was added in which the horizontal rudder (elevator) was interlocked with the mechanism that operated the wing-warping feature. In other words, rudder and aileron effect were linked for a combined action. By that time, too, the Wrights had worked out a design which eliminated the forward assembly that had carried the elevators, a change which greatly improved the overall appearance of the machine. This Model B was dubbed the "headless" Wright, and during a display at the Asbury Park, New Jersey, flying meet, it was noted that the control for horizontal flight was now mounted on the tail assembly behind the directional rudder. All this improved the general design of the biplane, but it was not until 1915 that the Wrights finally accepted the idea of an enclosed fuselage. Because of their hidebound determination to stick to the pusher-biplane type of aircraft, the Wright Company was never able to compete in the military field. True, a few Model B planes were purchased for the Army training schools, but were soon condemned as a result of several training-field fatalities.

This decision left the Army with only five airplanes that were even remotely suited for instruction. They were Thomas-Morse tractors, reminiscent of the early Curtiss trainers of that era. At this point Glenn Curtiss, who had sensed the military trend, hired a Britisher, B. Douglas Thomas, an engineer employed by the Sopwith Company, to design a tractor biplane that might conceivably take its place alongside the standardized trainers being used by the Royal Flying Corps. As was to be expected, Thomas produced a conventional biplane that bore several features of the Avro 504K in that it had a standard undercarriage with ski-type skids to prevent nose-over landings, but instead of a mount to carry a rotary-type engine, Curtiss demanded a design that would take his own 90-hp OX-5, a water-cooled V-type power plant.

In addition, Thomas's design underwent immediate "improvement" in the Buffalo plant of the Curtiss Company, and in its modified version turned out to be a combination of the earlier models listed as the Curtiss J and Curtiss N machines. The new trainer was listed as a JN, and the slurring of the two separate letters into a feminine name was inevitable. Thus the term Jenny. The fourth version of this aircraft—JN-4—was introduced as an early trainer. A few were sent to the Mexican border as observation planes, and in that manner became the Jennys used in World War I training schools. JN-4 was to undergo a double career, one as a military trainer, and then as a postwar barnstorming plane. It was this ugly duckling of wartime aviation that was to inspire the first fluttering of U.S. commercial aviation. The Curtiss Jenny, in spite of many shortcomings, was the aircraft that made possible the first air mail and pioneered the first transcontinental routes that were to spread into today's network of jet transportation.

World War I, which advanced the science of aviation and provided a new three-dimensional battleground, contributed greatly to today's worldwide network of commercial aviation. Prior to August 1914 the aeroplane was little more than the playboy's speedster employed in the search for the latest thrill, or a mount aboard which one could compete in flying competitions and in that manner gain personal renown or headlined publicity. Few considered the flying machine a possible medium of commercial transportation, and no wonder. After all, the contraption was nothing more than a body in which a man could sit, supported by a set of fabric-covered wings which, when thrust against fluid air by means of a propeller driven by a gasoline engine, would lift a certain amount of weight off the ground and then thrust it over varying distances at "mile-a-minute" speeds. It could stay aloft as long as there was fuel in the tank, and it could carry one or two passengers—if the wing surface was sufficient and the engine could provide the necessary push or pull.

But that was all. One could increase the speed by adding to the power, or by reducing the size or number of the wings. It could fly only in the most favorable weather and earn its keep only as long as groundlings would pay at the turnstile to witness the thrilling phenomenon. Only a relatively few people wished to fly, and those who were willing to take the chance had first to appear at some nearby stretch of level turf from which the machine could take off and land. Compared to the convenience of the motorcar or motorboat, both of which could stop or go at the will of the operator, the aeroplane was an illogical vehicle.

Fortunately, there were a few visionaries whose imagination took them beyond the limitations of the country-fair race tracks. They honestly believed the machine could be enlarged, modified, and turned into a means of scheduled transportation. Another group saw the aeroplane as a weapon of war, an adjunct to the cavalry to be used chiefly for observation. To prove this, brave photographers risked short flights over suburban areas and with their pocket Kodaks snapped pictures of the landscape over which they were flying. The results were interesting even though in most instances the prints were fuzzy and quite indistinct. The aerial camera with its long-range lens still had to be invented.

The military concept was totally ignored by most high-ranking officers—particularly the cavalrymen—whose arguments were that the machine was too noisy for efficient scouting, unreliable in weather that would provide cover for cavalry scouts, and, even worse, the damn thing gave off odors that offended the dignity of military gentlemen. Naval admirals placed the aeroplane in the same category as the upstart submarine, another odorous invention that assaulted the aesthetic nostrils of surface seamen. Still, there were a few military minds that were to introduce "bomb dropping" competitions at the flying meets, substituting paper bags of flour or oranges tossed out at circular targets chalked on the ground. In August 1910 Lieutenant M. S. Crissy was pictured holding a small "aerial bomb" in his hand while seated in an Army Wright biplane. Other belligerent types had themselves photographed sitting in the passenger seats of open-faced biplanes, aiming light machine guns at imaginary targets while the aeroplane was still sitting on the ground. There is no reliable record that any such weapon was actually taken into the air—and fired—until well after the outbreak of World War I.

While there always will be dozens of claims to have been the "first" to fly the mail, carry a paying passenger, set up a scheduled airline, and link one metropolis with another, few aviation histories have offered the details of what must be the first scheduled airline to be operated in the United States. This enterprise, believe it or not, began passenger-carrying operations on January 1, 1914, flying out of St. Petersburg to Tampa, Florida, using a Benoist XIV flying boat. The pilot on the inaugural run was Anthony Jannus and his lone passenger was A. S. Pheil, mayor of St. Petersburg. The company, for the record, was known as the St. Petersburg–Tampa Airboat Line.

It has been difficult to completely identify the Benoist aircraft, but from fairly reliable sources it was a two-seater biplane, powered with a six-cylinder 75-hp Roberts engine which gave a top speed of 70 mph. A later version of the XIV was modified to take a second passenger.

The trip from St. Petersburg to Tampa was simply a 21-mile flight up Tampa Bay and took about twenty-three minutes. The schedule called for two round trips per day, but special flights were made whenever there was the demand. A one-way ticket cost $5.00, and the passengers were allowed a gross weight of 200 pounds, including baggage. Anything in excess was charged at express rate, or $5.00 per 100 pounds.

The St. Petersburg–Tampa Airboat Line remained in business for about four months, during which time it carried 1,205 passengers and flew a total of 11,000 miles. It was said later that the business was disbanded because of the war in Europe, a point which remains unclear as the United States did not become a belligerent until April 1917. However, until a new claimant pops up, we shall have to award the scheduled passenger-carrying "first" to the St. Petersburg–Tampa Airboat Line.

As far as carrying the mail by air in a flight recognized by the U.S. Post Office Department, we must go back to the year 1859 when, on August 17, a man named John Wise planned to fly from Lafayette, Indiana, to New York City via free balloon. He also advertised he would carry a small cargo of mail, and many people in Lafayette eagerly penned letters to friends in the east and marked them "Aerial Post."

Wise filled his balloon at the local gas works, and the mail was placed aboard the basket beside the aeronaut's lunch. At noon the big bag, which had been christened *Jupiter*, was released, and it floated away with 350 pounds of sand, instruments, and provisions. There was little wind and the balloon moved slowly. After being aloft for more than two hours, Wise concluded he had traveled only sixteen miles, so he decided to make a landing and, as a novel idea, dropped his mailbag overboard with a parachute devised from a bedsheet and some strong twine.

Surprisingly, the mailbag and the balloon landed on a public road within fifty yards of each other, and Wise then discovered that he had flown to a point south of Crawfordsville. One hundred years later—1959—the Post Office Department officially recognized this effort as the first airmail flight in American history and commemorated it with a special airmail stamp.

Balloons also carried the mail (French) out of the besieged city of Paris during the Franco-Prussian War of 1870, an enterprise that also saw the development of the microfilm science. Invented by a Parisian photographer named Dagron and used to reduce the size of the messages, microfilming thus cut down the weight of the mail loads to be carried.

The idea of carrying mail from city to city seems to have been in the minds of men as soon as there was an aircraft that could fly a distance of one hundred miles. Who first conceived this service, or made an attempt to operate an airmail route, has never been clearly established. Many stunt shows in which small packages or bags of mail were flown from one point to another were carried out chiefly as a publicity feature and are not to be taken seriously. For instance, in November 1909 Hans Grade, a German engineer who is credited with building the first successful German airplane, a high-wing monoplane, made a flight of 55 minutes and carried four passengers and one piece of mail between Berlin and Potsdam. It is claimed that this was the first postal item ever dispatched by air.

The first piece of mail carried by air in the United States was flown from Albany to New York City on May 1, 1910, by Glenn Curtiss. The 142½ miles were covered in two hours, 50 minutes of flying time at an average speed of 54 4/5 mph. Curtiss also received the $10,000 prize money offered by the New York *World*. More than a year later in September 1911, Calbraith P. Rogers took off from Sheepshead Bay race track on Long Island in an attempt to win a $50,000 prize for the first coast-to-coast flight across the United States. It took him 84 days, and enough spare parts to build three Wright biplanes, but he was the first man to fly across the continent. He also carried small packets of mail from city to city, although this was not an authorized service.

On September 14, 1911, Earle Ovington carried a 15-pound pouch of mail from Sheepshead Bay, Long Island, to a post office in Jamaica, a few miles away. Postmaster General Frank H. Hitchcock had formally turned over the pouch to Ovington while Edward A. Morgan, Postmaster of New York City, had looked on. Amazingly enough, no one was photographed shaking hands. The flight was promoted by the Nassau Aviation Corporation, and the experiment was carried on for about a week.

America was slowly becoming "air conscious," a phrase that cluttered the news for the next few years, and whenever an exhibition flier appeared in a town of any size he was encouraged to make another "memorable" flight, carrying a small packet of mail. Dozens of such flights were recorded and many noted names appear in the records, such as Lincoln Beachy, Glenn Martin, Chance Vought, Charles Willard, Beckwith Havens, Charles Walsh, Farnum Fish, Harry Atwood, and several others of that period. Some of these flights ranged as far as ninety miles, some as few as six. In one instance Paul Peck claimed to have flown from Coney Island to California, but this was not another transcontinental flight. That Coney Island was a small town in Ohio, as was California. They are only four miles apart.

Amid this country-fair atmosphere it was to be expected that the promotors would soon introduce fliers of the gentler sex, and by 1913 a number of young women pilots were giving exhibitions and "carrying the mail" on any excuse that would draw paying customers to the nearby race tracks. Among them were Ruth Law, Katherine Stinson, and her sister Marjorie, who was "commissioned" to fly mail from San Antonio to Seguin, Texas. Of course this was just another stunt to add to the program. Ruth Law made the headlines by flying the mail in the Philippines. We shall meet Katherine Stinson again later in this record.

As will be appreciated, all these were publicity flights and had little or nothing to do with speeding up the mails. Few pilots who took part in these displays had any idea that within a few years, smack in the middle of a world war, the United States Post Office would establish an official airmail service, operating Curtiss Jenny JN4H (Hisso powered) planes between New York City and Washington. The first official mail-carrying flights were to take off on May 15, 1918, with President Wilson lending his prestige to the opening ceremonies. How this experimental innovation was contrived while American troops were fighting at Cantigny and the news that our leading ace, Major Raoul Lufbery, had been shot down and killed, is something of a mystery. Still, it offers an interesting story.

Initial credit for this brave experiment goes to Otto Praeger, then Assistant Postmaster General, a tough-minded, hard-working man. He had absorbed the best traditions of the Post Office Department which in earlier days had pioneered post roads, river-steamer routes, the overland stage, pony express, the railroad, and even motor transports for the carrying of mail. Praeger was among the first to see the possibilities of an airmail service, and as early as June 1910 Representative Morris Sheppard of Texas introduced a bill in Congress, the text of which read as follows:

Be it enacted . . . that the Postmaster General is hereby authorized and directed to investigate the possibility and cost of an
aeroplane or airship mail route between the City of Washington
and some other suitable point or points to experiment, and
report the result of said investigation to Congress at the opening
of the short session in December next, in order that it may be
definitely determined whether aerial navigation may be used
for the safe and rapid transmission of the mails.

This resulted in a number of stunt exhibitions, thirty-
one, in fact, that were staged by individual pilots, aviation
groups, and small-time businessmen who had a vague idea
there might be money in some form of commercial aviation. These exhibitions, however, were carried out with no
expense to the Post Office Department. Few knew that
Congress had appropriated $100,000 to pay for the experi-
ments suggested by Representative Sheppard. Unless this
money was put into circulation by July 1, 1918, the whole
suggestion would be withdrawn.

Captain Benjamin B. Lipsner, a nonflying member of the
U.S. Aviation Service, who in civilian life had been a skilled
mechanical engineer and an expert in big machinery lubrication problems, had just completed the development of an
aviation lubricant to replace the very expensive Castrol
being widely used overseas by front-line aircraft. His Liberty Aero Oil filled the bill at the time, and while awaiting
a new assignment he wondered what had become of the
half-remembered idea of establishing a Post Office airmail
service. Early in 1918 Captain Lipsner made an inquiry
through the office of George L. Conner, Chief Clerk of the
Second Assistant Postmaster General, as to whom he
should see about the idea of carrying the mail by aeroplane.

Conner was a very busy, but patient man, and after
questioning Lipsner concerning his background and other
qualifications, asked him to draw up a general plan including the actual cost of operation. Lipsner had tackled many
problems as an automobile test driver and as a mechanic

servicing aircraft of the period. He had provided maintenance for the Texas Oil Company's fleet of trucks and similar service for the Albert Pick Company. He assured Conner that he was capable of producing a full set of reliable figures.

The Chief Clerk left his desk and had a talk with Otto Praeger who had Captain Lipsner brought into his office. Within half an hour Lipsner had convinced both Post Office men that an airmail ulility was possible, and pointed out that if such a service had been started five years earlier, American aviation would by now have developed its own planes instead of having to rely on craft being supplied by the French and British. "We would have learned a lot about commercial flying and we would have a considerable reserve of pilots trained in long-distance flying," he declared.

Both Praeger and Conner agreed the summation was sound, and thus encouraged, Lipsner continued. "Today's Signal Corps is using planes and mechanics, and they are beginning to turn out hundreds of pilots, but they are being trained only for military flying. We could take a small number, train them over the cross-country routes and turn them into mail pilots. Today, the Army is using truck drivers who learned to drive for commercial firms before the war. A form of commercial aviation can have the same value for the future. An airmail service can produce a whole new era of transportation. If we can get a few Signal Corps planes and some of their pilots, we can fly the mail and improve the training of the pilots at the same time. In other words, if we begin now and move by easy stages until we have learned the operational procedures—and the costs—we can soon have an air-mail service running most efficiently."

Praeger was fascinated with the idea that Lipsner could install an airmail system and show the costs of operation and maintenance of the flying equipment. "How long do you think such a venture would have to be underwritten?"

Lipsner frankly admitted he didn't know. "Perhaps five

years," he said thoughtfully. He was somewhat shy of the mark. Private contractors did not begin to fly the mail until 1926.

Praeger pondered on the situation and then said, "This has been very interesting. Where can I reach you if we decide to go into this further?"

Lipsner explained that he had just finished an Army lubrication project and was awaiting a new assignment. Praeger nodded, and said, "Good!" With that the Army captain was escorted to the door. He hadn't expected much and probably felt he was getting what later became known as the "don't call us, we'll call you" brush-off. However, the next day William A. Parish of Texas Oil, who had originally picked Lipsner for the Army lubrication team, called to say that the Post Office wanted to borrow his services for a few days—something about organizing an airmail service.

"What about my Army responsibilities?"

"Forget them for the time being. Postmaster General [Albert S.] Burleson has obtained a temporary release from Newton Baker. You'd better trot over to the Post Office building and check in with Otto Praeger."

In that manner the U.S. Air Mail Service was established, at least as far as selecting a man to head the organization was concerned. From that point on all Lipsner had to do was wangle some Jenny trainers from the Signal Corps and obtain the services of a few pilots capable of flying a bag of letters from—well, from New York to Washington.

The idea of carrying the mails by air was as sound as any innovation in communications or transportation, as early in 1918 there began a widening pool of manpower. Pilots and maintenance men were being turned out by dozens of training centers all over the country. Manpower was no problem in the United States, but there was a lamentable lack of modern aircraft. For more than three years America had tried to ignore the war in Europe, and few realized the great development in all types of weapons, armored tanks, and particularly the aircraft which were being flown in the first war-in-the-air. Only a handful of military men, who had been sent across the Atlantic as neutral observers, had any idea what progress had been made in the development of single-seater scouts, two-seater fighters, and reconnaissance planes, or realized the extent multi-engined bombers were being used on long-distance raids against enemy-occupied cities, manufacturing centers, and vital communications. In early 1918 there was no such item as an American twin-engined military aircraft on the production line of any factory.

The number of men who were willing to risk their skills and finances on the development and manufacture of aircraft could be counted on the fingers of one hand. The Wrights had ignored the possibilities of a fighting plane. Glenn Curtiss had built a few birdcage biplanes for aerial competitions or for playboy sportsmen who could afford such luxuries, but at the time he was more interested in the manufacture of engines which might be suitable for aircraft propulsion. Curtiss was first of all a mechanical engineer and knew very little about the design of aircraft, but it must be stated that his firm was the first to produce a successful flying boat, one that flew on January 12, 1912. The following year the White and Thompson Company of Sussex, England, which had become the Curtiss agent abroad, had hired an ex-Royal Navy flier, John Cyril Porte, as its test pilot. Porte became involved in a British-American idea of developing a plane capable of flying the Atlantic, a venture later financed by a syndicate headed by Rodman Wanamaker. Whether the plans for this aircraft originated in Britain, or whether Porte took his idea to the Curtiss plant in Hammondsport, New York, is not clear, but a twin-engined flying boat, to be known as the H.4 *Small America*, was actually built and passed all its flight tests on Lake Keuka, using two Curtiss 90-hp engines. Unfortunately, when World War I broke out Porte had to return to his more important Royal Navy duties, and the transatlantic flight was abandoned.

Curtiss offered the plane to the British who accepted it gratefully, and, in fact, built many of the same design to patrol their vital coastlines. The blueprints were also turned over to the U.S. Navy, and it was this basic flying boat model that was eventually developed into the famous NC-4 which in 1919 made the first flight across the Atlantic.

For the record, there were several flying boats or hydroplane models being used by the U.S. Navy in 1918, but they did not suit the airmail plan, as Captain Lipsner intended to open his routes over land areas between key cities.

Donald Douglas, already considered a design genius, was putting the finishing touches to a twin-engined bomber to be built by Glenn Martin, although it never took off the ground until well after the Armistice. Chance M. Vought, an early pilot, had built a two-seater plane intended for military observation that was eventually developed into the Lewis & Vought V.E.7, and offered as an advanced trainer, many of which were to reach U.S. airfields in time to celebrate the end of hostilities. This V.E.7, powered with the 180-hp Hispano-Suiza engine, was far superior to the JN-4, and it is still something of a mystery why it was never introduced into the postwar commercial operations. It may have been that the Hisso engines were in short supply or that the manufacturing license agreement was about to be concluded.

Another important figure in the field of design, Grover C. Loening, tried to interest both the Army and the Navy in his ideas for military aircraft, but his plans were too advanced for the stodgy military mind. Before the war came to its close he had produced a two-seater, monoplane fighter that was armed with four machine guns—a military machine that might have ranked with Europe's best, had it reached the fighting front.

But with all the money available, the technical knowledge, and the enthusiasm generated by America's entry into the war, there was not a worthwhile basic design that could be quickly converted into a transport suitable for the hauling of mail over the wide open spaces of the United States. The best that could be obtained were four JN4H Curtiss Jennys borrowed from the Air Service training establishment.

2

Jenny Carries the Mail

Captain Lipsner, still in military uniform—including spurs on his polished boots—took up his assignment to organize an airmail route and develop the flight schedules. One amusing incident connected with the early project was typical of the comedy of errors that sometimes marked the hurried planning. It was argued that if the country was to have an airmail system, there would have to be recognizable stamps affixed to the letters flown by air. The Army man left that to the post office officials, believing they would produce something illustrative of the Mail Service.

They certainly did. A stamp, printed in two colors, offered a carmine frame through which a Curtiss Jenny was shown as a mail plane. It was an impressive engraving and marked to sell for twenty-four cents. All well and good, but, as though flaunting the service's future, the first sheet to be run through the press for the two colors came out with the airplane flying upside down! Before the error was noted a stamp dealer wandered into the Washington post office and requested a full sheet of "the new Air Mail stamps," and unwittingly purchased a philatelist's bonanza. Post Office officials tried to return his twenty-four dollars, but the buyer refused to part with them, and there was no recourse since the inverted stamps had been sold in a legitimate transaction.

In May 1969 one of these stamps sold for $31,000, twice the price a collector paid for it in 1964.

Six Curtiss JN-4 training planes, built to the specifications of the Army's wartime training program, were modified at the Curtiss plant in Buffalo and listed as JN-6H (Hisso) mail planes and shipped to Belmont Park, New York, where they were uncrated and assembled for the first pathfinder, or experimental, flights. The modifications included taking out the front cockpit equipment, installing larger fuel tanks to double the range, and building in a hopper to accommodate a few mail pouches. The Curtiss firm had agreed to have six such models ready in about eight weeks, but only four were available by the time the post office was ready to inaugurate its mail service.

Four Army pilots, Howard P. Culver, Torrey H. Webb, Walter Miller, and Stephen Bonsal, were among the first fliers to be assigned to what was then being called the Aerial Mail Service. Later on James C. Edgerton, who had just passed his primary training course, and George L. Boyle were added to the staff. Boyle's future father-in-law was Judge Charles C. McCord, Interstate Commerce Commissioner. Boyle was selected to fly the first mail flight from Washington to Philadelphia on May 15, the opening day of the service.

The full flight schedule was drawn up as follows: Lieutenant Boyle was to take off from the Polo Grounds in Washington and head for Bustleton Field, a 130-acre layout in North Philadelphia, some 128 miles away. There his pouches were to be turned over to Culver, who would haul them the remaining 90 miles to Belmont Park. While Boyle was heading northeast, Torrey Webb was to take off from the race track and head for North Philadelphia, where on his arrival at Bustleton his pouches were to be taken over by Edgerton and flown to Washington.

It was as simple as that. But, of course, one had to plan for pilot error and for tricks only a Jenny could play, and hope for a fair dose of miracle luck. So far, Captain Lipsner had had more than his share of ill fortune. In the first place, the pilots, grudgingly loaned by the Army Signal Corps, had had very little cross-country experience. From some accounts they were school instructors who had piled up many flying hours, most of them within a dozen miles of their training fields. When inclement weather turned up they wisely nosed down and sought the shelter of the hangars and the officers' mess. On the other hand, if they ran into fog or rain while flying this hare-brained airmail scheme, they probably would remember their flying school safety measures—and remain alive to fly another day.

This is the view Captain Lipsner probably took just prior to the opening of the new mail service, but it is not to be presumed that military officials had no interest in this home-service aviation project or felt that the post office was taking valuable men or aircraft from their training programs. A few farsighted men realized that an airmail service *might* develop long-distance cross-country flying in a manner that was beyond the scope of the military training plan, a point that was to be completely justified. But Lipsner was looking into the future too, and knew that unless this pioneer plan was carried out successfully it would be years before anyone would try again. These inaugural flights would have to be made without a hitch in order to attract the publicity such a scheme required. It was on this premise that President Woodrow Wilson and a group of distinguished guests were invited to be on hand at the Washingto Polo Grounds for the inauguration of the Aerial Mail Service.

In his personal story* Lipsner tells of the harrowing night he spent anticipating the many mishaps that could cancel

* *The Airmail—Jennies to Jets*, by Captain Benjamin B. Lipsner, as told to Leonard Finley Hilts, Wilcox & Follett Co., 1951.

out his airmail program. There could be the standard engine troubles, bad weather; compasses could go haywire; pilots might get lost; and, worse of all, President Wilson might ignore the invitation or be too busy to appear. Lipsner wondered if Otto Praeger was suffering the same torments.

Came the dawn, and a beautiful May day was promised. By 8:30 it was already clear, bright and warm. The Polo Grounds was hardly suited for a major flying project such as this, for it was surrounded by towering trees; but there was no other choice, and it was convenient for rushing the incoming mail to the post office building. Its surface was fairly level and the turf firm and neatly mowed. Lipsner hoped there would be some wind to help his pilots vault the trees, but by 9:30 not a zephyr stirred, and except for a few mechanics there were no people on the field. Finally, a police van chugged in and unloaded a few bluecoats who looked about for an anticipated crowd and then with a bored air of professionalism took up their positions near what mild activity was discernible.

A bulky man, flashing a Secret Service badge, arrived and demanded to know from where the airplane was to take off. In other words, he wanted to know where to park the President's car and where it would be safe for the Presidential party to stand. Lipsner was relieved to learn that the Chief Executive would honor the occasion with his presence, but now it was more imperative that his airmen get through with their mail pouches. The first was due in at 10:30.

A few minutes later there was the clackety-clack of an approaching aircraft which proved to be one of the new airmail Jennys being flown in for the Washington-Philadelphia leg by Major R. H. Fleet, in temporary command of the flying equipment to be used in the Post Office Department's venture. For some years Fleet claimed to be the nation's first airmail pilot, whereas he actually never officially carried a bag of mail. On this occasion he simply delivered a plane for the inaugural flights. About two weeks later he was transferred from the Washington area to Ellington Field in Olcott, Texas, and then to Brooks Field in San Antonio. In later years Fleet carried out important experimental work in the aircraft industry, but he never was an airmail pilot.

Fleet's ship was the one to be flown from Washington to Philadelphia, and news photos of the day show the major with his own map spread out on a lower wing, explaining the details of the route to be flown by Lieutenant Boyle. Other photographs present pertinent shots of Lipsner and Praeger handing the bags of mail over to Boyle, who was also being seen off by his sweetheart Miss Margaret Mc-Chord peering through an armful of roses.

While everyone waited for Boyle's plane to be waved off for Philadelphia, the President's party—which included Mrs. Wilson, Postmaster General Albert S. Burleson, Assistant Secretary of the Navy Franklin Delano Roosevelt, and a Japanese named Mr. Kambara, who was said to be the Postmaster General of Japan—spread out as a formal committee. Mr. Wilson was nursing a heavily bandaged hand on which, it was rumored, he had suffered a severe burn while clutching at a hot exhaust pipe during an Army tank demonstration a short time before. However, this did not prevent the President from dropping a personal letter addressed to Postmaster Thomas G. Patten of New York City into one of the pouches. This first-cover letter was to be auctioned off for the benefit of the American Red Cross with an opening bid of $1,000.

There were more photos, but no recorded speeches. Boyle fastened his safety belt and a Sergeant Waters began the engine-starting procedure: "Switch off!"

"Switch off . . . gas on," Lieutenant Boyle responded.

The Hisso was primed, and then Waters called, "Contact!"

The brand new Hisso was stiff and it took a chain of five

men to pull the propeller through. They did this several times, but nothing happened. The engine coughed, gushed smoke, but refused to start. The prop kicked once or twice, but always ended up perpendicular, and still. This went on for several minutes and then Otto Praeger appealed to Captain Lipsner. The spark plugs were checked, and they tried again. Someone asked whether there was any gas in the tank. Waters looked and saw that the gauge indicated a full tank, but he remembered that it could be relied on only when the plane was in its correct flying position—on the ground. He peered into the tank and discovered it was almost empty. Someone had forgotten to check the fuel after Major Fleet had landed the Jenny. As soon as some twenty gallons, siphoned from a British airplane standing nearby, had been poured into the tank of the mail plane, the Hisso started with no trouble at all.

Even Mr. Wilson smiled when the situation had been explained.

Boyle went through his flight checks, and then taxied out to the center of the field. He peered about for some evidence of wind, but finally took off and just cleared the trees with a few inches to spare. With that, the visitors began to climb back into their motorcars. It was at that point that Lipsner took a final look at the departing plane, and to his astonishment saw that Boyle, instead of heading for Philadelphia, was flying at top speed in the opposite direction. The pouches were safely aboard, the airmail plane was in the air and off on schedule, but the pilot was flying toward Fredricksburg—not Philadelphia!

Captain Lipsner sought solace by hurrying back to his office and resuming his desk work. He was advised that Torrey Webb had taken off from New York as scheduled. A few minutes later he learned that Webb had landed safely in Philadelphia and had turned over his mail pouches to Lieutenant Edgerton, who had taken off without incident and was expected in Washington shortly. Burying himself deeper into the paper work, Lipsner was next interrupted by a long-distance call from Waldorf, Maryland, about twenty miles southeast of Washington, to learn that Boyle was reporting in.

"My compass got a little mixed up," Boyle explained.

"Where's the mail?"

"I'm having it loaded on a car now, and I'll make sure it is rushed back to Washington. Sorry, Captain."

Some years later the Post Office Department issued a brochure on the Aviation Mail Service in which Major Fleet gave his version of this incident. In spite of the detailed information given him, Lieutenant Boyle became completely lost. He circled about and finally landed in a plowed field near Waldorf, Maryland. His plane stood up on its nose and broke the propeller. The Post Office Department gave him a second chance, and on this occasion Fleet escorted him in another plane for some distance over the same route to indicate the correct compass course. Believing the young pilot was well on his way, the major turned back for Washington. But Boyle became lost once more, ran out of fuel, and landed near the mouth of Chesapeake Bay. He refueled there, took off again, but crashlanded near the Philadelphia Country Club damaging a wing but suffering no injury to himself. He delivered the mail to Philadelphia by truck.

Despite these unfortunate mishaps, the Post Office Department requested that Lieutenant Boyle be given a third chance, but Major Fleet had had enough. He denied the request, relieved Boyle of his Aerial Mail Service assignment, and sent him back to flying school for further training. His place was taken by Lieutenant E. W. Kilgore.

For the record, the bags carried by Boyle on that first short flight brought in a gross revenue of $1,584. Three hundred of the 6,600 letters were destined for Philadelphia, 3,300 for New York, and 3,000 were to be distributed from New York. There is no record of who bought President Wilson's letter or where it is today. The rest of the day's flights were carried out without incident. The newspapers gave the inauguration a good play, but one or two editorial writers questioned the practicality of sending mail by air.

But, in spite of the stamps that were printed upside down, recalcitrant engines, and a treacherous compass, the airmail system soon settled down to its routine program. Take-off times were better adjusted to fit delivery to or from the base post offices, and within a short time the phenomenon of commercial flying so intrigued the public that great crowds began to gather at the three fields to watch the take-offs and landings. Lipsner had to call on the police to provide guards and roped-off protection. New flying equipment was introduced, and on the New York–Philadelphia run Curtiss R-4s, powered with Liberty 400-hp engines, were tried out. This over-publicized power plant had given American aviation its prize headache, but Captain Lipsner had some magic touch with the few assigned to his service and they gave little or no trouble. The Hissos used in the airmail Jennys were built at the Wright-Martin Aircraft factory in New Brunswick, New Jersey, under manufacturing rights obtained from the Spanish Hispano-Suiza Company.

The weather was exceptionally good, but there were days when the sun did not shine, when the wind was high, or when rain came down in torrents. Then, as in later years, military airmen were not expected to carry out flight operations unless weather conditions were exactly ideal, but the new airmail service found that the pouches piled up at the flying fields, regardless of weather, and the pilots were expected to haul them to their destinations.

Also, in 1918, meteorological science was hardly out of its infancy and any reports available were far from reliable. The best that could be expected was to ascertain in New York what conditions were like in Philadelphia or Washington. There was no way of learning whether it was raining over central New Jersey or upper Delaware except by random calls over the telephone. Any weather information which could be gathered was marked on a dispatch board devised by Captain Lipsner, and on this primitive device were chalked the three basic areas, the planes and their pilots, along with some sketchy detail of the weather conditions over each leg of the run.

Another point seldom appreciated today is that there were no maps suitable for aerial navigation. The state maps of New York, New Jersey, Pennsylvania, Delaware, and Maryland were all drawn to different scales and showed only political divisions with nothing of the physical nature except cities, towns, rivers, harbors, and perhaps railroads. The airmail pilots had to take a complete map of the United States and fold it into strips in order to have all areas on a uniform scale. Finally, Major E. Lester Jones, Chief of the Geodetic Survey, prepared more suitable guides for the fliers. This, indeed, was the era of seat-of-the-paints flying . . . and no parachutes!

Over the first two months of operations, May 15 to July 16, 1918, Lipsner was able to present a fairly comprehensive report showing that his pilots had completed 88 out of a scheduled 100 flights, which, considering the equipment and a complete lack of radio communication devices, was a remarkable achievement. The record over the first full year—May 15, 1918, to May 15, 1919—shows that the schedule called for 1,263 flights, only 55 of which had to be canceled. Of the 1,208 trips started, 53 were forced down by bad weather, and 37 were not completed because of engine trouble. In other words, 92.73 percent of all flights attempted were successful, and 128,255 miles were flown. The weather was braved in 436 cases when airmail planes took off in fog, rain and other forms of inclement weather.

There was a period when the pilots, if caught in a rainstorm, encountered alarming vibrations of their engines, and it was discovered that the wooden propellers could not stand the bulletlike effects of the rain. The leading edges of the blades often splintered and their all-important camber was badly damaged. Lipsner finally overcame this by covering the attack edges of the blades with a special tape. Later on he had his propellers manufactured with a thin metal covering to protect them from such storm damage.

Turnbuckles, used to tighten flying wires in the rigging, also gave considerable trouble. These had to bear the shock of instant tension, ranging from eight hundred pounds to four tons. As they were always being adjusted before or after every flight, the threads wore out quickly and the turnbuckles had to be replaced; but they were scarce, and Lipsner often had to fly to some Army airfield and filch handfuls when the Stores sergeant wasn't watching.

The engines—Liberties and Hissos of the day—were also sources of annoying trouble, mainly because they had been assembled hurriedly in wartime factories. Lipsner endured the distressing period of warped exhaust valves until it was discovered that the engines should idle for some time after the plane had landed. This gave the valve stems time to cool off gradually. Today, with the metal available and the improved cooling systems, this trouble has been eliminated.

As each week of flying was completed, the pilots became more familiar with the areas over which they flew. Their cross-country flying improved day by day. Next, there was an understandable desire to stretch out the schedule. Edgerton was the first to make a round trip between Washington and Philadelphia. Stephen Bonsal turned in several round trips over the New York–Philadelphia leg, and Lieutenant Torrey Webb made an exploratory mail flight from New York to Boston. This effort was something of an aviation epic. The run was intended only as an experimental flight to determine whether a regular route might be established. Carrying only seven pounds of mail, Webb took a mechanic, R. Heck, along for any mechanical emergencies. The trial flight was started on June 6, 1918, and shortly after take-off Webb realized his compass was inaccurate. He selected a level field near Hatton, Connecticut, and made a landing. After adjusting the instrument as best he could, he took off again and eventually landed on the estate of Godfrey Cabot at Saugus, Massachusetts, about seven miles north of Boston. Because the turf was soggy from recent rains, one of the plane's wheels sank in and the Jenny tried to stand on her nose. The propeller was splintered and much of the rigging system was strained. A Boston post office truck came out to retrieve the mail, and Webb and Heck remained with their craft until spare parts could be provided and the necessary repairs made.

Webb was not able to get away from Saugus until June 11, but on his return trip he carried 64 pounds of mail which had been specially stamped in Boston. All this airmail business so fascinated Postmaster Murray that he decided to fly back to New York with Webb and learn firsthand what flying the mail entailed. Mechanic Heck was quite willing to take the train back to Grand Central.

Webb ran into frightful weather and had to fly "blind" most of the way through fog, rain, and heavy mist. Taking no more chances than necessary, he made a landing in a small field near the West Hills home of Otto H. Kahn, to get his bearings. From there on conditions improved and they landed safely at Belmont Park.

It must not be presumed that the comparative success of the opening of this airmail service was greeted with enthusiasm in Washington. Shortly after the schedule got under way, Representative Martin B. Madden, chairman of the Ways and Means Committee whose duty it was to keep an eye on treasury funds, asked Captain Lipsner to call on him.

"So you're the bright young Army officer who, while we are engaged in a world war and are pressed for men and materials, has decided to start an airmail service, eh?" he exploded without polite preliminaries. "It's nothing more than a ridiculous, asinine venture, and if I had my way I would see that you were thrown into the Federal Penitentiary, and make sure the key was thrown away. Now get out of here!"

Four years later Colonel Paul Henderson was appointed Second Assistant Postmaster General and placed in charge of the Airmail Service. Colonel Henderson was the son-in-law of the same Representative Madden, and the connection gave the airmail pioneers a voice in Congress. Henderson was destined to become an important figure in air transport, an official who proved that the airmail planes could be flown around the clock. It was he who erected guidance beacons every twenty-five miles along what was to become known as the Columbia Route from New York to San Francisco, and near each beacon he planned to lay out emergency strips, known grimly as "crack-up fields." It was this Columbia Route, sometimes known as the Woodrow Wilson Airway, that became the backbone of America's commercial aviation.

Lipsner's primitive airmail service showed a startling profit in its first year of operations. The Postmaster General must have been astonished to receive this first breakdown of revenues and costs which indicated a surplus of $19,103:

Revenue from airmail postage		$159,700
Saving in railway transportation		2,264
Total revenue and saving		$161,964
Cost of operations	$137,900	
Loss: Plane No. 3, less salvage	4,961	
Total costs	$142,861	$142,861
Surplus		$ 19,103

These costs on a per-mile projection reveal that $0.2829 per mile was spent for overhead; $0.2029 per mile for flying; and $0.4081 per mile for maintenance and repairs.

These were the first-year figures for 128,255 miles of flying in which 193,021 pounds of mail were carried.

If comparisons must be made, let it be noted that the Pony Express of 1860 demanded $5 for the postage of a half-ounce letter, and there was no direct delivery to the home of the recipient. Paradoxically, it must be pointed out that for the same price today one could hire a private messenger to take a bundle of letters by air from New York to Washington and beat the present post office operation by a day or so.

Other factors of this twelve-month operation show that 35,930 gallons of gasoline were consumed and an average of 4.09 miles were obtained for each gallon. The pilots were in the air for 2,096 hours at a cost of $64.80 for each hour of flight time.

Regardless of these encouraging figures, it was soon obvious that this aviation experiment would have to be expanded. Although a profit had been shown, the planes had not carried the amount of mail of which they were capable. Actually, the public showed little interest in the venture, perhaps because it was thought that the war deserved wholehearted attention. Very few felt that any letters they wrote were important enough to send by air, considering the price demanded for this service. There had been no concerted effort to publicize the novel operation. At times Lipsner resorted to subterfuge and stuffed the mail pouches with ordinary first-class mail, thus encouraging his pilots to risk bad weather to get the loads through.

It was also argued that twenty-four cents to fly a letter from Washington to New York was too high, considering that sometimes ordinary mail by train was delivered as quickly as that sent by air. At that time letters bearing airmail stamps could not be dropped in any convenient mailbox—they had to be taken to the post office. The only stamp that could be used was the regular airmail stamp. All in all, the airmail system entailed a great deal of inconvenience, and, furthermore, the service related only to the key routes from New York to Washington.

Captain Lipsner, who has seldom been given full credit for his role in the development of the airmail system, decided to make a personal survey of the situation. The rate of twenty-four cents had been cut to sixteen cents, but the cost of postage wasn't the complete answer. Only a few imaginative businessmen in the east were able to make use of the service. If airmail was to become self-supporting, bigger and faster planes would be needed and the routes would have to be expanded. If the service could be extended from New York to the Pacific coast, or even to Chicago, much time would be saved and eventually a nationwide system could be set up.

Until midsummer of 1918 Lipsner was still an Army officer on leave of absence from his military duties. His pilots and planes were contributions from the Army, and he was to some extent shackled in his planning by the rules and regulations of a wartime military system. However, by July 15—at the suggestion of the Postmaster General—the Secretary of War, Newton D. Baker, finally relieved Lipsner of his military duties. He reverted to his civilian status and accepted the post of Superintendent of the Aerial Mail Service, the first such utility in any country in the world. It was this change of status that gave the former captain his chance to suggest that the service become a completely civilian organization. In order for the service to be expanded and put on a real paying basis, it would have to be released from military overseers and turned into a businesslike, civilian operation. Otto Praeger gave Lipsner his head with authority to order half a dozen more suitable aircraft and hire a number of experienced pilots to expand the route.

Lipsner announced publicly that the Aerial Mail Service was in the market for a fleet of planes which would suit the proposed expansion of the service. One response came from the Standard Aircraft Corporation of Elizabeth, New Jersey, which, at the time, was manufacturing a Hisso-powered biplane of its own design and building Caproni and Handley Page night bombers for the U.S. Army. Charles H. Day, chief engineer of the Standard company, suggested that their Standard biplane could be quickly modified to carry mail. The machine was a smart-looking affair, reminiscent of the French Bréguet, except that it was designed for the Hisso instead of the bulkier Renault engine and had Spad-like wings and typical Spad interplane struts.

The Standard JR1B Mailplane, as it came to be called, was to carry a pay load of 180 pounds plus the pilot. Powered with a 170-hp Hispano-Suiza engine, it was expected to show 100 mph low down and climb to 5,300 feet in ten minutes. With sixty gallons of fuel in the tank, it had an endurance of better than three hours. Considering everything, it was an ideal mount for the job. The Post Office Department ordered six of these planes.

While the aircraft were being assembled and test-flown, Lipsner was collecting a small group of civilian airmen. Among them was Max Miller, who had been an Army instructor at San Diego and had logged more than 1,000 hours in the air. Max resembled Charles A. Lindbergh, who was to become an airmail pilot some years later. Tragically, Max later died in a burning Junkers while flying over Morristown, New Jersey, shortly after he had married Daisy Thomas, the Aerial Mail Service's first stenographer.

Robert Shank was another keen, reliable pilot, who had put in 1,200 hours in Texas teaching Army students to fly. In turn, Shank recommended Edward Gardner, a former racing driver, who had taken up flying and had 1,400 hours in his logbook. Gardner was a most daring airman, one who performed with considerable flourish and style.

Maurice Newton, a man well over forty, was the fourth pilot to be accepted. In those days Newton's years were against him, but he had been a test pilot for the Sperry Gyroscope Company and had considerable experience in checking those important instruments. He was signed on and proved to be a valuable addition to the flight staff. The ground crew included Edward C. Radel of Buffalo, New York, who was taken on as Chief Mechanic at a salary of $2,000 a year. His assistants were William H. Read, Charles C. King, W. O. Beatty, A. C. Darniel, Henry Wacker, A. F. Cryder and E. N. Angel. Besides being a splendid mechanic Radel was also a skilled musician who played both the saxophone and the French horn. In his later years he joined Fred Waring and his Pennsylvanians.

Following the American tradition, there had to be a ceremony to commemorate the delivery of the six Standard Mailplanes. On hand for that occasion were Alan R. Hawley, president of the Aero Club of America; Henry Woodhouse, vice president of the Aerial League of America and editor of *Flying*, an aeronautical journal of the day. Standing in this small group was Captain Frederick Libby of Sterling, Colorado, who, while flying with the British Royal Flying Corps in France, had become the first American to reach the "ace" rank. Fred was back home on leave and was being icily ignored by the Washington crowd, although General Billy Mitchell had whisked him out of the R.F.C. to contribute his knowledge and experience to the U.S. Aviation Service. But bureaucratic chauvinism had taken over. As some people felt Fred had renounced his U.S. citizenship by volunteering to serve with the British years before America had joined the campaign, he had been left high and dry on the service tree. This point was never brought up when other Americans had volunteered for the French Foreign Legion. The fact that Libby had shot down twenty-four enemy planes while serving as an aerial gunner and as a pilot was never taken into account. For a time Fred seriously considered returning to the Royal Flying Corps, but Billy Mitchell persuaded him to reconsider. By the time American bureaucracy had found a post for this outstanding airman the Armistice had been signed.

Postmasters from all the surrounding towns were on

hand, the new mailplanes were inspected, and after a luncheon was served in the Standard Aircraft office, all concerned trooped back to the flying field. A few commemorative watches were presented "to keep the pilots on time," and Mr. Lipsner made an appropriate speech summing up his interest in commercial aviation and adding details of his plans for the Aerial Mail Service. President Harry B. Mingle of the Standard company presented silk American flags to each of the pilots. A stack of mail was postmarked on the field by Assistant Postmaster Morris of Elizabeth, and motion picture cameras ground away to record the beginning of commercial aviation. Two of the planes took off and landed in Philadelphia, a trip that took only forty minutes—something of a record for nonmilitary aircraft.

During the luncheon and the formal palaver, Lipsner had a brief opportunity to become confidential with Harry Mingle and explain some of his problems. "Frankly," he said, "I don't know how long these single-engine planes will fill the Aerial Mail Service requirements. We may have to adopt much larger aircraft. But where we are going to get them I don't know. I've seen the hull of a new Curtiss NC which could handle a couple of tons of mail, but it's a flying boat and it would be difficult to change our setup to work from seaplane bases, and so far we have no plans for transocean flying."

Mingle was delighted with the prospect. "Would you be interested in the Handley Page twin-engined machine? At present it's a bomber, but it could be modified to carry more than a ton of mail."

Lipsner admitted that any landplane capable of carrying that much cargo might interest him very much.

"Then, too," Mingle went on, "the Handley Page has two engines which would cut your power problems in half. We could have one ready for you to test out in a very short time."

"One plane wouldn't be enough. I'm thinking in terms of a whole fleet to carry out the schedule and route I have in mind."

Mingle turned on a knowing wink. "Don't worry. We have enough parts stacked away here to assemble four hundred of these big babies."

On the way back to Washington Lipsner reveled in the prospect of a twin-engined carrier, one capable of 90 mph with a range between 550 and 600 miles. He wondered how long it would take to train his ex-Jenny pilots to fly a British two-engined bomber. He planned to put the idea to Otto Praeger—and the Postmaster General.

The last runs of airmail to be flown by Army pilots were carried out on August 10, 1918. On August 12, the first civil airmail service began. On this occasion there were no formal ceremonies, for the President of the United States was otherwise engaged, and as far as Washington was concerned, the airmail service was no longer a novelty. By this time Lipsner had shifted the Capital base from the Polo Grounds to the flying field at College Park, Maryland, about twelve miles from the Potomac. On the opening day of the new service Max Miller left College Park at 11:35 A.M., carrying 222 pounds of mail, and landed at Philadelphia at 1 P.M. Maurice Newton took off from Philadelphia at 1:13 P.M. with 224 pounds of mail and landed at New York by 2:15 P.M. On the reverse flights Robert Shank left Belmont Park at twelve noon and landed in Philadelphia at 1:25 P.M. He hauled only 30.5 pounds of mail. Edward V. Gardner, carrying only 16.5 pounds of mail, took off at 1:30 P.M. and arrived at the Washington field at 3:30 P.M.

The difference in these mail loads indicated how well Lipsner had been drumming up airmail business in and around Washington, whereas no one in New York or Philadelphia had found time to encourage businessmen to make use of the service. Again, the problem was to prove that letters sent by air would reach their destinations well ahead

of those moved over the railroad facilities. But no matter
how the postal men switched their schedules, how often
the airmail was picked up and delivered to the flying fields,
and how widely the system was expanded, it was evident
that mail would have to be flown round-the-clock. During
the night hours mail piled up in post offices and in sheds at
the flying fields. In other words, as much as half the time
available, when the mail might be winging through the
skies at a speed up to three times faster than trains
chugged, was wasted. If the Aerial Mail Service was to pay
its way, night operations would have to be established.
Faster planes, longer routes and heavier pay loads were not
the final answer. The airmail loads would have to be
carried during the night hours if a letter written and posted
late in the afternoon was to be in the city of its destination
early the next morning.

This brought up the possibility of adopting a commercial
version of the British Handley Page 0/400 twin-engined
bomber. A Captain Brown, a Canadian, who was a member
of the new British Royal Air Force, had been assigned as a
test pilot to the Standard Aircraft Corporation to check out
the bombers as fast as they came off the assembly line. Captain Brown willingly gave Max Miller a test flight in order
to show how easy it would be to convert Lipsner's single-
engine pilots to the Handley Page.

After a few circuits of the field, the plane was brought in
and landed. Miller was delighted. "This big baby is as easy
to fly as our old Jennys." He beamed with glee. "I'm willing
to go solo right now."

Captain Brown admitted that he had let Max make the
landing Lipsner had just watched, and Lipsner suggested
that Max try again—an actual solo flight. Miller handled
the British bomber as though he had been flying it for
months. The superintendent of the Aerial Mail Service was
equally delighted.

After a long conference with Praeger and Postmaster

General Burleson, it was decided to check back with Harry Mingle to get figures on prices, delivery dates, and the possibility of taking over the plane Max Miller had already flown. Lipsner planned to have it on hand so the rest of the pilots could familiarize themselves with the machine. For a few days it looked as though the Aerial Mail Service would soon be flying giant twin-engined planes, but there was a Nippo in the ointment. When Lipsner next called on Harry Mingle to inquire about obtaining a small fleet of Handley Pages, Mingle seemed to have lost interest in the proposed deal. He intimated that the matter would have to be taken up with the head office.

"Head office? Aren't you the president of Standard Aircraft?" Lipsner was puzzled.

"Well, yes, I am, but there's a factor you should know about. Standard Aircraft is financed and controlled by the Mitsui Company of Tokyo, Japan. They have the manufacturing rights, and decide who may buy the Handley Pages."

This revelation toppled Lipsner's high hopes and elaborate plans, but he listened to Mingle's explanation and decided to be patient and see what would happen. Mingle felt that before long the Japanese owners would be more than willing to sell these British bombers to the Aerial Mail Service, if only to get rid of their heavy inventory. A few letters, telegrams, and cables were exchanged, but for some unexplained reason the Japanese owners of Standard Aviation decided to scrap their whole pile of Handley Page parts, rather than sell one model to the United States Post Office Department.

Lipsner pondered for years on this strange decision, for in all probability the Aerial Mail Service would have taken all the Handley Pages the Standard factory could have assembled. These advanced aircraft would have put the United States Aerial Mail Service months ahead of any foreign project. The twin-engined planes certainly would have been safer to fly, would have cut down on crashes and casualties, and would have sped the development of the service. In fact, the whole potential program of U.S. commercial aviation would have been advanced. There would have been coast-to-coast delivery months before that linkage actually was completed and, more important, it would have been most efficient and reliable.

3

The Hell Stretch

To regress in the history of the early airmail system: in 1917, after Woodrow Wilson had been elected for a second term, the Board of Governors of the Aero Club of America drew up on paper a transcontinental air route and named it the Woodrow Wilson Airway, after the former president of Princeton University. This was the forerunner of our present-day network of aerial highways which covers all sections of the United States. The Woodrow Wilson Airway comprised a zone eighty miles wide which, cutting through the states of New York, New Jersey, Pennsylvania, Ohio, Michigan, Indiana, Illinois, Iowa, Nebraska, Wyoming, Colorado, Utah, Nevada, and California, linked New York with San Francisco. A line drawn through this imaginary zone touches most of the important cities of the nation. It was conceivable that future air travelers flying over this route could reach either side of this zone in a half hour of flying, and any city or town located within the imaginary zone was mapped as being on the Woodrow Wilson Airway. A number of similar airways were linked into the main route, setting up a network of aerial routes. Landing places for aircraft and suitable identification marks were to be placed at important points along the direct line of the Airway, and later on each city and community was to be so marked.

All this imaginative planning was only in the minds of a few officials of the Aero Club, and furtherance had to be postponed for more immediate matters. President Wilson reversed his stand in April 1917 and asked Congress to declare war on Germany. From that date on, American interest in aviation was confined to the development of a military air service. Still, there was a map on which were drawn the routes of the Woodrow Wilson Airway, and by late August of 1918 Lipsner decided to make use of it. He called a meeting of his pilots and his chief mechanic, Eddie Radel, to discuss the possibility of extending their present airmail system. A copy of the Aero Club airway map was tacked up and used in planning the link between New York and Chicago.

Starting from the race track at Belmont Park, their proposed route would cross Manhattan, northern New Jersey, climb over the Allegheny Mountains of Pennsylvania— making stops at Lock Haven and Cleveland—and then cross the lower tip of Lake Michigan to land at Chicago. This promised certain difficulties for the pilots and their Standard Mailplanes, for there would have to be a number of emergency landing fields, properly staffed, to provide fuel, supplies, and routine repairs. But Lipsner's whole group flailed into the task with enthusiasm and industry while still carrying out their daily flights over the existing route. There was some loose talk of providing the pilots with electrically heated suits such as were being used by the British in France, but even more novel was the hope that the planes would be equipped with two-way radio sets, for it was rumored at the National Bureau of Standards in Washington that the British were actually using such equipment aboard their aircraft along the Western front.

(The fact of this rumor was that specialists in the Royal

Air Force were already building two-way radio-telephone sets with which flight leaders could talk to other pilots during their patrols or receive spoken messages from the ground. These electronic experiments were being kept fairly secret until standard sets could be built and fitted into the multi-seat aircraft then in use. Simple radio sets connecting the aircraft observers with mobile ground stations, using keys and Morse code, had been used to spot targets for the artillery since early in 1915.)

Lipsner did his best to obtain radio equipment for his proposed New York to Chicago run, but as long as there was a war on in France there was little or no chance of obtaining such important communications equipment for his pilots. Nor did the electrically heated suits materialize. However, such general discussion did afford subjects which inspired good publicity for the airmail service. It would need all it could get, for the planned route included a dangerous flight across the Pennsylvania mountains—a stretch that later became known as the "graveyard run,"— and for some years the hop over the Bellefonte range was declared unsafe for the transportation of air passengers.

All through August and early into September Lipsner and his pilots studied the proposed route to Chicago. Max Miller and Ed Gardner were selected to make the first experimental run, and from the beginning there was friendly rivalry between the two pilots, though they were bosom friends on the ground.

Lipsner had planned to send off two planes at the same time and hoped that at least one of them would get through. This arrangement caused some warm discussion because each pilot felt he was capable of making the trip on his own. He did not want either to follow or to provide a pathfinder plane for the other. Finally, Lipsner had to resort to the flip of a coin to see which man would have the honor of taking off first. Miller won the toss. Gardner smiled, extended his hand and said, "Good luck, Max."

With that, the rivalry seemed to have been quenched,

but it gradually built up each day, and instead of considering the run as an important pathfinder effort, it was being spoken of as a race. In the meantime a number of temporary fields were designated. Two planes were selected for the trip and in true American fashion an insignia to mark the planes was devised. This was Lipsner's idea. He objected to the "race" story then making the newspapers, explaining that Miller was to fly a Standard Mailplane while Gardner was to pilot a Curtiss R-4 powered by a 400-hp Liberty engine. He felt this was a good time to devise a new twist to the publicity. As he left his office one day he noticed a discarded Mail Pouch Tobacco wrapper. He picked it up and had an artist copy the illustration which was used as a service insignia on the sides of his planes. The design was used on most airmail planes as long as the post office service operated.

So far Ben Lipsner had been troubled only by the normal problems of running a commercial operation. He had weaned the service from military control and had been awarded the job of superintending an independent post office airmail service. Only equipment problems, weather, schedules, and the rivalry of pilots had given him trouble —which he handled as an executive should—but since the airmail service was about to expand and stretch its routes from coast to coast, the fine old law of politics began to show its hand. In the vortex of planning the pathfinder route to Chicago, a new figure fluttered into Lipsner's office requesting a job as a mail pilot. Dozens of others had applied previously and their names and records had been filed for future reference, but this was an unusual applicant, one with long curly hair, a smart summer dress, neat underpinning, and a shy smile.

"I'm Katherine Stinson," she announced with a flash of her pretty eyes. "I would like to fly the mail."

Miss Stinson, as mentioned previously, was a licensed

pilot, one of the first American girls to take up flying and compete in the hurly-burly world of exhibition and stunt flying. She and Ruth Law of Chicago were considered the darlings of the aviation set. Katherine had been taught to fly in 1912 by her brothers Eddie and Jack at the old Max Lillie Flying School on Chicago's Cicero Field. She had won the title Queen of the Air at the 1916 Sheepshead Bay Aviation Tournament when she was but twenty years old. She had toured the United States, Canada, and Japan. It is reported that she and her sister Margie eventually became U.S. Army instructors, training American and Canadian pilots, but we have never met any World War I airman who admitted he took dual-control time with either sister.

But here was America's Queen of the Air applying for an airmail pilot's job and arguing prettily that being a woman should have no bearing on the matter. Lipsner was experienced enough to know that exhibition flying over a fair ground or around a race track had little in common with guiding a load of U.S. mail through all kinds of heavy weather, and he gently, but firmly, turned her down, sending her away with, "Perhaps at some future time your application may be considered."

Miss Stinson seemed to accept the decision, showing no pique or disappointment, but she had hardly left the Post Office Building when Lipsner received a telephone call from the Postmaster General's office ordering him to place Miss Stinson on the staff of airmail pilots. Obviously, someone obeying the rules of political expediency had decided that this young lady stunt flier would be a valuable asset to the airmail service.

Several days later Miss Stinson turned up once more at Ben Lipsner's office and, after some cursory questioning, explained that she could only fly if her machine was rigged with Wright-type controls. She had never flown with the standard joystick and rudder. The Wright system combined two sticks, one on each side of the pilot's seat. One was used for the elevator, the other for the rudder and the wing-warping system.

Lipsner argued that it would be out of the question to modify a Mailplane in that manner, and again sent the young lady on her way. Within the hour his telephone rang again, and someone in the Postmaster General's office ordered him to provide Miss Stinson with a Mailplane equipped with Wright controls. There were no ifs, ands, or buts. Miss Stinson was to be provided with an aircraft she could fly.

Once these control changes had been made, Maurice Newton, flying a Standard Mailplane, agreed to escort Miss Stinson over the route from Washington to Philadelphia. She was to pilot her own particular model. The trip north was uneventful, but on the next day when the return was made, Newton gallantly permitted Miss Stinson to glide in and land first. Once she was down and taxiing up to the hangar, he made his touch down. That evening the Washington newspapers presented the experiment in the following manner:

KATHERINE STINSON BEATS
VETERAN AIR MAIL PILOT TO
WASHINGTON

It made a fairly interesting story, but that was the end of Miss Stinson's airmail flying. After all the top-level pressure, the expensive equipment changes, and the publicity, she decided that cross-country airmail flying was not her idea of a paying profession and that she could make more money performing simple aerial stunts over country-fair race tracks.

Meanwhile, plans were still being drawn up for the initial New York to Chicago flight schedules for September 5, 1918. A few days before, Lipsner had gone on to Chicago where he had a desk and an open-wire long-distance telephone set up in what is now the Federal Building. With this arrangement he hoped to keep in touch with the two pilots whenever they made a scheduled stop or had a forced landing. As it turned out, this communications system proved to be a timely inspiration.

Ben Lipsner was both hopeful and anxious the night before this historic effort was to begin. He was certain his pilots and planes were capable of making the flight. He also knew there were certain hazards over parts of the route. If a serious accident were to mar the initial attempt, it might put an end to the expansion planning. However, after a good night's sleep and some words of encouragement from Federal Judge Kenesaw Mountain Landis,* Lipsner settled down at his Chicago desk and awaited the first report from his pathfinder pilots.

The first report to come through advised that Miller and Gardner had arrived at Belmont Park and that the weather in New York was dark and threatening. By 7:08 A.M. Max Miller, having the luck of the toss, got away first and headed for the "hell stretch" over the Allegheny Mountains. He climbed to 5,000 feet, braving the leaden sky, passed over Newark, and from there encountered heavy fog. Over the next two hours he flew "blind" in more ways than one, for he had no instruments designed for such conditions.

Ed Gardner was scheduled to take their chief mechanic, Radel, with him in the Curtiss R-4, but by the time they were in their cockpits with the pouches of mail stowed away, a heavy rain came down. Radel growled at their ill luck, but Gardner fluffed it off with, "Forget it. A bad beginning can be a good ending."

Gardner started his run for a take-off, but was quickly signaled to cut his engine and turn back. Angered and frustrated, he learned he had broken a tailskid which would have given him considerable trouble had he continued on

---

* Judge Landis was the father of Major Reed Landis, who shot down nine enemy planes while flying with the U.S. Aviation Service in France. Judge Landis later became the High Commissioner of baseball.

for his first check-in. He bounced out of the cockpit, spite-fully mad, realizing Miller must be piling up a long lead. Another Curtiss stood nearby, and he ordered the ground crew to transfer the mail and spare parts to R-4 No. 39365. The field superintendent protested that the plane had never been tested. It had just been flown in.

"Is it full of gas and oil?"

"Well . . . yes, but . . ."

"Well, I'm flying to Chicago whether it's tested or not. Come on Radel, are you game?"

"You know me," the chief mechanic responded, and at 8:50 A.M., more than an hour and a half after Miller had taken off, Gardner and Radel were in the air. In their rush to get away, they had forgotten to transfer their lunch package and the fire extinguisher.

In the meantime, Miller in the lead plane was churning through a blanket of fog, anxiously clinging to his 284-de-gree compass course and trying to figure how far he had flown during his time in the air. He was supposed to make Lock Haven his first stop, but it was impossible to see any-thing in any direction. Taking a wild chance, he began to let down, foot by foot, fully expecting to see a full-sized mountain in his path at any time. When he finally broke through he discovered he was past the worst of the moun-tain range, and flying over a small river. He followed this for a few miles and then decided to circle the area and land. There was nothing anywhere that was marked as a landing field, but he carefully investigated and then landed on a half-mile-long stretch of open meadow.

He made inquiries of passersby and learned he was about a mile from Danville, Pennsylvania. Making certain of his position, he took off again, climbed up through the clouds, continued west, and about forty-five minutes later recog-nized Lock Haven and landed. Checking back over his map he saw that the river he had first noted was the upper reaches of the Susquehanna. In selecting Lock Haven for the first scheduled stop, Lipsner had picked a town that was almost completely hidden between two mountains.

Later on, Miller explained that had it not been for a spluttering engine which indicated he was running out of fuel, he would have continued on. But considering the weather, he had made a remarkable flight from New York with only a simple compass to guide him. At his first opportunity Miller called Lipsner and inquired about Gardner.

"Never mind about Eddie. Where are you?"

"I made Lock Haven, but I have a leaky radiator, and this field is no place for a beginner. Who selected this trap, anyhow?"

"Never mind. Get that radiator fixed—fast—and get out of there as quickly as possible. Call me at your next stop, and good luck."

It required about an hour to get Miller's radiator repaired, to take on fuel, and to transfer the mail. He also managed a light breakfast, something he had forgotten in his hurry to get out of New York. By 11:45 he was flying out of Lock Haven, clambering through murk, and still ruddering to keep on his new compass course of 283 degrees.

Gardner also had to bore through a terrific storm, encountering clouds and fog, as had Miller. In the slanting rain he drifted about thirty miles off his course, chiefly because of an unchecked compass, but in spite of the elements and the inability to correct for the drift, he managed to make a safe landing at Wilkes-Barre about forty-two miles northeast of Danville where Miller had first landed. He called Lipsner in Chicago.

"Where's Miller?" was his first question.

"Never mind Miller. Where are you?"

"I landed at Wilkes-Barre at 11:05 with a storm coming up. I'll take off for Lock Haven right away. Now tell me, where's Max?"

"He's all right. He landed at Lock Haven. Get going. You

might still catch him, but check your compass, or you'll never make that first control stop."

Ed Gardner did not get away from Wilkes-Barre until 12:02, or exactly seventeen minutes after Miller had taken off from Lock Haven. He had no sooner made a safe level than he ran into a violent thunderstorm and had to go down to a dangerously low altitude, just skimming the tops of the Allegheny peaks. He landed next at Bloomsburg, some fifty miles east of Lock Haven, first to find out where he was, and second to check some engine trouble.

Gardner and Radel took off again, and were next reported down at Jersey Shore, Pennsylvania, which still left them fifteen miles short of Lock Haven. Gardner called Lipsner, told him where he was and explained that they had found sand and water in their gas line. They finally staggered into Lock Haven at 2:16 P.M.

Gardner again inquired about Miller, and Lipsner had to tell him he had not been heard from since he left Lock Haven. The second lap of this crazy race was on, and Gardner roared out of the confines of Lock Haven and sped after Max. Actually, Max thought Gardner was either right behind him, or even leading him into Cleveland. A mechanic in Lock Haven had said he had heard a plane fly over at a high altitude some time before Max had landed, which intimated that Gardner might have found good weather somewhere and already was well on his way to the second check-in point—Cleveland. It never occurred to Max that the engine the man had heard was his own as he was circuiting to find the Lock Haven field.

As soon as Max had taken off he ran into a portion of the storm Gardner had encountered outside Wilkes-Barre. He hoicked for altitude, hoping to climb over the turbulence, but could not evade it since the storm clouds were higher than his Standard could climb. He managed 6,000 feet, but conditions there were no better. He not only was flying blind but was encountering very turbulent air. He stayed with his compass course for more than an hour before risking a lower level. He next noted a number of trees swishing past his wingtip and realized he was flying parallel with the side of a mountain. He ruddered, yanked the stick back, and climbed into the clouds.

At 1:50 P.M. his Hisso engine showed signs of overheating, and he knew he had to risk a landing somewhere. Again, he gingerly lost height through the murk and didn't come into the clear until his altimeter was registering about 200 feet. Quaking with dread, he first spotted a small farmhouse beside a picturesque field, and he glided in safely. When he had unfastened his belt and had started to climb down, he was met by an irate farmer who stood covering him with a shotgun. Max had heard of such situations, but hadn't believed a word of them. He tried to ignore the rustic and explain he was having engine trouble.

"You get that thing off my place, or I'll blow your head off," the farmer threatened.

"Look, mister," Max tried to explain. "This is a government mail plane, and I'm having engine trouble. Give me a couple of minutes to find what is wrong, and I'll be glad to get out of your way."

The farmer brought the shotgun up to his shoulder. "I heard all about you flying fellers. Think you can swoop down on anyone's property jest as you like. Well, you git out of here!"

There was no arguing with a fool holding a 12-gauge shotgun, so Max took off again and quickly landed elsewhere. This time he met a friendlier agriculturalist who listened and then explained that this was Jefferson, meaning Jefferson County. Max thought Mr. Friendly was referring to Jefferson, Ohio, and figured he had drifted somewhat north of his intended course. After filling his radiator from a rippling stream, he took off and decided on a revised course to the south that would take him into Cleveland. He flew in this direction until his engine showed signs of overheating again, so he landed for a third time on a suitable field and once more refilled the radiator from a nearby brook. There were no passersby to advise him where he was, and using the rule of thumb, Max thought he was near Newcomerstown, Ohio. He took off again and flew until he found a town of some size that proved to be Cambridge, Ohio, a township about one hundred miles *south* of Cleveland. He called Lipsner from there.

"Where's Eddie?" he began.

"Never mind Eddie. Where are you?" was the routine response.

"I'm down at Cambridge, Ohio. I was given the wrong direction by a farmer in a place called Jefferson in Pennsylvania."

Lipsner listened with unbelievable patience, and then explained that Gardner was still earthbound at Lock Haven and would be lucky to get away again in daylight.

Max said he would do his best to get to Cleveland by nightfall, and hung up. With that, the Aerial Mail Service superintendent sat back and awaited the next chapter of this comedy of errors.

Some temporary repairs were made on his radiator in Cambridge, and Max took off for Cleveland at 6:10. However, the repairs were not enough and he had to force-land twice more to fill up with water. It was well after dark when he reached the outskirts of Cleveland. He could not find the allotted field, and after circling for some time he landed at 8:25 in a prairie area seven miles from the city. He called up Postmaster William J. Murphy, who came out, picked up the mail pouches, and arranged for Max's overnight stay.

The next morning Max flew his plane to the Glenn Martin factory where the Hisso radiator was removed and properly repaired. Because of this further delay, he did not get away until 2:15 that afternoon. Ed Gardner also had to stay overnight in Lock Haven, and he took off at 10:45 A.M., breasting a 20-mile-an-hour wind and low-lying clouds, but flying conditions were on the whole satisfactory. At 6,000 feet he found a clear sky and he made considerable progress. He passed over Oil City and hit Franklin, Pennsylvania, well on course, and landed at Sharpsville at 12:45 to make certain of his position. He got away again in twenty minutes and soon caught his first glimpse of Lake Erie.

Approaching Cleveland, he sought the Glenn Martin field but found it difficult to locate. Had he flown directly there he might have seen Miller taking off, but he lost about thirty minutes in finding the field. He was in the air again by 3:59, less than forty-five minutes behind Miller. Lipsner in Chicago realized that his pathfinder trip could wind up as a keen but friendly competition that could do no harm to the airmail publicity. The weather was clear, though there was a strong headwind.

Miller next landed at Bryan, Ohio, a few miles from the Indiana state line, and took off again half an hour later—at 4:55—headed for Chicago. Six minutes later Gardner landed at the same field and could hardly wait to have his Curtiss refueled, but it was almost six o'clock before the necessary servicing could be completed so that Gardner and Radel could take off for the last leg.

Both aircraft were in the air on the home leg of the race to Chicago. Max made it in exactly two hours, arriving at Grant Park on the lake front where a crowd of people had been waiting behind the roped-off landing area.

This historic flight touched off a deafening cheer, and the police had difficulty keeping the crowd off the landing area. It was as though none of them had ever seen an airplane before. When postal officials moved in to take off the mail pouches, the crowd had to be pushed back. It had been arranged that Special Delivery couriers would personally deliver the mail to its various destinations that same night.

Once more the same inquiry marked Miller's clamber down from his cockpit. "Where's Eddie?"

"Right behind you . . . somewhere," Lipsner explained through pent-up emotions.

Max turned around, thinking Gardner was already on the ground, but gradually realized he was still in the air. "Am I really in first?"

"You sure are. Congratulations!"

Once he knew he had won this race, Max became apprehensive about Eddie. "When did you last hear from him?"

"From Bryan. He landed there six minutes after you left."

Max looked up at the sky. It was becoming darker and darker, and the bonfires that had been lighted to mark the field at Grant Park seemed to flame up higher and higher. A number of spectators broke through the police lines and begged Max to autograph copies of the daily newspapers. He put up with this for a few moments, and then began to fret about Gardner. He went back to Lipsner. "Listen, Cap, if Eddie realized he was that close behind me, he may have taken the short cut over the lake, trying to beat me in. He could be totally lost out on that side of the city."

"There's nothing more we can do about it. We have flares and bonfires alight."

"Listen, Cap. Let me have my ship again. I'll go up and try to find him and show him the way in."

Lipsner tried to calm Miller down. "Be reasonable, Max. You're tired out and you're not thinking straight. Why don't you get in one of the autos here and run over to the Union League Club and get some rest?"

Max argued that he'd not be able to rest until Eddie got in. "If I were lost up there, Eddie would do the same for me."

"I won't let you go," Lipsner said, but Max tried to make a dash for his Standard. Lipsner and others pinned his arms to his sides, and finally persuaded him the idea was futile. Just at that point a messenger from the nearby Columbia Yacht Club advised Lipsner that he was wanted on the club's telephone. With Miller at his heels, he raced over to take the call.

Gardner was at the other end and explained that he and Radel had been forced down by darkness in Westville, Indiana, but were both safe and were being given a wild welcome by the townspeople.

"Good! Glad to hear from you. Now get a good night's rest and leave early enough in the morning to have breakfast with us in Chicago."

Gardner and Radel arrived at Grant Park at 8:17 the next morning, and the great pathfinder effort came to its close. The first flight over a portion of the Woodrow Wilson Airway had been completed, but in the cold light of morning, it was realized that the effort had been far from satisfactory, regardless of the weather conditions through which it had been flown. Miller's actual flying time had been thirteen hours, forty-seven minutes. Gardner's figures were even less impressive.* Each plane had carried a total of around 400 pounds of mail, and, up to a few years ago, the spot on which Miller's wheels first touched down in Grant Park was marked with a battered piece of plumbing pipe. Today, within a few blocks, will be found the offices of all the major airlines.

A few notables were at the reunion breakfast held at the Union League Club. Among them were Augustus Post of the Aero Club of America; Dorr E. Felt of Beloit, Wisconsin, inventor of the Comptometer; Postmaster William Carlile of Chicago; William T. Donoghue, the Park Board

---

* For a comparison in time and distance, British Handley Page 0/400 bombers were at this time carrying out raids on targets more than 300 miles inside enemy lines. Each was loaded with 2,000 pounds of bombs, and the raids required nearly eight hours of flying. Chicago is 713 air-line miles from New York.

official who had issued the permit to use the Grant Park strip for the experiment; and Charles Dickinson, who headed a noted seed company. Dickinson had shown a lively interest in the aviation industry and later became involved in the early days of airline development.

Both pilots told their stories and, with fascinating candor and detail, related what it was like to fly the "hell stretch" over the Allegheny Mountains. This was to be the standard yarn for the next ten years, until the engine manufacturers produced a power plant which could cope with the problems of high-altitude flying through North American winters. Again, man had to provide the mechanical power to thrust his air frame through the air, no matter how far, how high, and how fast he wished to fly. Each change in the requirements demanded in turn an improvement of the power plant.

Miller and Gardner enjoyed two days of rest and renown while their planes were being checked and serviced for the return flight. It was agreed that Miller would again take off first, and instead of their racing each other they would race the clock. To make certain of this it was arranged for Gardner to rest through that day. So, on September 9, Max took off at 6:40 A.M. on a beautifully clear morning and headed for Bryan, 160 miles away. On this flight he carried only a small pouch of mail, which he intended to drop over the Bryan field instead of actually landing. He covered the distance in sixty-nine minutes. Going into a steep glide over the field, he tossed the pouch clear and saw it drop into a designated area. He zoomed and roared off for Cleveland.

Just as he was glorying in the boost of prevailing winds, a water connection to the radiator became loose and he was forced to land at Woodhill Park, about seven miles from the Glenn Martin field. This delayed him several hours, and he did not get off from Woodhill Park until 4:30 P.M. Almost three hours later he landed at Milesburg, Pennsylvania, to check his compass course for Lock Haven. He called

Lipsner in Chicago and asked permission to continue to New York, but the superintendent refused to let him take the risk and ordered him to stay where he was until the next morning. As a result, Max successfully completed his return trip at 11:22 A.M., September 10. He then proceeded to Washington to await further instructions.

All well and good, but Ben Lipsner was determined to prove that mail could be flown between New York and Chicago well within one day. He hoped Eddie Gardner would have better luck, but the next day produced a steady downpour that promised to continue for hours. Gardner was on hand, ready to go, but someone took a moody view of the situation and said it would be tempting fate to take off in such weather. Eddie took the hint and cut his engine. Lipsner moved into the picture and stuck a small package of mail into the cargo compartment.

"Are you kidding?" Gardner asked.

"No. You know the code of the airmail. It goes through, hail, rain, or shine."

Gardner still wondered if his boss was joking.

Lipsner ordered a number of policemen to clear the field for a take-off and then took Eddie aside. "Listen. I want you to land that packet of mail in New York tonight. Miller would have done it except for the bad break, that radiator. Here's your chance to ring up a new airmail record. Are you going, or not?"

Gardner still hesitated and reminded his boss that he had had no breakfast.

"If you get away now you'll be in Bryan—maybe Cleveland—in time for breakfast. Stop wasting time."

During all this Radel was carefully going over the plane, although by now the rain was pelting down in torrents. By the time the tarpaulin engine-covers had been removed and both men had climbed into their cockpits it was almost as dark as night.

The engine twirled beautifully, but Gardner still considered the ominous sky. He explained later that he was not worrying about himself, but hated taking Radel on this risky venture. Finally realizing that Lipsner was determined to get that packet of mail through, he showed his old determination and said, "Okay. We'll go and we'll sleep in New York tonight."

It was 6:25 A.M. when the Liberty-powered Curtiss took off and buried itself in the murk and fog over Lake Michigan. When next heard from, Gardner had dropped a small sheaf of mail, weighted with a monkey wrench, on the Bryan field, and had sped on for Cleveland. So intent was Gardner on making every minute count that he failed to phone Lipsner every time he landed for servicing. This left Ben suffering the agonies of an anguished taskmaster. Now and then he received vague telegraphic reports of the progress, but the suspense nevertheless built up.

That evening Lipsner's telephone rang and he took up the receiver hoping to learn that Gardner had arrived safely.

"This is the New York City News Bureau," a strange voice said.

"Good! Have my airmail boys arrived safely?"

"Well, no, sir. I'm afraid we have bad news for you."

Lipsner mopped his brow. "Well, let's have it."

"We have just received a flash that Gardner and Radel plunged 7,000 feet from the sky. Both are seriously, if not fatally, injured. They have been taken to a hospital on Long Island. The mail plane was completely demolished."

Lipsner thanked the News Bureau and then made plans to take the next train back to New York. Throughout his whole trip there was no further news from any reliable source. The newspapers carried no report of an airmail crash anywhere in the vicinity of New York. He sat it out all through the night, finally arriving at Grand Central. As he stepped off the train, he heard a familiar voice say, "Hey, Cap."

It was Eddie Gardner, standing unassisted and grinning through adhesive plaster strips that covered a cut across the bridge of his nose.

Lipsner could not utter a word. Eddie took him by the arm, picked up his baggage, and led him along the platform to the exit. Finally Ben whispered, "Where's Radel?"

In good spirits, Eddie laughed and said, "He's over there calling his home to tell them to cancel any funeral arrangements they may have made. He's all right. Just slight burns and a bruise or two."

"You're supposed to have crashed from 7,000 feet."

"I never knew our plane could make that height. Where'd you get that yarn? We fell only a few feet."

Radel approached and they guided Lipsner into a restaurant where they told their story over a luncheon.

In as few words as possible, this is what happened. Gardner got away from Lock Haven with no trouble and had no problems crossing the Alleghenies as night began to fall. By the time they had crossed New Jersey, the New York metropolitan area was a glittering fairyland with many kinds of lights everywhere. With so much commercial illumination they could not find the faint glares put out at Belmont Park. Gardner circled the city several times until his fuel began to run low.

Turning toward a safe area of Long Island, they found what looked like a clear spot below. Gardner went into a series of figure eights to lose altitude slowly and to ascertain exactly what was below. Actually, they were over Hicksville, and the open area was nothing more than a patch of low bushes, but neither Gardner nor Radel could make so definite an identification. When they dropped lower, Gardner thought they were skimming over a forest of treetops. Presuming that full-grown trees would be about thirty feet high, Eddie decided to make two more descents of about fifteen feet each and then go for a pancake landing alongside the wooded area. The idea showed sound thinking, but what they had seen was not treetops—it was the foliage of low bushes. When Eddie started his second fifteen-foot drop the mail plane bashed into solid ground, wiping off the undercarriage and skimming along on the lower longerons. There was a splintering crash and the Curtiss tilted on her nose and wound up on her back.

Neither Gardner nor Radel remembered much of what happened next. For a time the mechanic was trapped under the gas tank and lay screaming for someone to "take the engine off my back." Gardner dragged himself clear and struggled to get Radel out. By that time a small crowd had gathered. With willing hands to help, Radel was finally hauled out. He claimed his shoulder was broken, but a doctor in the crowd tried to assure him otherwise. The mechanic insisted all the way to a nearby hospital that he had "busted his shoulder."

Luckily, neither man had suffered serious injury, and both were elated they had brought the mail through from Chicago in one day—even though it had taken nine hours and eighteen minutes of actual flying time.

In this neck-or-nothing manner, Lipsner's airmail service brought out the many problems which were to be encountered in further extension of the present system. In going over Miller's and Gardner's reports again, Lipsner decided to rearrange the route into three definite sections. First, his planes would take off from Belmont Park and land at Bellefonte, Pennsylvania. Between these two points an emergency landing field was to be set up at Lehighton. Lock Haven, because of the difficult approach through the mountains, would be dispensed with. The next leg, Bellefonte to Cleveland, was to use an emergency field at Clarion, Pennsylvania. The last section was to remain as originally planned—Cleveland to Chicago with Bryan, Ohio, as the emergency stop.

But these pioneering plans could not be immediately

carried out. The flying equipment was inadequate, though Lipsner still hoped to get some of Harry Mingle's Handley Pages. He next engaged ten additional pilots and put them through cross-country training on the Washington–New York run. Among these were Dean T. Lamb, a soldier-of-fortune pilot who had been "war flying" in Mexico long before the United States had responded to the German threat; Ira O. Biffle, who later taught a youngster, Charles A. Lindbergh to fly; Trent C. Fry; Leon D. Smith; Carl B. Smith; William W. Harrison; Dan Davidson; Dunn K. Steel; C. C. Eversole; and Ed Hubbard. These men brought the total of airmail pilots to eighteen.

There was no further New York to Chicago airmail flying, at least on a scheduled basis, until May 15, 1919, some six months after the Armistice had brought a close to World War I. It was not until July 1 that year that the route went to regular operation. By then, too, the flying service was working in cooperation with the rail services. For instance, the Chicago and Cleveland gateway mail was dispatched from New York by plane. On delivery in Cleveland it was placed aboard trains which had left New York the night before and was carried on to cities in the Middle West. This saved about sixteen hours in mail delivery to that central area and about twenty-four hours to the coast. Eastbound flights over this route advanced the delivery of gateway mail out of Cleveland to New York in much the same manner. On the eastbound trips mail was flown from Chicago to overtake the mail train in Cleveland that was due to reach New York at 9:40 the following morning. Here, again, sixteen hours were saved in the delivery of mail to New York and the New England areas.

When in December 1918 the inside story of the Mitsui Company's control of the Standard Aircraft Corporation finally blasted Lipsner's hopes of obtaining Handley Pages, he made a few inquiries regarding a number of Army surplus aircraft. Unexpectedly, he was advised he could have all he wanted simply by picking them up from a storage area in Houston, Texas. There were a number of Curtiss R-4 planes there, powered with the Curtiss V2-3 engine, aircraft that originally were built as "heavy duty" two-seaters for the Mexican Border incident and modified later for bombing training. A few were converted to take Liberty engines and designated as R-4LMs. They had a wing span of 48 feet, 4¼ inches, an overall length of 28 feet, 11 inches, and a gross weight of 3,272 pounds. They were said to have a top speed of 90 mph.

Had a number of these R-4LMs been available, they might have filled the immediate bill, but only models with Curtiss engines were assembled for flight. When Lipsner took four of his best pilots—Max Miller, Eddie Gardner, Louis Gertson, and Lawton Smith—to Houston, they had no choice but to try out these ancient hulks.

The test program would have been a joke, had it not been so treacherous. Not one of the airmail pilots could get any of these gift planes off the ground. In fact, Gertson, who made the boldest attempt, wound up in the top of a small tree. That ended Lipsner's search among the Army's surplus stockpiles. However, he did obtain later a few of the Liberty-powered R-4LMs which he assigned to the New York–Chicago route.

Gertson's hair-raising, tree-nesting experience was only one of the increasing mishaps and accidents that were beginning to plague the project. Some of this was to be expected, of course, and considering the primitive equipment, Lipsner's determination to maintan a daily schedule, and the intermittent displays of pilot cantankerousness, the crash column was comparatively free of fatalities.

4

Politics and Pandemonium

Up until the end of World War I Ben Lipsner had guided his airmail operations with a fairly free hand. He had hand-picked his pilots, laid out his own routes, set up his schedules, and, considering the circumstances, had turned in a creditable performance. In fact, many people conceded he had made the basic plans for America's present-day network of domestic airlines. His several superiors in Washington had been too occupied with the war effort to take much notice of the strivings of the Aerial Mail Service. With the Armistice, preoccupation with Germany came to an end and politicians resumed their peacetime practice of catering to their constituents. For varied expediencies a great deal of pressure was brought to bear on the man who had for months been quietly running the world's first successful airmail system.

Thousands of young men were hurriedly brought home from overseas in answer to the clarion call of "Bring our boys home for Christmas." Some of these men were trained aviators with impressive records made in the sky over the Western front. A few had visions of continuing a career in the air, and of these the knowledgeable ones stormed the Washington ramparts to demand employment in the Aerial Mail Service. There were thousands who had learned airplane maintenance. There were men who felt the country they had "fought for" owed them a living, and they fully expected to obtain well-paying posts on many of the airmail fields.

History reveals that most of the airmen who had flown for any length of time against enemy opposition showed little interest in the possibilities of postwar aviation. They had had all they wanted of flying and were satisfied to be alive, to return home, to resume their college courses or go back to jobs they willingly had left in 1917. Generally speaking, the airmen and mechanics who had just completed their training or had served as instructors showed the greatest desire to continue flying or servicing airplanes. A few World War I aces were persuaded to stay in the Air Service; a few tried the barnstorming circuit but did not stay long with that shoddy business. Wiser heads among them entered more reliable professions—such as aviation insurance—and ignored the antics of the intrepid birdmen.

Ben Lipsner knew he was in trouble when the boys came home and learned that in their absence an airmail service had been established. The demands of the fence-fixing politicians soon multiplied his problems. Over the war months he had gathered a complete and reliable staff to carry out the schedules he had drawn up, but as the year 1918 flipped off the calendars, long lists of names were submitted from various Washington bureaus, all applicants for airmail jobs. Obviously, the manpower shortage was over.

Lipsner did his best to place men with suitable skills or flying experience where he could, but airman who had flown only French Nieuports, S.E.5s, and Spads in military operations were not skilled in the all-weather cross-country requirements. Mechanics who had serviced only rotary engines and machine guns were hardly suitable in the maintenance of Curtiss or American-built Hisso engines. In fact, few Air Service men in any category fitted the specialized requirements of the Aerial Mail Service (shortened later to Air Mail Service).

Gradually, to Lipsner's consternation, applicants whom he had politely turned down, appeared to have political influence and were appointed without further interviews or explanation. In most cases, these men were assigned to service the mail planes. This further endangered the lives of the pilots, who were trying to prove that the routes could be flown daily in any weather on regular schedules. Free of the easy discipline of wartime fields, the new appointees refused to accept the strict rules of this peacetime organization.

Also, for reasons known only to himself, Otto Praeger— who had been Lipsner's soundest support in the Post Office Department—had cavalierly discharged Eddie Gardner and E. Hamilton Lee for refusing to take off in a heavy fog that had cut visibility to less than 25 feet. Lipsner investigated and learned that Gardner had made one attempt to carry out his flight but had been completely lost for more than an hour and was lucky to get down in an open area five miles from the Belmont Park field. When he refused to take off again Praeger ordered his immediate dismissal.

It required time, but eventually Lipsner was able to rehire Eddie Gardner and put him back where he was needed. However, in September 1920, while flying county-fair stunts at Holbrook, Kansas, Gardner was killed. E. Hamilton Lee later became United Air Lines' senior pilot with more than 4,400,000 flying miles without an accident.

This discharge of Gardner late in November 1918, less than three weeks after the Armistice, marked the beginning of the end for Lipsner. His relations with his superiors deteriorated rapidly, and men totally unfit for the service were hired without his being consulted. Others were removed to make a place for more recent applicants. Then someone in the Post Office Department suggested that the airmail service might consider enlarging the scope of operations by flying the mails at night during the worst of the winter months. Lipsner, of course, had been considering this, but he realized that with the available equipment, night flying over the well-established Washington–New York run would present many difficulties and hazards. However, he was willing to consider opening a daily New York–Chicago flight by May 15, the anniversary of the first flight of his Army airmail service. By that date he might have more reliable aircraft, and the weather would certainly be more clement over the mountain areas.

But the bureaucrats had decided that while Lipsner could still run the Aerial Mail Service—and assume all the responsibilities—he could no longer make the major decisions. In December 1918, Praeger issued a news release stating that the Aerial Mail Service was about to purchase a fleet of special mail planes at a cost of several million dollars, and that the New York–Chicago service would be started at once. Ben had been advised of none of this. In the same release he read that a number of new appointments had been made which, from Lipsner's point of view, were men not qualified for these jobs that carried certain responsibilities. He requested a personal interview with Otto Praeger and stated that because of his continued interest in the cost of operating the service he felt he should have been consulted in the matter of spending great sums of money for specially built aircraft. Many military planes, originally designed as bombers, were available at virtually no cost; modifications required would be comparatively cheap, compared to the cost of brand-new equipment. Lipsner also objected to opening the New York–Chicago route before the coming spring.

Praeger listened politely and stated that the plans were already made, that future extensions of the routes would be carried out with the augmented Aerial Mail Service staff. Lipsner bowed to the inevitable, went home, and wrote his resignation which he planned to submit to the Postmaster General the next morning. Additional copies were passed on to the press. Whether this was wise or ethical must be decided by the reader.

Early the next day Lipsner's resignation was handled as front-page news and his service was lauded in all the important papers, but the Post Office Department went ahead with its plans. A railway man with no previous experience with aircraft was named the new Supervisor of the Aerial Mail Service. A former $1,600-a-year clerk in Lipsner's office became Chief of the Maintenance Section although he was not an engineer.

One appointment did have merit. A son of the Purchasing Agent of the Post Office Department, a former Air Service pilot, became chief of the flying section. It was his duty to test all aircraft, carry out routine flight experiments, and assume full control of all in-air activity. Whether his military experience was sufficient to enable him to take over and perform this job efficiently was long debated. Finally, two former postal clerks were named aerial mail divisional superintendents. Amid all this backing and filling fourteen of the regular pilots, who had been flying the Washington–New York run, threatened to resign or go on strike. Lipsner wisely persuaded them to stay on and keep the service in operation.

As was expected, there followed a series of accidents and embarrassing incidents to some extent due to hurried arrangements and the inexperience of the new staff. On December 16, 1918, Carl B. Smith—who had put in eleven years of flying, mostly with the U.S. Navy—was killed while piloting an American-built de Havilland-4 at Elizabeth, New Jersey. He was testing the plane that was to be used in the opening of the New York–Chicago route. Two days later, Leon D. Smith—no relation—was scheduled to fly a Curtiss R-L biplane from Belmont Park to Cleveland. He experienced engine trouble and an abortive start. Finally airborne, he was forced down at Bellefonte, the small industrial town in central Pennsylvania. Then, Michael Ebersole, taking off from Chicago, had an emergency landing only a few miles out of Chicago.

The same east-west schedule was attempted again on December 19, but the jinx was on and neither plane reached its first refueling field. A third attempt was even more embarrassing for neither plane got off the ground and the widely advertised New York–Chicago opening was postponed for ten days, or until all planes could be overhauled.

By December 27 the fanfare was revived and another attempt was made, but once more failure disrupted the effort and the Post Office Department postponed plans to open this extended route of the service. It will be seen that Lipsner was justified in his previous caution, for by May 15, 1919, only the Chicago–Cleveland leg of the New York–Chicago route was being flown with any degree of regularity. The "hell stretch" in and out of Bellefonte was too much for the pilots and the equipment available. The complete route was not in operation until July 1, 1919.

In his home in Chicago Ben Lipsner read of these vicissitudes, but parried the many questions put to him by members of the press. He explained he hoped to organize a passenger-carrying air service between New York and Chicago, an announcement which resulted in bold-type front-page display in newspapers all over the country. Almost immediately a number of financiers and reputable bankers wired him that they would supply all the capital necessary to finance his passenger-carrying service. This yet-to-be-organized Aerial Navigation Company of America also attracted the interest of a number of his former pilots, and before the end of 1919 Lipsner had formed the company with a $1,000,000 backing. He declared that his new service would begin operations between New York and Chicago by the following May 15. A charter was acquired for the Aerial Navigation Company of America. The wartime ban on civilian flying had not yet been lifted, and Lipsner could do nothing to remove the restriction. So the Aerial Navigation Company of America, the first air transport company to be issued a charter, had to close its doors. The United States was not yet ready for passenger-carrying aviation.

Still upset over the many mechanical failures experienced in the Aerial Mail Service, Lipsner decided to develop a reliable aircraft engine, for by now he realized the key to successful commercial flying rested in the efficiency and reliability of the power plants.

During the postwar years Lipsner's contribution was acknowledged by several important institutions. On one occasion the Aerial League of America presented him with the Winged America Trophy for his pioneer work as the first superintendent of the Aerial Mail Service. In 1939 he was given the First Airmail Pioneer Award by the same Aerial League of America, and on one National Airmail Day, Captain Lipsner was guest of honor at a wreath-laying in Grant Park at the spot where Max Miller's first airmail plane had landed.

In order to appreciate the post office's contribution to America's progress in commercial aviation, we must in all fairness also relate its successes, which were to prove that commercial flying could be made a profitable operation.

Once the complete New York–Chicago flight became a routine operation, 1,906 miles were flown every day and more than 30 percent of the trips were made through fog, rain, and other forms of inclement weather. It was fortunate that during these anxious months a parachute pack was made available to airmail pilots. During 1918, both the United States Air Service and civilian inventors had experimented with a neat pack 'chute that could be used to escape from disabled aircraft. More than 1,500 successful experimental "jumps" were carried out before the device was fully developed and made suitable for the limitations of the average cockpit. Prior to this, Italian, German, and Russian wartime airmen had been provided with a sort of parachute widely used during the latter months of the war. French, British, and American airmen had shown little interest in the device since they felt that anything as bulky as a parachute would be more of a hindrance than a factor of safety. They, of course, were familiar only with the kite-balloon parachute which was carried in a large leather cone and hung outside the basket. However, by 1922 the United States Air Service had adopted the Irvin seat-type 'chute and it was compulsory for all airmen whenever they were on flight operations. Presumably it was this U.S. Air Service type that was adopted by the Air Mail Service. Charles Lindbergh was to take to his 'chute three times while flying the Chicago–Minneapolis route before he became world renowned for his 1927 solo flight across the Atlantic.

Step by step, the airmail network was widened. By May 15, 1920, a new segment was established which linked Chicago, Iowa City, and Omaha. Three months later, airmail pilots were flying still another route between Chicago and St. Louis, and by December 1, 1920, a run, linking Chicago and Minneapolis, was put in operation.

By now, a letter mailed in New York and addressed to someone on the West Coast would be flown to Omaha, there transferred to a mail train, and carried to its destination. In this manner at least one day and sometimes two were saved—time important to many businessmen. Eventually, the last leg of the transcontinental route—Omaha to San Francisco—was flown with stops at North Platte, Nebraska; Cheyenne, Rawlins, and Rock Springs, Wyoming; Salt Lake City, Utah; and Elko and Reno, Nevada, by September 8, 1920.

The first westbound run of this final leg, carrying 16,000 letters, attained an average speed of 80 mph and arrived in

San Francisco without incident twenty-two hours earlier than the best possible time by train. This advantage of twenty-two hours meant delivery on the West Coast two days ahead of schedule. Unquestionably the Air Mail Service had become a communications factor to be reckoned with.

Overseas, no such success had so far been reported. In March 1919 the British R.A.F. had established an airmail service between Folkestone and Cologne, Germany, for their army of occupation, but this was hardly a scheduled operation. In August of the same year the British Air Transport and Travel Company was flying from London to Paris, but the business had to close down within three months. The KLM Royal Dutch Airlines was founded in October, and, in November 1919, the British opened an airmail route between London and Paris. The American Aeromarine West Indies Airways, an international air passenger service, flying between Key West and Havana, was inaugurated November 1, 1920. Far across the Pacific the Queensland and Northern Territory Aerial Service (QANTAS) was formed to provide airtaxi and joyriding flights in Australia. KLM did not open its thrice-weekly service between Amsterdam and London until May 17, 1920.

The post office's transcontinental service disclosed the fallacy of flying the short New York–Philadelphia–Washington run, and along with the Chicago–Minneapolis and Chicago–St. Louis routes, was dropped. By comparison, they were not true time-savers. However, politics may have played a part in this. President Harding, posing as an economy-minded executive, decided to cut down on the postwar spending spree and Congress followed suit refusing to vote appropriations for these short air hauls although they could have provided valuable training runs for many new pilots.

The crux of this matter will be found in the Harding administration's halt to further expansion of the airmail. It began to seek out means of transferring the entire service from government to private interests, arguing that the direct operation of air carriers by the post office was a departure from American tradition and out of line with a businessman's administration. Railroad men were especially outraged by the government's competition with their lines, and the Kelly Bill, introduced by Representative Clyde Kelly of Pennsylvania, was in part the Congressional voice of the railway mail clerks.

The complete transcontinental mail route was flown only in the daytime. Sacks of mail were transferred to the rail service during the night, a practice that took some of the glory from the operation. Still, someone had to prove the potential value of the system and plans were laid for a through flight from San Francisco to New York, an effort that would require both day and night flying. Although hazardous, it was seen as a prime publicity stunt for the Air Mail Service, and if successful would eliminate the train-relay linkage which was both time-consuming and expensive.

This epoch attempt was to be made at a time of year when bad weather could be expected over almost any sector of the route. The actual date was February 22, 1921, when two planes and pilots were to leave New York and two more would take off from San Francisco. There still was nothing in the way of reliable instruments. They carried no radios. There were no lighted airways, and emergency fields were few and far between. Why February was selected has never been explained, but some men have pointed out that February 22 was Washington's birthday. However, aviation was still the newspapers' pet headline subject, one that could be relied on to furnish an extra edition whenever circulation could stand another boost.

The war had been over for nearly three years, and in the wild postwar era an American Navy flying boat had completed the first air crossing of the Atlantic. A British R.A.F. pilot, John Alcock, had thrilled the world with his nonstop

flight over the same ocean. The first lighter-then-air transatlantic voyage was made by the British R-34 dirigible.
Keith Smith and his brother Ross successfully flew a Vickers "Vimy" twin-engined bomber from London to Australia.
A U.S. Army Air Corps crew, headed by Lieutenant Colonel
R. C. Hartz, made a 9,823-mile flight around the United
States, taking in thirty-one states, ninty-five cities, and
twenty-nine national forests. Before 1920 had ended another crew of Air Corps pilots had carried out an air-
mapping tour of Alaska—covering 4,345 miles—and Lieutenant John A. Macready had flown a single-engined biplane to a new altitude record of 37,800 feet.

All these efforts were comparatively successful, but over
the same period of time there were many disasters. Barnstormers, who were flying surplus Curtiss Jennys, were
cracking up faster than the newspapers could record the
fatalities. Harry Hawker and Mackenzie Grieve, two British
airmen, tried a nonstop flight of the Atlantic, covered only
about 1,100 miles and then plopped into the sea. Nothing
was heard from them for about a week, when it was reported that the Danish steamer Mary had picked them up.
Since she carried no wireless set she could not report their
rescue for several days. Her skipper finally had signaled
the good news by semaphore to a coastal station off Scotland. Needless to state, the newspapers milked that "disaster" for all it was worth.

When Assistant Postmaster General Otto Praeger sensed
the Air Mail Service was in trouble, particularly with the
new administration, he conceived the idea of making a
day-and-night demonstration of flying the mail from coast
to coast. It was later learned that he had hoped to have
this effort completed on Washington's birthday, which was
considered the tag end of winter, and in that manner
arouse new nationwide interest in the work of his flying
postmen.

But bad luck plagued the effort from the start. One of

the two pilots taking off from New York was forced down after he had been in the air for only a few minutes. The second pilot did make it as far as Chicago, but was then grounded by a sudden snowstorm. The first eastbound plane, taking off from Crissy Field in the shadow of the Golden Gate, was flown by Captain W. F. Lewis, who crashed in Nevada and was killed. The second plane, another DH-4 flown by Frank "Farr" Nutter, left San Francisco at 4:29 A.M. and climbed to about 12,000 feet to clear the Sierras. Nutter braved the bitter cold and swirling updrafts and safely reached Reno. The plane with its load of mail was taken over by Jack Eaton and J. P. Murray, and, in that relay manner, the mail from San Francisco arrived in Cheyenne at 4:57 that afternoon. By that time the shades of a winter night were falling, but Frank Yager bravely hauled the load through to North Platte, Nebraska, landing there at 7:50. By now the mail pouches had been in transit for fifteen consecutive hours.

In landing at North Platte, Yager broke a tail skid. The next courier, Jack Knight, was delayed almost three hours before he could roar off for Omaha. The de Havilland clambered into the inky blackness at 10:44 and headed across the wide waste of the Nebraska plains. There was a layer of broken cloud drifting along at 2,000 feet, making the task of contact flying the more difficult, but full details of the transcontinental effort had appeared in all the early evening papers and public-spirited citizens in Lexington, Kearney, and Central City built great bonfires to act as guides for the airmail pioneer. Knight related afterward how grateful he was for the welcome illumination.

After flying 276 miles through a bitter cold night with a few bonfires to guide him, Knight finally touched down at Omaha at 1:15 A.M. He was chilled through and almost exhausted. Adding to his discomfort, the airport manager, Bill Votaw, told him the pilot who was to meet him in Omaha had been grounded by a snowstorm in Chicago.

This appeared to put an end to the overall effort; the mail pouches would have to be shipped through to Chicago by train. All the planning, flying and braving the elements by five airmail pilots went for nought.

To Jack Knight, who had just flown this last leg to get the mail half way across the continent, it made no sense to turn it over to the railroad. "Check my tanks," he said, still slapping his gloved hands together. "I'm taking my load to Chicago."

"You're crazy, Jack!" Bill Votaw declared. "You've never flown the Omaha–Chicago leg, even in the daytime."

"What's the difference? If they'll keep a string of bonfires going, it should be easy. Remember, that snowstorm will be heading east—not west." He sipped a mug of black coffee and stamped his feet to arouse some warmth in his chilled frame. Then they went to an all-night diner near the hangar where Knight studied an automobile road map and worked out an elementary course.

In spite of Bill Votaw's protests, Jack Knight took off from Omaha shortly after 2 A.M., heading out on a compass course for Des Moines. He encountered a strong crosswind out of the north and he had to put the sluggish de Havilland into a crabwise course which made navigation most difficult. Every few minutes he studied the Rand McNally road map with the aid of a pocket flashlight, checking overside for some evidence of a distinctive road or a curve in a railroad. Using the flashlight cut down his night sight, and low clouds added to his problems. If any bonfires had been lighted they were nowhere in evidence on his course.

However, despite snow flurries, stretches of cloud, and some gathering fog, he finally spotted the dome of the Des Moines capital building. After one circuit of the city, he decided there was too much snow on the ground. He elected to go on to Iowa City which he found by following a railroad track, but as he switched over to his gravity tank, he realized there was no one in attendance at the emergency landing strip. There were no lights or even a bonfire, so he circled the field, gunning his Liberty engine to arouse some attention. As he looked below he saw that it was sleeting in Iowa City, which made him the more determined to get the mail through.

Suddenly a red glare blazed out on the ground, and Jack went down and made a fairly decent landing. An old man, obviously a Swede, who said he was the caretaker, had heard the roaring engine and had floundered out of his hut just in time to guide the de Havilland in.

"We heard the flights were off," he explained, "but when I hear your engine, I run outside and I light a fuse anyway."

"Well, thanks," Knight said. "Do you have any gas? My tank's about empty."

"Sure. We got gas."

Together, they rolled out a rusty metal drum, and with five-gallon cans transferred enough fuel to fill Knight's tanks once more. The old caretaker set off two more flares to mark a take-off run, and Jack roared away, heading for Chicago. It was still sleeting, but he climbed through the murk and found a cloudless sky that was dotted with silver stars, so he settled back, praying his engine would last the route. Gradually, a new dawn tinged the horizon, the fog layer broke, and below him glowed some lights that he sensed came up from Maywood Field in Chicago from which the airmail planes were now operating. The Liberty began to cough and miss, but Knight knew he had enough height to glide in with a dead stick, if necessary.

He aroused himself to carry out a normal landing. His watch showed it was 8:40 A.M. He was too exhausted to climb out of his cockpit. He watched his mail pouches turned over to J. O. Webster, who would fly them to Cleveland. There they were to be picked up for the final lap to New York by Ernest Allison, who put down at the Hazelhurst Field on Long Island just 33 hours and 21 minutes after Pilot Nutter had taken off from San Francisco. The actual flying time over the whole 2,629-airline-mile route was 25 hours, 16 minutes. Jack Knight's epoch-making flight, which is still one of the classics of commercial aviation, had made this record possible. More important, it had saved the airmail system from the budget-slashing ax of the politicians, for Congress next passed a list of laws regulating civil aviation and then appropriated $1,250,000 to continue and expand the airmail service. This included a complete lighted system over which the mail was to be flown. Very encouraging, but it took some four years to accomplish, and only a handful of people realized that it was Jack Knight's valiant flight that enabled the stumbling aviation industry to survive a serious crisis.

Over those next four years, while radio communications were being improved and hundreds of guidance beacons erected, the airmail pilots continued to fly "by the seats of their pants," forcing modified warplanes through what has become a legendary period of civil aviation. They flew their routes in weather that a decade later no pilot in his right mind would have attempted to face, with equipment that already was more suited for the shelter of museums or aviation exhibitions. But they unquestionably built up the techniques that were to make United States air transport the pace-setter for the rest of the world.

With the continued development of the radio system, airmail flights were carried out on the guidance and weather information supplied by the Marconi system, which certainly made commercial flying much safer. These weather reports were also of importance to many government agencies, the Department of Agriculture in particular.

Facts and figures on these various extended routes make interesting reading. During 1921 the Post Office Department spent $476,109 for new aircraft or for modifying warplanes donated by the Army. This arrangement was closed out by July 1, 1921, when the de Havilland 4B, as the American version was known, was assembled with the Liberty-12 engine as standard equipment. By now, the once unsatisfactory engine had been fitted with stub-tooth gears, drilled pistons, and an improved oil pump. It was fairly reliable, particularly when mounted in de Havillands that had been built for the U.S. Navy. These new planes were made more suitable for night operations with luminous instrument dials and running, or navigation lights comparable to those on ships at sea. Special landing lights, similar to the automobile headlight of the day but much more powerful, were built into each wing. Also, two parachute flares for emergency use were fitted into each plane and could be released by the pilot to locate a suitable landing strip, should he be forced to land at night. These flares furnished about 30,000 candle power and would burn for nearly seven minutes, giving illumination over a radius of one mile from an altitude of 1,000 feet. These de Havillands carried 500 pounds of mail with reasonable speed and reliability and were comparatively easy to fly.

The beacon lights that were to be set up over the main routes of the airmail system gave new impetus to the reliability of schedules and the safety of the pilots. A master light consisted of a 36-inch, high-intensity-arc, revolving searchlight of 500,000,000 candlepower, mounted on a 50-foot tower, located at all regular fields. On a clear night the beam could be seen from a distance of 130–150 miles. At each emergency field was erected an 18-inch rotating beacon of about 5,000,000 candlepower set on a windmill-type tower, which on clear nights was visible from 60 to 70 miles.

The main landing fields were lighted by large searchlights, similar to the 36-inch arc beacon, but were fitted with a special lens that spread the beam fan-shaped across the strip. At the time, pilots felt they were landing under near-daylight conditions with true perspective for their approach.

The first lighted airway system in the United States was set up in 1921 by the Army Air Corps over an experimental stretch between Dayton and Columbus, Ohio, a distance of about eighty miles. It was put in operation and tested for many months, after which the Army placed all its findings and recommendations at the disposal of the Post Office Department. Manufacturers of special lighting equipment also contributed valuable knowledge and offered their fullest co-operation.

Employing this Army information, the Post Office Department erected a chain of beacon lights between Chicago and Cheyenne, and several emergency fields were illuminated and suitably marked. The main terminal fields were laid out and set up for flight and postal efficiency, and the landing strips clearly lighted. As a result, over a period of four days during August 1923, a regular schedule was flown between New York and San Francisco, simply to test the system. The experiment included a night flight between Chicago and Cheyenne, just as Jack Knight had flown it two years before, but on this occasion the experiment was carried out over a lighted and well-marked air route. The result of this test was most satisfactory, and the operation of a regular schedule was decided on after another full thirty-day check was flown and the flights carefully analyzed.

To further promote the airmail system the postage was reduced to eight cents an ounce for each zone through which a letter was transported. At the time the route was divided into three zones: New York to Chicago, Chicago to Cheyenne, and Cheyenne to San Francisco. Under this system a letter sent from New York to San Francisco still required twenty-four cents in postage, but one sent to Chicago cost only eight cents. Later this complicated system was dispensed with and a new rate of ten cents per half ounce was adopted.

All through 1923 and well into 1924 the Post Office Department worked on a transcontinental service schedule that would have a loaded plane depart from an initial terminal in the morning and arrive at the far end of the route in the following afternoon. With the success of this transcontinental run a new demand arose for a special overnight service between New York and Chicago, one that would deliver a letter written during the business day to the other terminal in time for the first delivery the next morning. This overnight service was established July 1, 1925.

During the summer of 1924 the lighted airway was extended eastward from Chicago to Cleveland and westward to Rock Springs, Wyoming. A Cleveland–to–New York guidance system was soon added, as was an illuminated route from Rock Springs to Salt Lake City, but in this latter instance, only after overcoming the most difficult planning. These two stretches had to be carried over rugged mountain ranges in areas where emergency fields were few and far between, but eventually the full lighted airway was stretched from New York to Salt Lake City, a distance of 2,045 miles, at a cost of $542,000.

Success rewarded these aerial pioneers. Of course there were some losses intermingled with the heroic efforts of the pilots—who almost daily made dramatic flights so that the mail would go through. Some pilots were daredevils, throwbacks to the legendary era of the Early Birds; some were castoffs from the military service; a few were willing to accept the new doctrine of instrument flying and be guided by beacon lights and radio aids, but many still preferred to fly by the seat of their pants. The standard commercial pilot was not yet being cut from some rigid template. It takes years to develop such a man, just as it had taken centuries of a mechanical civilization to create the skipper of a transatlantic liner or the engineer of a luxury passenger train.

By 1926 the varied chapters of success, the steady increase of mail loads, and the continuing demand for more speed made it evident that a plane capable of carrying larger loads was required. Several contemporary manufacturers were pleased to submit designs and offer bids for an improved mail carrier. The Douglas Company was the first to produce a suitable model—an aggressive-looking biplane, powered with a water-cooled engine, sometimes listed as the M-2. This cargo carrier would haul twice the load carried by the de Havillands, and at greater speeds.

On a demonstration trip between Chicago and New York an M-2 carrying a 1000-pound load, covered the run at a speed of 167.5 mph—with a favorable wind. Six weeks later on January 30, 1927, the run between Chicago and Cleveland was made at 175.1 mph. The greater cruising range of the M-2 eliminated the necessity for fuel stops at Bellefonte, Bryan, and Rawlins on the westward trips, while Iowa City, North Platte, and Rock Springs were deleted from the eastward run. From all accounts, this was the last mail plane contracted for by the Post Office Department, for by December 31, 1927, the Air Mail Service was closed out and the route operations turned over to a number of private agents.

In 1922 and 1923 the Post Office Air Mail Service was awarded the Collier Trophy for the most important contributions to the development of aeronautics. The Harmon Trophy was awarded to airmail pilot Shirley Short in 1927 for his remarkable record of flying 718 hours in all kinds of weather through all four seasons without an accident. Forty percent of this record was flown at night.

The pilots of the Air Mail Service had flown more than 12,000,000 miles, and by 1927 probably were the finest group of commercial airmen in the world. Of course, they were fortunate to have a 3,000-mile-wide country to operate over with no international boundary problems and customs regulations that at the time obtained over Europe and South America. The airmail pilots were well paid and possibly set the wage scale for the rest of the world. As an instance, by 1927 pilots with 2,000 flying hours to their credit, who had averaged 800 hours per year of which 35 percent was night-flying, were paid $10,000 per annum.

The expenditure of running the Air Mail Service from its beginning in 1918 until August 31, 1927, amounted to $17,411,534. Over that same period about $5,000,000 worth of airmail postage was sold, which would indicate that there had been a loss of $12,000,000, but it might be well to concede that the experience gained, and the impetus given commercial aviation, was worth every penny of the deficit.

Regardless of the financial figures, it will be seen that the Post Office Department's Air Mail Service had operated for a sufficient length of time to demonstrate the practicality of commercial aviation, and the Post Office Department realized it was about time to invite private enterprise to enter the field and eventually take over the whole operation. By 1926 several contract-mail routes were put in operation, and the contracts for several more about to be awarded. On July 1, 1927, the lighted airway and the radio service of the Air Mail Service were formally transferred to the Department of Commerce, and arrangements made for the transfer of terminal airports to the municipalities in which they were located. The same procedure was followed where buildings such as those in Chicago, Omaha, and San Francisco, that were on property owned by the War Department, reverted to the Federal government.

By December 31, 1927, the Post Office Department's interests in the Air Mail Service were completely closed out at all fields, and the last flight flown by an Air Mail Service pilot was made on September 9, 1927. Beginning in June of that year a number of private companies took over the various routes on contract. Forty-three post office pilots were laid off and about 600 ground and office employees placed on the discard heap. How many were taken over by the private companies has been difficult to ascertain.

5

The Gifts of the Guggenheims

No story of commercial aviation in the United States would
be complete without a general history of the Daniel Guggenheim Fund. It has been responsible for the sound and
scientific development of aeronautical engineering, aircraft safety, blind flight, and the investigation of a more
reliable meteorological service. Daniel Guggenheim and his
son, Harry F. Guggenheim, have probably contributed more
to America's peacetime air supremacy than any family in
this country. Unquestionably, the Guggenheim Fund established the United States' early leadership in commercial,
and, to a great extent, military aviation.

The Guggenheim fortune was built on a series of South
American mining ventures. Long before the trite word
philanthropy became general, the Guggenheims were shar-
ing their wealth through a pattern of foundation grants
and providing financial assistance to many worthy young
men. It was natural that both father and son would early
see that a new field of such programs lay in the conquest
of the air.

During a conversation between Daniel and his son Harry

—who had flown with the United States Navy in England, France, and Italy, and who later was on active service in World War II—the idea of raising a sum of $500,000 to set up an aeronautical school at New York University was brought up. After further investigation Daniel agreed to subscribe the complete sum himself, and from that early discussion the Daniel Guggenheim School of Aeronautics developed and was quickly integrated in the N.Y.U. curriculum.

But that was only the beginning. The N.Y.U. school was intended only for the training of engineering students. As soon as classwork began it was obvious that progress in aeronautical development outside the school was practically at a standstill—and had been since the close of the war. To punctuate the importance of commercial aviation Harry Guggenheim obtained an interview with President Coolidge at the Executive Mansion, where he outlined his father's new plan. He reminded the President that commercial aviation had a great future in the United States and that both manpower and funds were available to initiate a broad program for the advancement of peacetime flying. President Coolidge, a shrewd New England businessman, saw the value of the project and called in Herbert Hoover, his Secretary of Commerce. Over a White House luncheon, these three men discussed the Guggenheim plan, continuing their talk later in the President's study.

A short time after, January 16, 1926, Daniel Guggenheim wrote a letter to Secretary Hoover in which he announced his intention to establish the Daniel Guggenheim Fund for the Promotion of Aeronautics. He outlined the Fund's intent to demonstrate the possibility of blind flight, improve the science of meteorology, raise the safety of aircraft, and broaden the study of aircraft engines. Portions of the grant were to go to the universities and technical institutions for research and practical experimentation, part to the support of libraries and aeronautical associations here and abroad. In that manner documentation of the science would be extended.

One paragraph read:

There are indications of a great change in the last few months which has given impetus to plans for developing American civil aeronautics that is bound to produce permanent results. The extent of our country, its physical characteristics and its intimate contact with Canada, Mexico and the West Indies are such as to make air service highly desirable. The success of the transcontinental air-mail service operated by the Post Office Department and the general approval which has greeted its operations indicate that the choice of a method for developing civil aeronautics in the United States is the question demanding immediate solution. There is every reason to hope that before the end of the present year [1926] civil aviation in the United States will have taken a long step forward toward a position of permanent security.

Further on in the letter he wrote:

In these circumstances I have decided to establish the Daniel Guggenheim Fund for the Promotion of Aeronautics and to place at its disposal the sum of $2,500,000. The Fund will be administered by a Board of Trustees composed of men of eminence and competence.

I shall place the sum of $500,000 immediately in the hands of the trustees to defray the expenses of their studies and any work they may decide immediately to undertake. In addition, I will hold myself in readiness to supply any additional sum, up to a total of a further $2,000,000 as and when the judgment of the trustees may indicate that the money can be wisely used to promote the aims of the Fund.

Needless to state, the generous offer was gratefully accepted.

The immediate intent of the Guggenheim Fund was to erase the effects of World War I aviation—a military spree that over more than four years had built up a frantic demand for more and more warplanes, regardless of the cost. With the end of the war, the science of aeronautics and the aviation industry were in a state of stagnation and depression. Leftover military machines were dumped on a limited market at giveaway prices, erasing all incentive to develop civil types for air commerce. In other words, World War I was followed by an era of improvisation with surplus and generally unsuited equipment, rather than a sound development of aircraft that would fill postwar requirements.

Several members of the Fund made trips abroad to learn how far European designers had progressed. With open minds, they visited most of the recognized aeronautical experts and asked many pertinent questions. In England they found that the immediate interest was in aerodynamic safety and in the problem of controlling aircraft at speeds near the stalling point. The Handley Page slotted-wing was one example of how close the British were to some success in this particular field. British scientists were also well along in the development of a tailless, or pterodactyl, type, which promised a solution to stability and control at low speeds. Harry Guggenheim was especially interested in the performance of Juan de la Cierva's autogiro, and every member of the Fund's trustees was impressed with the diligent search for aircraft safety, as it was being conducted in Great Britain.

It was noted with interest that though European operators were already carrying passengers on modified bombers which accommodated a limited number of patrons, business fell off during the winter months. This was not because of inclement weather but because there were few American tourists with the funds to use the city-to-city airlines. Thus, it was obvious that in the United States there was a ready-made patronage for passenger airlines, but in 1926 there was no such travel convenience. Americans were willing to fly and pay extra for the service, but only in Europe were there any carriers to accommodate them.

Europe was showing the way in civil aviation. But more important, the major countries were focusing their interest on the development of safety rather than on the immediate revenue from commercial flying. Safety was the fundamental problem for the Guggenheim Fund to study, and top priority was the necessity to eliminate the hazards of inclement weather and various degrees of poor visibility with a combination of new techniques, experimentation, and more precise instrumentation.

The Guggenheim Fund approached this problem, knowing that until fog and bad weather were conquered, reliable schedules for commercial aviation would be out of the question. To slow down a plane because of poor visibility meant inevitably that speed would be reduced to the possibility of a dangerous stall. Though this may not have been fully realized at the time, it was eventually discovered that flying blind accounted for the bulk of accidents and fatalities brought on by an involuntary stall.

The Fund had suitable aircraft, a full inventory of flight instruments, available test fields, and the money for such a project. All that was needed was a reliable, courageous pilot who would be willing to carry out the hazardous experiments. By great good fortune a Lieutenant James H. Doolittle was willing. He brought the sound knowledge of an engineer, daring skill of a pilot, and a personality worth a million dollars to the Fund.

Doolittle, who had graduated from Rockwell Field, San Diego, in March 1918, was denied the opportunity to go to France and fight the German Flying Circus. He was transferred, instead, to Love Field, Texas, as an instructor. He was best remembered there for his spectacular stunting and unauthorized exhibitions of wing-walking, and there was a time when he was threatened with dismissal from the Army, but soon after the Armistice he was assigned to the Border Patrol, presumably to keep an eye on Mexican bandits.

Between patrols he attempted a number of long-distance flights from A to B, usually winding up in some restricted area completely out of fuel. Once, he came down in a mountain pass eighty miles below the Mexican border. To atone for this indiscretion Doolittle collected a mule train, then loaded it down with a new engine, some spare parts, and a couple of what-the-hell mechanics. Together they repaired the plane, and Jimmy flew it home to the States. There is no record as to whether the mechanics and mules ever reported back.

In 1922 Lieutenant Doolittle successfully made a flight from Florida to California, for which he was awarded the Distinguished Flying Cross. Several other spectacular flights were completed, and then the authorities shipped him to the Air Service Engineering School at Dayton. For a year he put in some heavy study while also carrying out a program of experimental flying.

He then took a course and a sheepskin at the University of California's School of Mining—which led to two years at Massachusetts Institute of Technology. Another three months of test-piloting at Dayton fitted in somewhat as a vacation. With all this, Jimmy Doolittle qualified for a Master of Science degree and a Doctorate in the field of Aeronautical Engineering. Following that skull practice, Jimmy went back to the more giddy forms of aviation, taking part in stunt-team exhibits. In one of these, three planes were linked together and flown through a program of aerobatics.

In 1925, flying a Curtiss seaplane, Doolittle won the Schneider Trophy Race at Baltimore by roaring around a triangular course at a speed of 233 mph—and was awarded the job of demonstrating Curtiss military planes in Chile. Before the actual demonstration flights could be started, Jimmy broke both ankles in some gymnastic horseplay at an officers' club, but within two weeks, still wearing plaster casts and braces, he was flying a P-1 Hawk through its paces. Once these sales requirements were completed, he flew another Hawk from San Diego to La Paz, Bolivia, and back, crossing the 15,000-foot Andes in both directions. A week later he flew a demonstration flight from San Diego to Buenos Aires.

Lieutenant Doolittle became a featured star at all aviation expositions and air races and always could be relied on to afford a thrill. On one occasion in St. Louis, while flying a "mystery" plane, he experienced engine trouble and piled up smack in front of the grandstand. Fortunately he was able to walk away from the wreck. At the Cleveland Air Races he had to take to his parachute when the wings of the aircraft parted company with the fuselage. But after climbing out of his harness, determined not to disappoint the crowd, he demanded another airplane and carried on with his announced program of aerobatics.

This Army pilot continued this type of career until the trustees of the Guggenheim Fund asked him to head their new Full Flight Laboratory. To this assignment Jimmy brought all his skill, daring, and broad understanding of aeronautical engineering. By now he was not only a resolute pilot, but one who could apply his skills and scientific knowledge to the Fund's program of practical investigation.

In the long search for a system of blind flying, Doolittle was greatly aided by Professor William Brown of M.I.T., and by Lieutenant Benjamin Kelsey, who acted as Jimmy's check, or safety, pilot throughout the many flying tests. The Full Flight Laboratory work was carried on for nearly a year before the outside world knew what was taking place, but on September 24, 1929, the Guggenheim Fund announced:

As a result of tests successfully conducted this morning at Mitchell Field, the Daniel Guggenheim Fund for the Promotion of Aeronautics is able to report a solution of the hitherto unsolved last phase in the problem of flying through fog. Under conditions representing the densest fog, reaching from any altitude to the ground, Lieutenant James H. Doolittle, conducting the experiment, was able to take off from the airport, fly from it and return to a given spot and make a landing.

According to a more detailed announcement from the Fund, the test plane used in these experiments was a Consolidated NY.2, fitted with a completely covered cockpit. Unable to see outside, and guided entirely by his instruments, Doolittle took off from Mitchell Field, flew away, turned around, recrossed the field, turned again, and came back, landing a short distance from the starting point. In the place of the natural horizon by which the pilot usually keeps his plane at a stable and safe flying attitude, and which would be invisible in fog, the pilot used an artificial horizon built into a small instrument, which indicated the longitudinal and lateral attitude of the airplane with relation to the ground at all times.

With stability thus assured, the pilot was able to locate the landing field by means of the direction-finding radio beacon already in use at Mitchell Field. This particular beacon governed the immediate approach to the field since it transmitted a beam 15 to 20 miles in length in either direction. On the instrument board of the plane, a visual radio receiver—consisting of two vibrating reeds tuned to the radio beacon—enabled the pilot to determine the location of the beam and thus the landing field. If he turned off his course to the right, the right reed showed excessive vibration, and vice versa. By keeping the reeds equilibrated the pilot could fly directly down the path of the beam to his landing. The sensitive altimeter, which showed his exact altitude, made it possible for him to calculate his landing to within a few feet of the ground.

The demonstration eliminated the last great hazard to the reliability of airplane travel. It indicated that a principle had been developed which, when perfected for commercial use, would make the aircraft comparatively independent of weather conditions. Also, this principle is not limited to one level of travel and can take advantage of a number of approaches to the destination, as it is not confined to a congested roadway or channel.

This early form of blind flying was achieved with the aid of only three instruments, all of which were standard equipment in most aircraft. The commercial practicality of the development was thus assured from the start, but the trustees of the Fund did not harbor the illusion that this method of blind flying could be applied immediately to all commercial aviation systems, and so a program of further research for the perfection of the method was drawn up and put into operation.

Doolittle and his aides next worked on extending the radius of blind flying by making use of the standard aural type of beacon, in addition to the short-range visual beacon used in the initial demonstration. For instance, it was proposed to adjust the two beacon beams so that they would intersect a short distance from the field. At this point of intersection, the pilot would turn down the course of the visual-type beacon, assured that its vibrating reed would lead him to a safe landing—at least as far as the local terrain was concerned.

It was also hoped that the pilot could be provided with an indicator to register distance, some device which would operate on the signal strength along the radio beam. If indicating beacons could be installed at the boundaries of the airport this would give the pilot a better indication of his position when searching for his landing area. The idea of the "bent," or slanting, beam to indicate the correct path down which his final glide could be made, was already under study by the Bureau of Standards at College Park, Maryland.

In a final word from the Fund it was stated that the problems of blind flying could be completely overcome only by furnishing pilots with suitable instruments and ensuring that every pilot was trained in their use.

With the chief problems of blind flight thoroughly understood and with the first sound approaches made toward
solving them, the Fund next turned its attention to another
poser of aviation—that of aircraft safety, particularly the
behavior of planes while flying at slow speeds. The Fund
announced it would appropriate $200,000 for a Safe Aircraft
Competition which would be open to designers and manufacturers of aircraft all over the world. No such competition had ever been arranged before, but to the amazement
of the trustees of the Fund there was little or no interest
on the part of foreign manufacturers.

There may have been some justification for this. During
the lengthy discussions concerning rules and basic requirements of the entries, most potential contestants either mis-
construed the intent of the detailed tests, or felt that the
competition would attract only a collection of freak aircraft.
As in today's automobile industry, any reference to or men-
tion of safety immediately triggered opinions that no basic
aerodynamic hazards could be overcome without undue
sacrifice of the practical utilitarian features of the aircraft,
or the application of freakish devices of unreasonable com-
plexity. Actually, this Safe Aircraft Competition was to lay
the foundation for the development of high-lift devices and
sound aerodynamic methods of improving the longitudinal
and lateral stability of airplanes, not only in small, private
aircraft, but in the giant land and sea transports that were
to come.

The details of this and other Guggenheim Fund contributions to the development of aviation will be found in
Reginald M. Cleveland's *America Fledges Wings** where
space allows a comprehensive presentation of the Fund's
history.

Abroad, only the aeronautical scientists of Great Britain
appreciated that the Guggenheim Safe Aircraft Competi-

* *America Fledges Wings* by Reginald M. Cleveland, Pitman Publishing Corporation, New York, 1942.

tion could produce the desired results. They realized it was not being made to encourage the design of any specific type or class of commercial aircraft, but that its objective rested in safety features that could be adapted to any commercial plane. Major R. H. Mayo, the Fund's representative in England, visited Paris and Berlin—first to test the pulse of reaction, and second to explain the details and intent of the competition.

The French showed little understanding of the plan. The Germans, though viewing the contest with professional interest, felt that under the circumstances their manufacturers would not have the money required to design and build any possible entries. Actually, the Germans were more interested in further development of their established airlines and in designing new types of aircraft than in expensive research directed toward aerodynamic safety.

The planning and discussions were taken up again in New York, and the opening date for entries was set for September 1, 1927. Four British firms were to be represented by standard fixed-wing machines, while a fifth planned to enter an autogiro. Unfortunately, by the time the competition opened, only the Handley Page slotted-wing entry appeared. The autogiro could not be modified in time to take part. There were no German or French entries, but Italy was represented by the Societe Italiana Ernesta Breda concern.

American manufacturers entered twenty-seven machines, but only fifteen of these appeared at Mitchell Field to take part. By then it was realized that the time between the opening date for the entries and the closing date—September 1, 1929—allowing time for designing, building and pretesting, was too long a time to maintain fervent interest. Also, several manufacturers had the impression that the first five planes which satisfied the safety requirements would be awarded the first five prizes—in the order of their presentation for examination and test. Another mistake was in deferring the tests until the early winter months, instead of running them in the more favorable summer season.

However, the full program of tests was carried out, with each entry given every chance to show its capabilities. The maximum speed requirement—110 miles per hour—proved to be something of a stumbling block to seven of the entries tested, although speed was not a major part of the safety conditions. As the competition proceeded, only the Curtiss Tanager, Handley Page, Fleet, and Command-Aire showed any prospect of completing the competition. Actually, only the Tanager and Command-Aire passed all the qualifying tests. The Handley Page failed to provide adequate accommodations for a pilot and an observer, but because of its excellent aerodynamic features and the probability that it would meet the safety-flight requirements, it was permitted to remain in the contest.

Both the Tanager and the Handley Page maintained level and controlled flight at speeds below 35 mph, but the Command-Aire failed this test by more than 11 mph.

In the end the Curtiss Tanager was proclaimed the winner, although the margin over the British entry was very slim; the Handley Page slots, though automatic and effective, were not considered as reliable as the manually operated flaps on the Curtiss. In other features there was little difference, but in the end everyone agreed that the major prize of $100,000 had gone to the better airplane. Each of the first five competitors to satisfy all of the safety requirements was to receive a token prize of $10,000.

The Safe Aircraft Competition made a great contribution to the development of commercial aircraft, even though the immediate results could not be predicted. The day of universal flying had not yet arrived—and certainly the competition had not produced the foolproof plane—but it did arouse promise of an aircraft that a pilot could fly with satisfaction, security, efficiency, and, above all, some degree of safety. Within a few years the Ryan Company had produced its WY-51 (Dragon Fly), a liaison plane that had an incredibly low landing speed. Military planes built by Stinson did not stall above 29 mph. Ercoup was turning out spin-proof ships with a tricycle landing gear. It must be remembered it was safety aircraft of this type on which student military airmen were first taught to fly, and many early transports which embodied the high-lift devices and safety-design factors of the Fund competition were carrying passengers in comparative luxury from coast to coast.

The Guggenheim Fund continued its excellent work by financing good-will tours—several of which featured Floyd Bennett, Admiral Richard E. Byrd, and Charles A. Lindbergh—all of which contributed to the growing interest in commercial aviation and the country's air-mindedness. Through these appearances and displays, the American public was able to view modern aircraft, and, absorbing the well-timed newspaper publicity, come to understand exactly what a commercial airplane was capable of. But, unfortunately, in the period following Charles Lindbergh's epic transatlantic flight there was still no commercial airline in the United States offering true passenger convenience and scheduling.

The airmail service, while still in the pioneering stage, had accumulated considerable ground and in-air experience, and there was no question concerning the future of basic organization. The main drawback was in the development of suitable commercial equipment. The Guggenheim Fund, responsible for aroused interest in flying, soon realized it had created a demand for passenger transportation, which could not be met with the available equipment. The airmail services had concentrated on single-engined cargo planes which were unsuitable for carrying passengers, whereas in Europe—where government subsidies had had an important part—concentration had been placed on passenger-carrying services, with multi-engined aircraft having been brought to a high standard of efficiency. To repeat this in the United States meant that airline operators would have to risk large sums of money for a project that was highly speculative.

The Guggenheims, father and son, decided that they were saddled with a certain amount of responsibility in this situation, and Daniel's practical mind saw clearly that passenger-carrying would soon become the important factor in commercial aviation. He called a meeting of airmail contractors and sent return railroad tickets to assure their appearance.

Paradoxically, the men who had been eking out a precarious living from the airmail contracts were, almost to a man, against Guggenheim's suggestion that he finance the establishing of an experimental passenger-carrying airline. Their argument was that because mail-carrying under subsidy was not too profitable, carrying passengers without government support would lead to bankruptcy. They pointed out also that any accident involving air passengers would reflect on the airmail routes and cut down the general use of the postal runs, mileage, and cargo loads.

Fortunately, there were two operators with a modicum of optimism and imagination—Harris M. Hanshue and Walter T. Varney. Hanshue was a former racing driver and automobile dealer who had become involved with a mail-carrying company on the West Coast. Varney was a war pilot who had gambled on operating an airmail line, running from Elko, Nevada, through Boise, Idaho, and on to Pasco, Washington. Both men jumped at the opportunity to obtain equipment loans from the Guggenheim Fund in order to break into the business of carrying passengers.

The two Guggenheims dismissed their guests and talked the matter over further. They remembered that such equipment loans had been used to establish American railroads and street railways. Why not apply the same financing to commercial aviation? The trustees of the Fund were called in to discuss this new project and decide how much money should be risked on it. The trustees were fairly responsive to the plan, and it was agreed that a certain sum would be advanced to one or several operating companies "for the purchase of the most modern, multi-engined planes of maximum safety and comfort so that an actual demonstration of performance and safety can be presented as an incentive for further development of passenger airlines in the United States."

It was recognized that such aircraft were expensive to buy and operate, and that it was because of lack of financial support that this phase of commercial aviation had been so retarded. However, any loan granted was to depend on compliance with definite requirements concerning the aircraft to be bought. There was no carte blanche to purchase any aircraft the operators might consider for their particular requirements. The Fund's equipment loan was to be offered on a broader base, one designed for the ultimate benefit of the passengers rather than the immediate benefit of the operator. The chief stipulation was that the planes were to be multi-engined, capable of continuing flight should one engine become disabled. Here was a safety requirement that so far had not been imposed on any of the European lines.

The advantages of multi-engined planes had been argued pro and con for a number of years, and the requirement for continued flight with less than full-engine power had never been clearly defined or practiced. In fact, European airliners, powered with three engines, were usually burdened with maximum loads that still permitted a take-off, and in more instances than not the loss of one engine in a three-engined transport set up a forced landing. In fact, multi-engined design, considering the reliability of the power plants of the era, was not an assurance of ability to maintain altitude if one of the engines cut out. There were many experts who argued that the multi-engined plane might provide a greater risk, for if one engine failed, it might set up a problem of instability. The Fund trustees, however, insisted on a multi-engined aircraft that could maintain altitude with a full load in spite of the loss of one engine.

It was also stipulated that the routes over which this new equipment would be flown were to be approved for passenger carrying by the then Aeronautical Division of the Department of Commerce, and that the routes selected be equipped with up-to-date communications and a reliable meteorological service. After a further survey of the existing mail routes by the Fund and the Department of Commerce, Western Air Express was selected on October 4, 1927, as the first model airline—which, by that time, had been flying mail and a few passengers over the Los Angeles –San Francisco route.

A formal announcement by Harris M. Hanshue, then President and General Manager of Western Air Express, read in part:

Establishment of a model passenger airline between Los Angeles and San Francisco as an actual demonstration of performance and safety has just been made possible. Planes purchased with money obtained under an equipment-loan plan will be the most modern, multi-engined design for maximum safety and comfort. They will have a cruising speed of about 120 miles per hour with a capacity cargo of nearly two tons.

The air-line distance between Los Angeles and San Francisco is 365 miles and the time necessary for flight over this route will be approximately three hours. Planes will leave either terminal at 10:30 o'clock in the morning and will arrive at the other terminal at 1:30 o'clock in the afternoon. Airports in both cities are situated within thirty minutes of the business sections so that office-to-office movements may be completed within four hours as compared to 13½ hours now required by railroad.

Western Air Express will provide the latest conveniences for its passengers. Lunch will be served in the air, and magazines, newspapers, radio entertainment, and market reports will be available.

After much consideration, it was decided that the Fokker F-10 three-engined transport, powered by Pratt & Whitney 400-hp Wasp engines, would be selected for the new venture. This airplane was designed by Anthony Fokker, Dutch engineer and manufacturer who had provided several types of fighter aircraft for the German Air Force in World War I. He now was top man of the Atlantic Aircraft Corporation, an American firm. The F-10 offered comfortable accommodation for ten passengers, and Fokker further guaranteed that safe flight could be maintained with any one of the three engines inoperative.

Three new Fokkers cost $50,000 each, and it was agreed that Western Air Express should purchase them with $150,000 loaned by the Guggenheim Fund, with all rights in them assigned to the Fund. Western Air Express further agreed to deposit securities as a safeguard to the Fund against damage to the aircraft. The loan was to be repaid over a period of two years, together with an interest rate of 5 percent. On completion of repayment, the three transports were to become the property of the airline. It may be of interest to note that the loan and full interest were repaid in the specified time.

The passenger service went into operation in May 1928, and was well patronized. Development of the line also initiated a new model weather service, and encouraged by the success of the Los Angeles–San Francisco run, other passenger air services were established, until the present network became the model for the rest of the world. Further details on the original organization and early development of Western Air Express will be presented in a later chapter.

6

Private Operations

How much the changes in government administration
played in the development of and the phasing out of the
Air Mail Service will always be debated. The Army's first
efforts at carrying the mail began in Woodrow Wilson's
second term, his World War I years. The service was taken
over by the Post Office Department in August 1918 and was
continued through the shortened administration of Warren
G. Harding and the administrations of Calvin Coolidge, who
remained in the White House until March 3, 1929. A new
Postmaster General, Harry S. New, acting under the authori-
zation of the Kelly Bill of 1925, began a gradual closing
down of the government Air Mail Service with the idea of
turning the complete operation over to private contractors.
He placed explanatory notices in the major newspapers
and called for bids on eight sections of airmail routes.
Knowing full well that any would-be operator would need
more than a few airplanes and a corps of pilots, he decided
the first contracts would be let only for short feeder lines.
Not until the contractors had proved their capabilities
would any important segments of the transcontinental run
be turned over to them. In other words, the Post Office

Department would deal only with responsible operators. No one-plane barnstormers need apply.

This was not exactly a new idea. The U.S. government had begun considering the prospects of commercial aviation as soon as World War I ended. The response introduced a man who was to became a tremendous factor in American aviation industry—William E. Boeing of Seattle, Washington. William Boeing, who was fairly well off through timely purchases of Northwest timberlands, became mildly interested in flying after watching Terah Maroney fly a Curtiss hydroplane—a biplane on a single float—on the Fourth of July, 1914. To celebrate the day, Bill Boeing and Conrad Westervelt, a former U.S. Navy pilot, decided to take a flight with Maroney. After beholding Puget Sound from the height of a few hundred feet, Boeing became intrigued with the financial rewards in the manufacture of airplanes. From that day on, timber and timberlands took second place in his business interest.

He bought a seaplane from Glenn Martin, who had a small factory in San Diego, and soon completed the requirements for a pilot's license. Boeing realized the European war might spread and engulf the United States, which would create a demand for military machines by the Army and Navy. He decided to open a shop and go into the business.

By 1916 he had taken on Westervelt as a partner, and together they designed a floatplane which they advertised as the B&W biplane. For a time there was some mild interest in this model, and Boeing hired a force of twenty-one men to build a number of these "military" aircraft, many of which were offered to the United States Navy as trainers. While naval officialdom was making up its mind, the Boeing team produced still another floatplane, powered with a Hall-Scott engine. This was listed as the Model C and was considered a much advanced contribution to naval aviation. Several were turned over to government test pilots for their appraisal, but Model C did not fulfill the required specifications or performance demanded by either of the military services. Before these requirements could be complied with the Armistice stirred up a wave of canceled contracts and Bill Boeing had to seek other outlets for his flying machines.

The era of peace triggered the idea for an exposition in British Columbia. A Vancouver business man, E. S. Knowlton, asked his postmaster, R. G. MacPherson, if a sack of mail might be flown from Canada to the United States as one feature of the planned exposition. MacPherson was interested and made a very flowery message that closed with, "When we mount upon the wings of eagles no line of demarcation then shows between Canada and the United States. May the first airplane mail be the harbinger of thousands more to follow."

Knowlton asked Bill Boeing if one of his machines could fly a bag of mail from Vancouver to Seattle. The American manufacturer assured him such a flight would be easy, and he selected Eddie Hubbard, one of his pilots, to fly one of their Model C floatplanes. Bill went along to keep a tally of the operation.

The flight up to Vancouver almost ended in tragedy, for shortly after leaving Seattle they ran into a black cloud area that became a snowstorm. They flew blind for half an hour, hoping they were skirting the eastern shore of Puget Sound. Finally there was a break in the murk and Boeing recognized the town of Anacortes below. They thankfully went down and landed, remained in town overnight, and when the weather improved the next day flew on to the Royal Vancouver Yacht Club basin where final arrangements for the formal opening of an international mail run were made. Carrying a small packet of sixty letters destined for American recipients, they took off for the 125-mile trip back. This was too much for the fuel capacity of the Model C, and they had to land at Edmonds just north of Seattle to take on another tankful of gasoline.

Because of this delay it required three hours to complete the first international airmail run, but March 3, 1919, has been credited with being the date of the first such flight.

Eddie Hubbard was so intrigued with the idea that he later obtained a Boeing B-1 flying boat, continuing the Seattle-Victoria run until 1927, and no little prestige devolved on the Boeing Company as the result of this early airmail project.

During the years 1920–25 several small operators were awarded contracts for short-haul mail runs, several for making last-minute ship-to-shore connections, using flying boats or floatplanes. Then the aforementioned Kelly Bill encouraged others to make bids for a number of routes during late September 1925, and by the beginning of 1926 contracts for the takeover of twelve airmail routes had been awarded. These, with starting dates, were listed as follows:

New York to *Boston*—Colonial Air Lines, June 18, 1926.

Chicago to *St. Louis*—Robertson Aircraft Corporation, April 15, 1926.

Chicago–Dallas–Fort Worth—National Air Transport, May 12, 1926.

Los Angeles to *Salt Lake City*—Western Air Express, April 17, 1926.

Elko, Nevada, to *Pasco*, Washington—Varney Speed Lines, April 6, 1926.

Detroit to *Cleveland*—Ford Air Transport, February 15, 1926.

Los Angeles to *Seattle*—Pacific Air Transport, September 15, 1926.

Chicago to *Twin Cities*—Charles Dickinson, June 7, 1926.

Atlanta to *Jacksonville*—Florida Airways Corporation, September 1, 1926.

Pueblo, Colorado, to *Cheyenne*—Western Air Express, December 20, 1926.

Cleveland to *Pittsburgh*—Clifford Ball, Inc., April 21, 1927.

Clifford Ball, awarded the Cleveland–Pittsburgh route, was one of the more interesting characters of those pioneering days. He had begun his career as a barnstormer, flying a Waco biplane out of a cow pasture known later as Bettis Field, in Pittsburgh. The 127-mile route was soon in operation and Ball dubbed it the "Path of the Eagle." Its first paying passenger, who willingly rode on top of the mail sacks, was a vaudeville performer named Will Rogers. Ball's actual base was the McKeesport Flying Field near Pittsburgh and his scheduled flights began April 21, 1927. Over his first year his OX-5-powered Wacos flew nearly 60,000 miles and carried 19,600 pounds of mail at a revenue of $59,000.

By 1928 the Wacos were replaced by a 5-place Ryan Brougham, a high-wing monoplane powered with the new Wright Whirlwind engine. The airliner was patterned after Lindbergh's *Spirit of St. Louis*, and passengers who risked the hop over the mountains between Pittsburgh and Cleveland were thrilled to learn they were flying in a plane "just like Lindy's." The fare was $20 each way.

By the end of that year three Fairchilds and a Travel Air were added to the equipment, and during 1928 Ball's line flew 725 passengers, 3,600 pounds of express, and 54,852 pounds of mail. The firm employed sixteen men, including four pilots. By 1930 the Clifford Ball line was taken over by Pittsburgh Aviation Industries Corporation and listed as Pennsylvania Airlines.

The Colonial Air Lines had the honor of receiving the first airmail contract, but it was the Ford Air Transport, owned by Henry Ford, that actually carried the first domestic mail under contract. As far back as 1923 Ford had been interested in the activities of William B. Stout, inventor and head of the Stout Engineering Laboratories which had worked with many of the Detroit automobile companies. Stout had taken a page from the book of Hugo Junkers, the German engineer. Junkers had developed an all-metal bomber for the Kaiser's Air Force and a monoplane wing that was braced internally—a factor that was to bring about the end of the biplane with its struts and external bracing. The Detroit Flivver manufacturer was so interested in the Stout experiments that he and his son each invested $1,000 in the firm, and a year or so later when Stout's first all-metal aircraft proved to be a success, they bought the entire factory.

The first Stout monoplane, popularly known as the "Flying Washboard" because of the corrugated sheet used in the wings and fuselage, was powered with a Liberty-12 400-hp engine and had accommodations for eight passengers and two hundred pounds of freight. When it was first used on the 140-mile Detroit–Grand Rapids run it covered the distance in about two hours. Passengers paid a fare of $18 one way, or $35 for a round trip. When the Wright Whirlwind radial engine had taken the premier position in the aircraft engine field because of the publicity inspired by Lindbergh's transatlantic flight, the Stout plane was enlarged to take three of these engines, and, as the Ford Tri-Motor, assumed an outstanding position in civil aviation. Some aviation writers described the plane as a Giant Air Pullman, for besides a cavernous cargo area it had wicker seats, a carpet down the aisle, and a form of air conditioning provided by windows which could be slid open sideways. (Shades of pressurized cabins!) The Tin Goose was the pioneering work horse until it was superseded by more efficient low-wing, twin-engined transports of the early 1930s —the Boeing 247 in particular. However, the Tri-Motor, or Tin Goose as it became known, was still being flown over Alaskan air routes as late as 1951.

The Ford Air Transport organization was not originally set up to bid for a commercial service, but was started as a private airline for the use of the Ford Company's many executives. However, from the beginning it had operated on a regular schedule between key cities of the nationwide organization. Thus, when the Postmaster General invited bids, the Ford Company had a service completely set up and ready to go, with much experience and certainly with sound financial backing. But after the two Detroit–Cleveland and Detroit–Chicago contracts were signed, the Ford organization took its time and did not start carrying the mail until February 15, 1926 when the first Detroit–Cleveland mail run was inaugurated.

Generally speaking, the other operators mentioned did not begin carrying mail until Ford Transport had been working for about three months. Most were small companies, precariously financed and using equipment that at best promised only a wild adventure. Most of these operators had made their bids with doubtful aircraft, a few ex-barnstormers, and a slatternly air base. Few had had any experience in carrying out scheduled runs or discipline of day-by-day operations. There was very little passenger carrying, except by hit-and-miss charter flights. There was no orderly ground organization or efficient maintenance. Few of the pilots had flown at night, and by the opening of the Kelly Bill era, there were few lighted airways to guide the airmen to their destinations.

Still, the post office had to rid itself of this aviation service now that it was established and in operation. They could no more continue and expand the facilities than they could lay down their own tracks and run a mail-carrying railroad. But by the spring of 1926 the companies awarded mail contracts were facing their moment of truth and wondering how they could fill the post office requirements.

For instance, consider Charles Dickinson, who had won the Chicago–Twin Cities (Minneapolis–St. Paul) route. When his contract came through he had five planes of assorted vintage with which to carry out his commitment. He sent his first mail load off on June 7, 1926, in extremely bad weather. His pilot, believe it or not, was named Elmer Partridge. It will be recalled that it was Dickinson who had argued against Eddie Gardner's taking off in a heavy rainstorm on the return trip of the New York–Chicago survey flight. But this was a different situation and

Partridge took off from Chicago. Just south of Minneapolis
something went wrong—the storm proved to be too much.
Partridge lost control of his craft and apparently spun in.
The plane was completely demolished and when a rescue
party reached the scene, Elmer Partridge was dead.

Within four months Dickinson had lost three more
planes, and all but one of his pilots decided to quit. Dickinson gave his terminal notice and withdrew from carrying
the mail.

The Twin Cities route was taken over by a company calling itself Northwest Airways, Inc. Among the stockholders
were Bill Stout and David L. Behncke, the latter of whom
was to become head of the Airline Pilots Association. Today,
the company, known as Northwest Orient Airlines, also
claims to be the second oldest carrier in the United States.
It made its start with the Chicago–Twin Cities route on
October 1, 1926, and continued this straight mail-carrying
operation until July 1927. Then it inaugurated a passenger-
carrying service which booked 106 passengers in the next
three months before suspending for the winter. The next
season Northwest began its first expansion, reaching westward through the Dakotas, Montana, and Washington. By
the 1940s its planes were flying to the East Coast cities
and westward across the Pacific—but more on this remarkable airline later.

Another example of the rags-to-riches history marking
these early mail-carrying days will be found in the record
of Harold F. Pitcairn, who, from a small shop set up on an
airfield outside Philadelphia, built a number of aircraft for
use in country-fair shows. In a half-hearted gesture, he put
in a bid to carry mail over a 595-mile route linking Atlanta
and Miami for $3 a pound, and to his surprise received a
signed and sealed contract to do just that. Prior to this,
Pitcairn admittedly had never picked up a U.S. Mail sack,
nor had any idea what such a container looked like.

In this contractual comedy of errors, Pitcairn—without

knowing it—found the Atlanta–Miami run was tied in with the New York–Atlanta hop. This additional mileage doubled the potential of his intitial contract. There was nothing to do but put his factory, known so far as Pitcairn Aviation, on a three-shift program and prepare to carry the mail with a handful of out-of-work war pilots. Amid all this confusion Pitcairn Aviation was changed to Eastern Air Lines.

All well and good. The shop work was concentrated on a stubby-looking biplane which Pitcairn called the Mailwing. This craft was powered with a Wright Whirlwind radial and easily passed the post office requirements. All that was needed now was the completion of a string of airway beacons, covering the whole New York–Miami route. To while away this delay, Pitcairn's pilots gave flying instructions to airfield gawkers, practiced their old wartime combat antics and took up sightseeing passengers who were delighted to make themselves comfortable in the mail-sack compartment.

Finally, in April 1928 Pitcairn's Eastern Air Lines began mail carrying. Over the first eight months, the Mailwings flew 338,532 revenue miles, met 93 percent of their schedules, and carried 111,428 pounds of mail. On July 10, 1929, less than four months before the stock market crash, Pitcairn sold his airline to North American Aviation, Inc. for $2,500,000, switching his interest from mail carrying to the development of the autogiro.

It will, by now, be appreciated that these small, pioneer airline operators were not particularly interested in carrying passengers since there seemed to be little demand for such service. First of all, the planes available lacked reliable engines. They were not capable of heavy pay loads, nor could they offer the convenience and comfort to which the traveling public was accustomed. There always was a hazard quotient, and to the man on the street, commercial aviation appeared a risky enterprise, carried out by fliers who were often advertised as daredevil war aces or refugees from the barnstorming clan who could always provide the newspapers with a new example of gory demise.

But there were some men connected with more stable means of transportation—railroad and motor buses running over statewide routes or affording commutation facilities for city dwellers—who saw that the airplane would one day take an important role in the passenger-carrying business and perhaps attract a certain percentage of their loads. Little did they know that within a few decades the transport airplane would put many of the passenger-carrying railroads out of business. But in the years 1926–34 there was a definite gamble in commercial aviation. Only a few of the most daring and foresighted would risk their money.

The early development of what became United Air Lines is a particular example of how the courage and drive of one man could lead to a billion-dollar enterprise. In his interesting book,* Frank J. Taylor gives a complete, flight-by-flight account of the development of United Air Lines and the amazing career of Vern C. Gorst of North Bend, Oregon, who early in 1915 was striving to organize a network of busline routes throughout Oregon. Vern Gorst became interested in flying in much the same manner as Bill Boeing, —and, like him, took lessons from Glenn Martin and bought a pusher biplane from Martin's Santa Ana, California, factory. Following the Boeing script, the Martin floatplane was cracked up and Vern was painfully injured. During his convalescence he read everything he could get on the subject of aviation, while at the same time continuing to direct the management of six jitney-bus lines he was operating in Oregon and California. In these alone were enough problems to keep several men busy, but between various crises, Vern realized the airplane was here to stay and that there

* *High Horizons*, by Frank J. Taylor, published by McGraw-Hill, 1955, 1958, 1962.

was a good possibility it one day would find its way into passenger transportation.

At a meeting of his partners in which the usual problems of motor bus transportation were discussed, Gorst broke in with an unusual observation—travel by air. "What I'm thinking of," he explained, "is the possibility of airplanes taking over our passenger business. They're already flying some of the mail."

It was just another of Vern Gorst's wild ideas, interesting and all that, but there were more timely matters to be considered. Not until 1925, when Vern learned the post office was calling for bids by private operators to fly feeder lines over the airmail system, was the subject introduced again. One of these feeder lines was to link Los Angeles with Seattle, a route that cut through their present motor-bus network. Gorst proposed that the operators pool their money and bid for the contract. Surprisingly, the idea was taken up immediately and a sum of $1,100 raised for Gorst to make a survey of the route.

Vern went to San Francisco. There he hired R. B. "Pat" Patterson, who owned a 90-hp Swallow, to fly him out of Crissy Field to survey a typical route up as far as Vancouver, British Columbia, and back again over an alternate course. The time of the year was November-December, but in spite of high winds, snowstorms, and tricky mountain passes, Patterson and Gorst flew over and selected a series of emergency areas and fair-ground strips, landing with no previous knowledge of the terrain. The whole trip was made without accident or major repairs at a cost of $43 for gasoline and $5.25 for oil. On the basis of this sketchy survey, Gorst announced on his return that the mail could be flown from the Mexican to the Canadian borders with no trouble. To make his point he bedeviled his busline operators to pledge $14,000 for stock in a $500,000 Pacific Air Transport Company he planned to organize.

Fourteen thousand dollars turned out to be a mere drop

in the bucket, so Gorst went all over Oregon and California, punching doorbells to raise more, and in this manner scratched together about $175,000—which included $40,000 of his own money raised by selling all but one of his bus lines. He also persuaded Ralph Virden, a stunt pilot, to sign on—plane and all—to become a member of the Pacific Air Transport Company. He hired ten pilots from a group of about two hundred barnstormers who were anxious to take jobs and eat regularly. Most of them had to take part of their wages in stock.

When the time came for submitting a bid for the Los Angeles–Seattle route, the Gorst combine suddenly learned it faced opposition from a group of California financiers headed by Harris M. Hanshue. Previously, Hanshue and two other gentlemen—Harry Chandler, a publisher, and William M. Garland, a real estate dealer—had resented the fact that the first proposed transcontinental route would link New York and San Francisco, ignoring Los Angeles completely. With their civic pride aroused, these three men had no trouble raising $250,000 to put their fair city on the aviation map. With that money they organized Western Air Express, the operation that was to be selected by the Guggenheim Fund to become the industry's model passenger airline. But at first Western Air Express proposed to bid on all mail routes that were to terminate in Southern California.

Amid all this financing, still another group appeared to get into the airmail activity. Allan Bonnalie, an aviation enthusiast who had been watching the moves made by Gorst and Hanshue, quietly interested a group of Southern Pacific executives in his proposal. Bonnalie pointed out that it would be wise for the railroad to arrange a working association with the growing aviation industry: first, to improve its own communications network; and second, to get a head start on any competition in the same field. The Southern Pacific group intended to bid on the Los Angeles–

Seattle feeder run, but when the overall proposal was placed before William Sproul, President of Southern Pacific, he canceled it at once, saying he doubted the airplane would ever become an important feature in commercial transportation.

Four decades later airliners had eliminated Southern Pacific's crack passenger train service, and seemingly put an end to that form of luxury travel.

Sproul thus banished the Southern Pacific threat, and Hanshue, after considering the topographical problems of the West Coast route—particularly the forbidding Siskipu Range—decided to tie in with Gorst's Pacific Air Transport Company. In that discussion Hanshue suggested they play safe and bid only on the less hazardous section south of the mountains. Gorst made the most of Hanshue's timidity and boldly put in a bid to fly the complete route—Los Angeles–to–Seattle.

The fiscal experts of the Post Office Department looked over the limited finances of PAT and suggested that Gorst raise its resources to at least half a million dollars. Vern had no idea where this money would come from, but he agreed to try to raise that much as quickly as possible. With that, Postmaster General Harry S. New awarded the contract to Gorst, who promptly turned it over to the Pacific Air Transport Company in return for 250 shares of its Class B common stock. Since there were only 500 shares of this voting stock Gorst found himself in full control of the company.

So far, so good. Pacific Air Transport was in business, and all Gorst had to do was to set up an airway, engage pilots, and find a few airplanes that could negotiate the hops. First, he persuaded a number of towns to lay out community airfields. With a truckload of discarded automobile headlights, he had a Goldbergian chain of beacons rigged up—some were set on the highest buildings, some rigged on beanpoles, and some were bolted to windmills or to the peaks of slatternly barns. He had the officials of the Standard Oil Company paint the names of their towns on the roofs of the company buildings so the PAT fliers would know exactly where they were.

His pilots, selected from a group of daring and in most instances wild-flying barnstormers, proved to be most resourceful and reliable.

Gorst next hunted for airplanes. On his first sally he picked up two Travel Air planes—a Swallow and a Waco—and three spare engines, for the cost of getting them out of the clutches of sheriffs or other lien-holders. But the workhorse-to-be of his fleet was a new Ryan monoplane, powered with the Wright Whirlwind engine. This aircraft had been developed by Claude Ryan of San Diego and when the first experimental model, M-1, was shown to Gorst, he was so impressed that he contracted for the first ten to come off the production line. These planes cost $3,500 apiece. The new Whirlwind added another $5,000 to the total cost.

As an aside, the Ryan concern began its operations in 1925 as a fixed-base depot to modify war-surplus aircraft, and under its original name, Ryan Airlines, Inc., began flying passengers on a regular schedule between Los Angeles and San Diego. As such, it must be credited with being the first year-round scheduled passenger service in the United States.

Ryan's first aircraft was a conversion of a World War I Standard biplane which was so extensively rebuilt and repowered—it had a 150-hp Hispano-Suiza engine, plus a four-place cabin set forward of the pilot's cockpit—that the company felt justified in listing it as a Ryan-Standard. The Los Angeles–San Diego service became popular and soon paid its way, so Ryan purchased a Douglas Cloudster, originally built to U.S. Air Service specifications but modified to a ten-passenger transport. With equipment of this type, Ryan Airlines continued its daily schedule until 1927, when it was taken over by a West Coast syndicate. The firm switched its interest to the manufacture of their M-1 mono-plane. It might be mentioned here that Ryan monoplane No. 16 of the early lot was sold to a young airmail pilot, Charles A. Lindbergh, who, in honor of his Missouri backers, named it the Spirit of St. Louis, and aboard it made the first solo flight across the Atlantic.

But it was not all beer and skittles for the Pacific Air Transport Company. Actual mail-carrying flights did not begin until September 15, 1926, and before their first winter had passed, three of the original ten pilots had been killed, including R. B. Patterson, who had flown Gorst over the first survey run. Eddie Near apparently fell asleep in the air and flew into the ground at Turlock, California. Art Starbuck crashed and suffered fatal injuries. However, despite the publicity attendant on these fatalities, there were dozens of men *and* women who demanded transportation by air and were willing to sit huddled in the mailbag compartment. The flight from Los Angeles to Seattle took 18.5 hours and the movie-theatre type tickets cost $132.

But the mail contract was almost the undoing of Gorst's PAT for the airline was to receive only 75 percent of the money paid for airmail stamps. Seemingly substantial at first, it proved to be insufficient to meet the overhead. Pilots had to take stock certificates as part of their pay. The petroleum companies also accepted stock for gasoline, and in many instances donated oil for aviation test purposes. Though president of the company, Gorst was living in a cheap Mission Street hotel in San Francisco, and more often than not was taking part of his salary in stock.

Much the same conditions were encountered by other air pioneers who were trying to build up an airline on the feeder mail runs. Consider Walter T. Varney, who had learned to fly with the U.S. Army in World War I and apparently retained some of his enthusiasm for flying. First of all he opened a flying school in his home town of San Mateo,

California, and from that branched into running an air service across San Francisco Bay and an air express between San Francisco, Stockton, and Modesto in California's desert valley. In all these operations he trained his flight students to pilot his planes, and his school mechanics to service them, as part of their training.

After a year or so of this hand-to-mouth existence, Varney learned of the post office feeder line contracts. He decided to bid for the 460-mile route between Elko, Nevada, and Boise, Idaho, and from there link up with Pasco, Washington, thinking no one else would be interested. After all, on paper this looked like an airline that flew from nowhere over hazardous mountains and deserts to nowhere. Varney put in a bid of eight cents per ounce and, since no one else had shown any interest, the post office made a special deal and agreed to pay him 80 percent of the postal revenue. Varney eagerly signed. Fortunately, he had an indulgent father who headed the Varney & Green billboard company, and on the strength of his family backing Varney was able to order six small single-engined Swallow aircraft for his original fleet.

Varney rushed to get his mail-carrying Swallows into the air. On April 6, 1926, Leon D. Cuddeback, who but a short time before had been a rookie student at the Varney school, took off from Pasco, Washington, and quirted his 90-hp plane over the mountains to Elko. That memorable flight put Varney in the records for making the first airmail run by any operator in the western area, and the first by any of the feeder lines that were later to be merged into the United Air Lines system.

But Varney was to have much the same trouble that plagued Gorst. The Swallows were not powerful enough to vault the mountain ranges—or his pilots were not skilled enough to get the best out of their engines—and he had to request sixty days of grace, explaining he hoped to get a few 150-hp Wright engines. The extension was granted, and at that point Vern Gorst came to the rescue and agreed to let Walter take the first three Ryan planes destined for the Pacific Air Transport fleet, a gesture that put Varney back in the air again by June 1. This gave him a fresh start toward building up an airline that was to weave a network over a million square miles of the Pacific Northwest.

In his second start Varney moved his southern terminus from Elko to Salt Lake City. This provided a better connection with the main intercontinental, or Columbia, route, as it was then known. But it also made a convenient connection with Western Air Express which was sweeping out from Southern California. The post office raised Varney's airmail tariff to three dollars a pound, practically doubling his original rate, and as a result the Varney Air Lines began to prosper. Within a short time Varney ordered a number of faster Stearman planes, which carried greater mail loads. When the Post Office Department put the Spokane-to-Pasco-to-Portland route up for bids, Varney was able to take that over also, and thus established a short route from the east to the Pacific Northwest, gathering in a number of good-sized cities at the same time.

This new arrangement of payment by the pound soon led a few crafty operators to mail themselves hefty mail-order catalogues, and even neatly packaged building bricks, addressed and stamped, since they could be sent airmail for considerably less than the post office was paying for carrying them from terminal to terminal. This ingenious trick was perpetrated for some time.

At this point, Clement M. Keys, a former editor of the *Wall Street Journal*, had decided to quit writing about financing the new aviation industry and get into the business himself. Fortunately, he was in touch with many influential businessmen and was quick to organize, and head, a dozen multimillion-dollar corporations. He backed the new Curtiss Aeroplane and Motor Company, the North American Aviation Company, and was to become an im-

portant figure in Eastern Air Transport. Keys and Carl B.
Fritsche of Detroit, who was managing the Aircraft Development Corporation, had at one time conceived the idea of
turning Detroit into the air transport hub of the country—
and almost succeeded.

Varney's success in the Pacific Northwest soon attracted
the attention of Keys, and he organized the Aviation Corporation of California to back Varney's venture. But he
arranged that one of his most reliable associates, Colonel
Paul Henderson, would become a director in the Varney
combine. It was about this time, too (late 1929), that
Walter Varney nurtured the idea of carrying passengers
over his routes, linking up his aircraft at Salt Lake City with
Bill Boeing's Air Transport Company, which had taken over
the San Francisco–Chicago airmail contract. With this idea
in mind, Varney ordered nine four-place Boeing B-40s to
handle the anticipated passenger loads. This feature of the
air-carrier business failed to materialize, but on the other
hand Varney's planes were carrying a million dollars worth
of air mail annually.

So far, the Varney interests seemed to run on greased
guides, and had the management been content to move the
overall operation cautiously and hew to the straight business line, all might have gone well. But Varney was imbued
with advanced ideas seen over distant horizons, rather than
consolidation of his unusual gains. He made himself chairman of the board of Varney Air Lines and appointed Louis
Mueller, an attorney in San Francisco, as president. He
traveled widely and handsomely, usually taking a number
of friends along as his guests, which can be costly. Then,
too, the influence of the Keys' interests indicated that the
Varney group was planning to move into the Pacific Northwest, or at least take over the greater portion of that lucrative area. This soon convinced the Boeing organization
that the Varney network would have to be bought up and
taken out of competition.

7

The Giants Preen Their Wings

To appreciate the tempo of these frantic times, it should be recalled that the mid-1920s introduced a state of the nation that outraged the moralists and the establishment of the prewar days. The various programs of flying still retained the neck-or-nothing attitude of the 1914–18 era, and even with the promise of enclosed cockpits no airman would consider climbing into an airplane without helmet and goggles, flare-cut riding breeches, and a long scarf knotted at his throat, for he was expected to continue the tradition of the intrepid airman. His social companions had assumed the flapper role, a pose adopted from the London party girl of pre-Armistice days. During those prohibition days she swished short skirts, rolled her stockings below the knee, and wantonly displayed generous lengths of bare thigh—all of which added to the prestige of the illustrator John Held, Jr. Corsets were dispensed with and long tresses were clipped in the style of Irene Castle to frame expressionless faces daubed with layers of odorous cosmetics. The original glamour of femininity had been replaced by an epicene form suggesting sexlessness. To prove they were fully emancipated, tribal ceremonies known as petting or necking were standard practice among youthful couples.

This was dubbed the Jazz Age, the decade of the beautiful and damned, and when Sinclair Lewis's *Babbitt* depicted the "stuffy hypocrisies" of the day, the jazz babies held up the volume and screamed, "You see! This is what we are against. This is the world you oldsters have made and want us to accept, and we say the hell with it!"

Does this page of history have a familiar ring?

The state of the nation, and in fact the world, was perfect for the further growth of commerical aviation. There was a high tempo of go-go in the air; a frantic desire to get somewhere else fast; there was no time for delay or interruption; the race for the almighty dollar had to be speeded up. What better medium than the airplane?

The Boeing saga began when Bill Boeing decided to replace the cracked-up pontoon machine he had purchased from Glenn Martin. At the time he had wished only to fly from one lake or river to another in pursuit of fish and game. We have outlined in a previous chapter the beginning of Boeing's commercial flying venture when he and Eddie Hubbard carried a token bag of mail from Victoria, British Columbia, to Seattle, Washington, after which Hubbard went into the business of carrying airmail for himself.

Boeing's planes, initially intended for the United States Navy, were bolted together in an old boat-building shop on the Duwamish River just west of Seattle. In order to form a basic working staff, Boeing took on Philip Johnson, Clair L. Egtvedt, and Roland Mayer, members of a recent graduation class of the University of Washington. Johnson became a shop foreman and salesman. Egtvedt was a dreamer-designer. Apparently Mayer did not stay with Boeing very long, but transferred his interests to lighter-than-air, becoming a Navy blimp pilot.

Bill Boeing returned to his lumber interests, leaving the building of airplanes to Johnson and Egtevdt, but kept his hand in by occasionally flying the Orient-bound mail from Seattle to Victoria on days of steamer sailings and picking up mail bound for the United States from Canadian Pacific liners just in from legendary Cathay. These short hops across Puget Sound kept Hubbard in funds and nourished Boeing's interest in aviation. Then, late in 1926, Hubbard heard of the Postmaster General's plan asking for bids from private operators to fly the mail over two important segments of the transcontinental route, one of which was the link between Chicago and San Francisco.

Hubbard talked over the project with Clair Egtevdt, who was still building fleets of aircraft on his drawing board. "I wonder if Bill Boeing would be interested in making a bid for the San Francisco–Chicago run," he asked. Egtevdt pinned a new sheet of paper to his table. "There's no use asking him until we have some figures to show," he mumbled, realizing that a mail run would require a cargo-carrying landplane. "Let's see what we can work out."

Over the next two days Hubbard covered page after page with figures showing how much revenue might be expected from the contract and what it would cost to operate a scheduled airline between the two key cities. He realized that whatever money might be forthcoming would not be sufficient to finance an efficient airline, but he also believed that with suitable publicity and intensive advertising the airmail revenue might be doubled. Hubbard continued to figure how many planes and pilots would be needed, and concentrated on the actual operations' costs. Egtevdt hunched over his drawing board to work out the details of an aircraft capable of vaulting the Sierra Nevada range and the Rockies, carrying a load of mail—and at least two passengers.

The figures and rough sketches finally fell into an encouraging pattern and both men felt they could fly an airmail route profitably for $1.50 per pound per 1,000 miles. With these conclusions and a rough outline of a new cargo plane, they cornered Bill in his office and outlined their plan. Boeing listened with only mild interest until Egtevdt suggested that such a venture might provide a new market for more planes, but at no time did Bill seem interested enough to reach for his checkbook. Hubbard and Egtevdt went back to the boat yard with little hope of enlarging their production line.

Later that day Bill talked over the new idea with his wife, who thought there was much to be said for a commercial airline, and she encouraged him to set up an organization to be known as Boeing Air Transport. After some probing telephone conversation with Phil Johnson, who was on the road peddling floatplanes, Bill decided to go ahead with Hubbard's figures and Egtevdt's rough sketches and make a bid for the San Francisco–Chicago route. While awaiting confirmation, he made Johnson president of the new organization and saddled Hubbard with the dual load of vice-president and general manager.

When all bids were opened it was found that Boeing's was considerably lower than that submitted by Harris Hanshue's Western Air Express. Boeing had bid $1.50 per pound for the first 1,000 miles and 15¢ per pound for each additional 100 miles which amounted to $2.98 per pound to fly a bag of mail from San Francisco to Chicago. Hanshue had bid $2.24 per pound and 24¢ for each additional 100 miles, as Western Air was already receiving $3 per pound for carrying the mail over the Los Angeles–Salt Lake City route. From all these comparative figures, conservative minds in the industry felt Bill Boeing would go broke within a few weeks. The post office also had reservations, and demanded an $800,000 bond to guarantee the opening of operations, although Senator Wesley Jones of Washington assured the Postmaster General that Boeing was a reliable businessman. Six months after the contract had been awarded, Boeing Air Transport was in the air with a number of Egtvedt's new Boeing 40-A mail planes.

The secret of Boeing's success lay in the fact that his 40-A biplane was powered with the new Pratt & Whitney Wasp air-cooled radial engine that produced 410 hp and had a cruising speed of 125 mph, carrying 1,200 pounds of mail, two passengers, and the pilot. Luck also slipped into the picture, for Boeing was able to buy a number of these engines when no other manufacturer could obtain one for test purposes. This came about when Bill remembered a prep-school companion, Frederick D. Rentschler, who headed the Pratt & Whitney factory in Hartford, Connecticut. This firm had developed the Wasp chiefly for a number of Navy fighter planes. During the summer of 1926 Bill went east and persuaded his old friend to induce the Navy to divert twenty-five of these engines for his airmail planes.

The Navy was amenable, and by the time the first airframes were assembled several of the Pratt & Whitney engines were already in Seattle. Clair Egtevdt quickly modified the engine mount to take the radial power plant. This change in design increased the 40-A's pay load from 1,000 to 1,500 pounds, which added $400 to the income from each trip. Two passengers were seated in a small cabin set between the wings, given two blankets, wads of cotton for their ears, large containers of coffee, and a charming view of a schematic maze of struts, guy wires, and control surfaces which flipped up and down. It was hardly luxury travel, but it beat the railroad's time by 56 hours. The pilot sat in an open cockpit set well down the fuselage, for no one believed a plane could be safely flown from any other position. The idea of putting a pilot under a transparent canopy was, in many quarters, considered suicidal. Two cargo hatches were built in between the passenger cabin and the pilot's cockpit.

Vice President Hubbard set up the company's headquarters in Salt Lake City, from where Western Air Express was carrying out its Southern California operations and the Varney Air Lines their Pacific Northwest routes. Hubbard first hired D. B. Colyer, an ex-Army pilot who had been Second Assistant Postmaster General in charge of airmail, to act as superintendent of operations. Colyer also knew many old Post Office mail pilots, and hired several veterans who had been flying the route day and night for the past three years.

As a result of this businesslike cooperation *and* Egtvedt's 40-A mail plane, the airline showed immediate success. By the end of 1927, after six months of operation, 525 passengers and 286,712 pounds of mail had been safely flown; all but 19 of the 372 scheduled flights were completed over a run that included intermediate stops in Iowa, Nebraska, Wyoming, Utah, and Nevada. Daily round trips left Chicago at 7:50 P.M., and San Francisco at 6:00 A.M. which permitted daylight crossing of the mountains. The westbound trips took about twenty-four hours, the eastbound two hours less. The one-way passenger fare was $200.

Another independent route that operated between Los Angeles and San Diego for about two years was the Maddux Air Lines, operated by J. L. Maddux. This was a remarkable organization for it offered its passengers a reasonable amount of comfort, safety, and convenience. Ground transportation was provided and the schedules usually were started and completed on time. The aircraft were Ford Tri-Motors, and in the Maddux model, besides the wicker seats and windows that opened for air conditioning, there were overhead luggage racks, individual reading lights—and a lavatory!

Maddux began his operation on July 21, 1927, and with only two Ford transports maintained a daily round-trip schedule between Los Angeles and San Diego, a distance of about one hundred miles. By 1928 this run was so popular the fleet was enlarged to thirteen Fords, and operations were expanded to include round-trip service between Los Angeles and San Francisco, Los Angeles and Phoenix,

Arizona, and an additional service south and east into Mexico and the Imperial Valley. The Maddux combine soon attracted the attention of more important operators, and on November 16, 1929, it was taken over by Transcontinental Air Transport and eventually became part of Transcontinental and Western Air or what is known today as TWA.

As practiced by shrewd businessmen and financiers, the intricate maneuverings of big business—imagination, greed, and natural inclination to extend any operation—gradually resolved into a definite pattern which left those on the fringes of the aviation industry gasping. The airplane, once the mount of the barnstormers, the winged charger of the pulp magazines, and still something of a country-fair sideshow novelty, was coming under the control of Big Business. If the truth be known, it was being manipulated by the monied interests just as the railroad networks had been in the days of the Vanderbilts, Goulds, Harrimans, and others who had flouted the intent of the Anti-Trust laws half a century or so before.

By late 1928 Egtvedt's 40-A mail planes had proven that an airline was only as good as its flying equipment. Furthermore, the Boeing Air Transport Company was reflecting the importance of sound business administration and a conservative level of operations. In contrast, Vern Gorst's Pacific Air Transport was experiencing a definite decline in revenue. Some people felt the Maddux Air Lines with its Ford Tri-Motors, and a splinter company of Western Air Express known as the West Coast Express, were taking considerable business from Gorst's line, but they were carrying only passengers. Obviously, new equipment was the answer. Gorst and his chief pilot Grover Tyler indicated an interest in purchasing a few Boeing 40s, but learned to their astonishment that they cost $25,000 apiece—a figure previously unheard of. Already awash in red ink, the PAT was unable to raise the money to buy one for trial purposes.

Learning of Gorst's financial predicament, Harris Hanshue of Western Air Express—who had been outbid for the San Francisco–Chicago route by Bill Boeing—moved to buy Gorst's controlling B stock for $250 a share, chiefly to take possession of the airmail contract. Other members of PAT opposed this move, and W. A. Patterson, acting as a voluntary financial adviser, suggested that the Boeing company buy up all of PAT's stock and merge the two airlines. This proposed merger was consumated after Bill Boeing offered $200 a share for all voting and nonvoting stock, and further agreed to keep on all of PAT's employees. As the result of this remunerative venture, Patterson was later persuaded to become Phil Johnson's assistant manager.

Still the gambler, Vern Gorst took his stock check of $94,000 and spent $30,000 of it on a Boeing flying boat. He opened a Seattle to Alaska airline which he operated for the next five years, hoping that one day the post office would reward him with a lucrative contract to fly mail over that route for about $450 a trip. Just when matters began to materialize for this deal, Juan Terry Trippe, head of the recently organized Pan American Airways, eased into the picture and picked up the contract for $4,000 per flight! There was more to this deal than meets the immediate eye.

Juan Trippe was an ex-Navy pilot, who, on returning to Yale to finish his education, organized a flying club at New Haven. He also edited the *Yale Graphic* and played football. Since his father, Charles White Trippe, was a well-known Manhattan banker and head of a family which had come to America in 1664, Juan was always in contact with the "right" people. Having never lost interest in his early experiences as a pilot, Juan soon left his father's bank and single-handedly set up what he called the Long Island Airways, a free-lance operation that carried out charter flights—in any direction. Next, he tied in with John A. Hambleton—a Baltimore banker who was an ex-war flier—and Cornelius

Vanderbilt Whitney. This threesome yearned for bigger and better things and put in a bid for the New York–Boston airmail run in opposition to the highly respected Colonial Air Transport (Colonial Airways Corporation). They failed in that, but by some neat manipulation in 1927 eventually acquired the old Aeromarine Airways route. This had operated between Key West and Havana, and had used a small fleet of Fokker ten-passenger planes for this 90-mile route. The company was renamed Pan American Airways.

Financed by United States and Cuban contracts to carry all first-class mail, Pan American couldn't lose. During November and December of 1927, Trippe's line gathered in $20,000 for flying 49,576 pounds of mail, express, and passengers. By September 1928 Pan American had moved to a new Florida international terminal in Dinner Key, a complex which offered hangars, customs, and immigration facilities. Over that year Trippe's pilots flew 297,000 passenger miles, carried 350,000 pounds of mail and express over a route he had extended into profitable areas of the Bahamas. It was evident from this that Trippe was looking ahead to the time when his Pan American Airways would spread out and become Pan American World Airways, and Gorst's Alaskan trail-blazing provided the link into the Northern Pacific routes.

Gorst never recovered from that disappointment. For a few months he operated a charter flying service for sportsmen, but eventually had to complete his destiny and return to running one of his original motor-stage lines between North Bend and Marshfield, Oregon. The luckless Vern Gorst died on October 18, 1953.

As stated before, the air combines were beginning to close ranks and take on a recognizable formula. In Detroit, Clement M. Keys and Carl B. Fritsche were pooling their wits—and any money they could raise—in an attempt to turn the Motor City into America's hub of aerial transportation and thus nudge Chicago out of the planning. In the course of this mild conspiracy they organized the Aircraft Development Corporation, one of the many investment groups of the time. Previously, in 1925, they had raised $2,000,000 to organize an airline that would link New York and Chicago. Keys, with his *Wall Street Journal* connections, had no trouble raising half of this sum in New York after talking with several so-called wartime profiteers, who had made large fortunes building aeronautical equipment for the Allies and later for the American forces. Thus, the first million was soon in the bank and Fritsche promised to raise the rest from a few Detroit automotive financiers, including the Fords. But to his amazement the motorcar men were not too impressed with the prospects of commercial aviation and only $500,000 could be raised there. So Chicago was brought into the planning and the additional $500,000 was quickly subscribed with Windy City enthusiasm. Thus, it must be assumed that for a mere half million dollars, Detroit missed out on becoming the aviation hub of North America.

With the $2,000,000 in hand, Keys and Fritsche organized the National Air Transport that was to have an authorized capital of $10,000,000—a backlog unheard of in aviation circles. Howard E. Coffin, vice president of the Hudson Motor Company, became chairman of the executive committee. Among the vice presidents were such figures as Charles L. Lawrence, president of the Wright Aeronautical Corporation; Wayne Chatfield-Taylor, a Chicago capitalist; and Eugene W. Lewis of Detroit. Colonel Paul Henderson, who had once been a Second Assistant Postmaster General and in some circles was looked on as the "father of the night mail," was named general manager. Fritsche took over the secretarial job. A small group of flight cadets, straight out of Kelly Field, was engaged, given conversion courses on civil-type aircraft, and taught that "neither snow, nor rain, nor heat, nor gloom of night

stays these couriers from the swift completion of their appointed rounds." Cadets or not, they were far better airmen
than those who had been honorably discharged from the
wartime military services.

Big Business was now crowding out the small-time independent promotor. Pioneer romance had had its day. As
has been shown, the wartime flier, who had attempted the
commercial venture, had risked his life, and to some extent
blazed a trail, was not a good businessman—and he seldom
had sufficient capital to justify his ambitions. He was soon
nudged out when it became evident commercial aviation
required a sizeable bank account. Wall Street wizards who
seldom left their swivel chairs, stock promotors more skill-
ful in finding investors than boring their way through
turbulent skies, and efficient cost analyzers with no interest
in shortening the risks between key cities, were taking over
the business of aviation.

National Air Transport began operations in May 1926,
flying ten Curtiss Carrier Pigeons, a conventional biplane
that was hurriedly designed for cargo-carrying. Powered by
government-surplus Liberty engines, the Pigeons were supposed to haul a thousand-pound pay load over the New
York–Chicago–Detroit route, but the Detroit contact was
ignored. All eastbound flights originated in Chicago and
headed south by way of Kansas City to Dallas, Texas, making contact with a dozen population areas along the west
Mississippi valley. The original plan to fly from Detroit to
New York did not materialize until one year later when
NAT managed to bid successfully for the 995-mile airway
route over the Columbia stretch.

But the fulfillment of this contract was no sinecure.
Other operators were moving in with plans to grab wads of
this airmail money. Keys and Fritsche quietly arranged
several shrewd deals which would enable them to submit
an additional bid for the entire San Francisco–New York
route. With that began a frenzied, if undercover, scheme

—to tie in, first, with Western Air Express. But Hanshue shied off from any merger with NAT, feeling his company would lose its identity if gobbled up by this voracious eastern combine. As a result, this series of negotiations came to nothing.

Next, NAT cast a greedy eye in the direction of Colonial Air Transport, which at the time appeared to be interlacing a network to serve the prime cities in New England and threatened to become a rival bidder for the Chicago–New York mail contract. Negotiations were initiated, but again neither side could agree on the details, so both planned to submit bids for the same route.

During all this, North American Airways, Inc., a hole-in-the-wall combine, put in a bid that was one cent lower than NAT's $1.24 per pound. North American Airways was headed by Charles A. Levine, a New York junk dealer who had gained some doubtful prestige after financing Clarence C. Chamberlain for a transatlantic flight during the Roman holiday period of transocean hopping. Again, the tactics and strategy of what seemed like bucket-shop finance amused the onlookers, who had no conception of the profits involved.

On learning the difference in the two bids, Levine announced he had been awarded the contract. The post office officials were so bewildered they suggested that NAT and Levine's North American Airways merge and operate the route together. The parties concerned met in a hotel. As an opener Levine demanded that NAT first buy a half interest in his NAA, and then supply the management. In turn, he agreed to turn over the airmail contract and a number of pilots who had previously flown the route for the post office. It was revealed later that he had obtained a signed agreement with the airmen to take blocks of NAA stock in payment.

In some manner the Postmaster General learned of this shady deal, and was also advised that Levine was being in-

vestigated by the War Department about some salvage contracts. He therefore canceled NAA's bid and handed the
contract to Colonel Henderson for NAT. Henderson immediately hired the post office pilots who were familiar with
the Alleghenies hop, had them checked out on Curtiss
Pigeons, and by September 1, 1927, NAT was flying the
Chicago–New York route. No immediate attempt was made
to establish a passenger-carrying business on the theory
that mail hauled at $1.24 a pound was more profitable than
a 150-pound patron paying only $200 for the same 724-
mile flight. Besides, passengers were a nuisance. In open
cockpit planes they would have to be provided with a helmet and goggles, coveralls—and a parachute! And consider
how much time it would take the pilot to show a passenger
how to use the damned thing!

However, NAT had to accept the problem of passenger-
carrying, if only to accommodate those crazy Westerners
delivered to them by Boeing Air Transport. For this they
first adopted a Travel Air cabin plane which had space for
three passengers, but this service was offered only on the
Chicago–Kansas City link. During 1928 NAT carried
1,560 people over this route, but eventually this passenger-
carrying schedule was turned over to another company,
originally known as Transcontinental Air Transport.

This new aviation venture had been organized by C. M.
Keys and financed with money provided by the Pennsylvania and Santa Fe railroads. Its early promotion happily
coincided with Charles A. Lindbergh's sudden world-wide
prestige following his solo hop to Paris, so Keys decided to
bring Lindbergh into the TAT picture. The Lone Eagle, as
he was popularly known, was given a large block of stock in
TAT and listed as its technical advisor. Overnight, TAT
was advertised as the "Lindbergh Line."

Transcontinental Air Transport went through an interesting period of operations as a result of being "forced" into
carrying passengers. The grim dread of the Hell Stretch

over the Alleghenies still remained, so passengers booking flights out of New York for the west were given real Hollywood service, made up of equal parts of ballyhoo and buncombe. First, they were put aboard a luxury train at Pennsylvania Station, and after an overnight run, were detrained at Columbus, Ohio. In the special dining car they ate their meals from gold plates, and were presented with gold fountain pens with which to write letters back home telling of their Great Adventure. They were carried from the stations to the airports in teardrop Aero-cars, and there usually was a movie star of some magnitude to spread her personality.

From Columbus, Ford Tri-Motor transports flew them on to Waynoka, Oklahoma, in broad daylight. On arrival, they were again picked up by Aero-cars and put aboard a Santa Fe train, which, overnight, took them to Clovis, New Mexico. There, another Tin Goose gathered them up and bore them into Los Angeles. This plane-train journey took about forty-eight hours and cost $480 per trip, but it was far from a paying proposition and TAT lost $2,750,000 in the first eighteen months of this operation, and a fair share of this was National Air Transport's money. They had bought 50,000 shares of TAT stock for $1,000,000, which in turn had given NAT a ten percent interest in the Lindbergh Line.

The corporate management of Transcontinental Air Transport recalls an interesting and seldom-remembered feature of those days—for TAT actually was a holding company, operating under the cover of an airline while holding blocks of stock in competing airlines. In fact, TAT was in the position to take airmail contracts from NAT, since Colonel Henderson, who managed NAT, also directed the operations of TAT. This was done by spreading the management very thin and allowing Henderson to be considered "the Keys Group." This complex maneuvering held for some time, until more youthful and straightforward management was brought to bear by men who had begun from the cockpits and hangars of the postwar years.

Among the early employees of the TAT group was John A. Herlihy, a graduate engineer and an ex-Navy pilot responsible for the design and layout of company airports over the route. Sometime early in 1930 Herlihy was fired by the TAT management but, fortunately, he was hired immediately by E. P. Lott, superintendent of flying for NAT, and became a night-flying pilot over the New York–Cleveland route.

To add to this corporate charade, it should be explained that Lott had been an aviation mechanic in World War I. On his return home he had bought a surplus airplane and taught himself to fly. He became a gypsy barnstorming flier, and before joining NAT had pioneered in aerial mapping. Together, Herlihy and Lott teamed up to make NAT one of the soundest operations in the aviation industry. Later, John Herlihy took charge of United Air Lines' nationwide operations, and headed all engineering and maintenance as United's senior vice president.

8

The Lindbergh Influence

Taking off from Roosevelt Field, Long Island, in the early morning of May 20, 1927, a youthful airmail pilot, Charles A. Lindbergh, flew alone across the Atlantic. He touched down on a grassy field outside Paris 33½ hours later, completing the first solo nonstop flight between New York City and France's City of Light. Unquestionably, it was the finest effort in aviation's history—a display of courage, flying skill, and the ultimate in confidence. But the grueling trip by this twenty-five-year-old American transformed him overnight into the archetypical airman and elevated him to the pedestal of a young god who was to arouse an amazing sociological phenomenon.

Only those old enough to remember the historic weeks and months that followed Lindy's landing in Paris and his triumphal return to his homeland can appreciate the impact his epic flight had—first on the nation, and second on the immediate growth of commercial aviation. To many sage thinkers, Lindbergh was the sole catalyst who aroused the vital interest in the airplane as a reliable and popular means of transportation. And yet, no more controversial

figure ever stepped into the spotlight of a national industry
—a strange, complex man, who seemingly never understood his fellows nor was ever fully appreciated by those
who vainly tried to know him.

How, then, could so complex a personality have such a
profound influence on Big Business of aviation?

The psychiatrists will take their favorite theory, flip the
pages of their Krafft-Ebing, and point out that Lindbergh
was from his early days the victim of an unhappy home.
His father was an indolent lawyer and a widely detested
politician whose first wife had died, leaving him with two
small girls; a third had died in infancy. In March 1901
Charles A. Lindbergh the elder married Evangeline Lodge
Land, a lively graduate of the University of Michigan, who
had been teaching science in the Little Falls, Minnesota,
High School. After an extended honeymoon with relatives
in California they returned home and the second Mrs. Lindbergh gave birth to a son in Detroit on February 4, 1902.

In the years that followed, Lindbergh senior took an
active interest in politics and won a seat in Congress. He
immediately took up the gage for the farmers in their struggle against an economy controlled by the railroads, the big
trusts, the tight grip on currency by private banks, and the
financial panic of 1907. Representative Lindbergh had also
become a militant isolationist, an opponent of war and of
any diplomatic entanglement with European powers. The
Spanish-American War had left on his soul a mark which
was to fester into a one-man crusade against the world war
that, less than twenty years later, was to engulf the United
States.

There was a natural liaison between Lindbergh and his
son. The father was determined to make a man of him and,
despite his aversion to war, he gave young Charles a 12-
gauge shotgun and a single-shot .22-caliber rifle when he
was seven years of age. He was taken into the fields and
taught the law of the hunt and how to handle firearms
properly. Those early years must have been idyllic, and

some time later when the Lindbergh marriage began to crumble, it was natural that the son would take his father's side. None of this was immediately apparent to relatives or neighbors, and Charles and his sisters lived a perfectly normal life—or so several biographers have depicted.

Lindbergh's schooldays reflected the happy-go-lucky routine we have long imagined as a typical Midwestern education in a town that was hardly an urban sprawl. The fields, forests, and waters of the Minnesota countryside were always nearby. Charles Lindbergh was not an outstanding pupil, except in such subjects as mechanical drawing and chemistry, in which he was graded VG (very good). During his vacations he cultivated the Lindbergh acreage with a tractor, one of the few in Morrison County. He cared for the stock, and worked diligently at anything which justified the use of machinery. In his last year in high school he possessed an Excelsior motorcycle, and for weeks outraged the neighborhood with his reckless antics.

By the time he was ready for college, the world was recovering from the bloody impact of World War I. Soldiers were still returning from the occupied areas. The Eighteenth Amendment had been put into effect, followed by gangster violence, bootlegging, and all forms of illicit traffic in alcohol. The Ku Klux Klan was revivified. Sinclair Lewis had put Main Street on display for the edification of the jokesters, and Warren Gamaliel Harding was urging a return to normalcy. In 1920 Lindbergh's mother, who was again teaching science at the Little Falls High School, encouraged him to enter the University of Wisconsin.

Again, Lindbergh proved to be no academic marvel and was impatient with scholastic routines. He was a practical joker of the lowest order—some of his tricks bordered on the malicious. His idea of fun was to leave frogs in the beds of companions, to drop cats out of second-story windows to see if they really landed on their feet, and secrete a cow in the room of a man terrified of bulls.

Charles lasted only into his second semester and then,

free as a bird, headed for the Nebraska Aircraft Corporation in Lincoln, a firm which manufactured Lincoln Standard aircraft and promised flying instruction as part of its sales promotion. From this point on we skim over Lindy's early flying career, including learning to fly. After one dual-control landing, he bought a new Curtiss Jenny and barnstormed all over the Mississippi valley, with various degrees of financial reward. To appreciate the full story of Lindbergh's early flying days, one should read *The Hero**** in which Lindbergh's background and career are presented in high key. The work is meticulously researched and presented with scrupulous regard for fact.

In 1924 Lindbergh applied for Army Air Service training, was accepted by the examining board at Chanute Field, Rantoul, Illinois, and ordered to report to Brooks Field, San Antonio, Texas, by March 15 of that year. Here was unfolded another chapter of wild adventure. One hundred and four candidates started this course, but only thirty-three completed the Brooks primary program for advanced training at Kelly Field. Of this handful only eighteen stayed long enough to receive their wings in March 1925. Nine days before he was to graduate Lindbergh was involved in a mid-air collision, and for the first time in his wild career had to take to his parachute.

On this occasion he was in a nine-plane formation of World War I S.E.5s. During a simulated air fight against a D.H.4 target ship his plane collided and locked wings with one flown by a Lieutenant McAllister. Both pilots decided to take to the silk and both landed safely. (This was the first of four occasions when Lindbergh had to leave a disabled aircraft.) Of the eighteen graduates, commissioned second lieutenants, most of them, including Lindbergh, resigned from any probable active service and became members of the Air Service Reserve Corps. After a farewell

* *The Hero—Charles A. Lindbergh and the American Dream*, by Kenneth S. Davis, Doubleday & Co., Inc., 1959.

dinner in San Antonio, Lindbergh boarded a train for St. Louis.

The man who was to become known as Lucky Lindy returned to civilian life and during his train ride had time to consider what kind of world he was reentering. Today the 1920s are presented under various titles. They were the Golden Twenties to the sport fraternity, the Flapper Age to the habitues of what became cafe society, the Age of Ballyhoo to show business, and the years of the Tabloid Press, which to many people marked the end of decent first-class journalism. To Lindbergh his world must have appeared a dreary morass that shocked his Midwest standards of social behavior, but, motivated by his love of flying and warmed by some vague remembrance of the earlier Kelly Bill, he mused over the possibility of turning his Air Service training into a civilian skill which would be both remunerative and worthy of his keen interest.

Further investigation disclosed that a number of small operators were preparing to bid for the advertised airmail contracts, and in St. Louis Lindbergh discovered that two wartime fliers, William B. and Frank Robertson— whom he had met at the 1923 International Air Races— were still in business as the Robertson Aircraft Corporation. This stick-and-string organization had been capitalized for $15,000, much of which was represented by a Curtiss Jenny and an extra OX-5 engine. The Robertsons liked Lindbergh, explained that they had put in a bid for the Chicago–St. Louis "feeder" run, and half promised that if they were lucky he could join the organization as a pilot.

While awaiting word from Washington, the Robertsons continued their business of repairing government-surplus aircraft, flight instruction, country-fair joy hops, and occasional charter flights. During this same waiting period Lindbergh obtained an OX-5 Standard and went off on a barnstorming trip through Illinois, Missouri, and Iowa. He joined a flying circus outfit, did stunt flying and some in-structing, and entered the Caterpillar Club for a second time when an experimental plane he was testing refused to come out of a tailspin. During these exhibitions he was billed as "Beans" Lindbergh—The Flying Fool. The nick-name referred to his voracious appetite for the famed Boston legume.

He put in two weeks of active duty with the Army at Richards Field, Missouri. Following that he joined the Mil-Hi Airways and Flying Circus at Denver, where he was hired to put on a program of stunt flying and to pilot char-ter flights. He also booked some reserve time with the 110th Observation Squadron, giving lectures on military flying to ex-war pilots who had volunteered for National Guard duty.

Early in 1926 the Robertsons were awarded the Chicago St. Louis mail contract. Lindbergh was hired immediately, and because of his skill, daring, and experience was named Chief Pilot. He flew the first load of Robertson mail out of Chicago on April 15, 1926. At the time the Robertson Air-craft Corporation was equipped with fourteen D.H.4Bs, powered with Liberty engines; and two Curtiss Orioles.

During that summer Lindbergh enjoyed all the flying he could wish for under reasonably clement weather condi-tions, and was well paid for his work. But as the summer gave way to an early autumn the Robertson pilots began to encounter sleet, snow, and early darkness. On September 26, 1926, after taking off from Peoria, Lindbergh headed for the Maywood Field in Chicago. Almost immediately a ground fog rolled in, covering the country northeast of the Illinois River. Over Chicago the fog covered the area up to a height of 900 feet, and though every resource known to aviation at the time was set up—upturned searchlights and drums of burning gasoline—nothing pierced the fog. Lindbergh circled the area, awaiting a break, until his en-gine cut out for lack of fuel. He quickly switched over to the reserve tank which held enough to give him about twenty minutes of flying time. It was soon evident he had no hope of getting down through the fog, and the gas gauge needle was moving down to the pin, so he climbed his aircraft to 5,000 feet and for the third time took to the silk, drifting slowly earthward. He presumed the D.H.4 would continue on a direct flight out of the area, but as he hung in his 'chute harness in the silence of the inky-black night he could hear the plane apparently circling on the few ounces of fuel left. He realized he had left the engine switch on, and knew that the airplane would fly until the last drop of fuel was sucked into the carburetor. As he descended, aiming his flashlight at the heavy bank of fog, he suddenly saw the abandoned de Havilland roaring toward him. There was nothing much he could do, and he had to hang there helpless as the big biplane passed him with only a few yards to spare. He manipulated his risers to make the 'chute slip away, hoping to keep clear of the erratic circle the plane must be flying.

Five times the roaring aircraft threatened him, but always at the last minute of approach it seemed to wag its coffin-shaped nose and veer off. Then, to Lindbergh's relief, it straightened out and disappeared into the darkness. He landed safely in a cornfield, and, after rousing some farmers, found his plane hardly damaged in a cornfield less than two miles away. He retrieved the mail, put it on a train at Ottawa, Illinois, and made certain it was headed for its destination in Chicago.

In mid-November, Lindbergh took to his parachute for the fourth time in less than twenty months. In this instance he was on the northbound run at night when he again encountered a blinding fog. Twenty-five miles beyond Springfield he worked his way beneath the vapor bank, flying at about 400 feet, but the fog gradually lowered so that it was impossible to make his mail drop at Peoria. He continued on toward Chicago, hoping it would break in time for him to get down.

Springfield was blotted out, but when he reached the Chicago area he found a break and decided to release a magnesium flare. The flare ignited properly, but the parachute intended to delay its fall caught on the de Havilland's tail assembly and was torn to shreds. The burning flare dropped like an incendiary bomb.

There was nothing further to do, so he once more climbed for altitude and waited until his reserve tank was empty. Then—after snapping the ignition switch—went over the side from about 14,000 feet. Once he was clear and with his 'chute properly open, he saw he had jumped in a snow squall. The silk canopy began to oscillate wildly for about five minutes. Finally, he dropped into a sable-dark area and found the snow had turned to rain, making his 'chute oscillate at a greater rate. His flashlight indicated he was at about the 500-foot level, and before he could determine what the ground below was like, he found himself straddling a barbed-wired fence. Fortunately, his flying suit was heavy enough to protect him from the barbs, and he climbed off, collapsed his 'chute, and rolled it into a manageable bundle. This time he made his way into the town of Covell, Illinois, where the proprietor of a general store promised to have a crew of men search for his plane. It eventually was found, completely wrecked. The mail, except for some oil soaking, was intact, and was delivered to its destination.

Lindbergh continued his mail runs for the Robertsons on schedule, but also did some free-lance flying, putting on exhibitions all around St. Louis. Here, despite his seemingly wild displays and practical jokes, he gradually gathered in a few friends—men who were important in their particular circle of business or society. Flying men all agreed that he was one of the outstanding airmen of the country, and all were amazed at his ability to defy wind, storms, and rain over the Chicago–St. Louis route. They all concurred that

Lindy was a natural flier, one who loved to fly, but who used good judgment whenever an emergency arose. Whatever the faults of his social behavior, he was a meticulously accurate flier who delighted in beating bad weather at its own game. Unquestionably, he was an important factor in the success of the Robertson Aircraft Corporation. By the end of 1927—after eighteen months of flying airmail schedules—three new Douglas Mail Planes (presumably M-2s) were added to the fleet. Over their first year Robertson pilots completed 97 percent of their 513 scheduled flights and carried 34,722 pounds of mail, for which the company was paid $138,714. Ten paying passengers were also carried on an experimental basis.

Lindbergh left the company early in 1927 to buy an airplane and compete for the Raymond Orteig Prize of $25,000, put up for the first nonstop flight between New York and Paris. His epic success need not be detailed here, for it is now high in the Golden Deeds of aviation history. Overnight Lucky Lindy became America's Lone Eagle hero, but he failed to live up to the expectations. For one thing, it took a presidential command to get him home from Europe. He was enjoying himself, flying every type of civil and military plane available in France, Britain, and Germany. He displayed a distinct dislike for crowds, presentation banquets, interviews, and formal social affairs. With laconic politeness he turned down dozens of promotional offers that would have brought him thousands of dollars. He refused bids from Hollywood, ignored pleas to sign testimonials, and at the same time avoided any form of scandal, behaving as a farm boy who has suddenly found himself in the peak position of a national industry. His one great defense against all these pitfalls was to do and say nothing.

Once the general furor over his transatlantic triumph began to abate, Lindbergh flew a public relations tour of the United States under the auspices of the Daniel Guggenheim Foundation for the Promotion of Aeronautics.

This series of personal appearances made the United States the most air-minded country in the world, and in retrospect would seem to be the Lone Eagle's greatest contribution to the industry and the eventual success of commercial aviation in this country. Later, when tragic circumstances and world events forced him to leave his native land, Lindbergh buried his grief in working with Dr. Alexis Carrel of France on several scientific experiments. In the meantime TWA had deleted the phrase "The Lindbergh Line" from their advertising and from the sides of their commercial aircraft. Later Lindy became a consultant for Pan American Airways and is said to have laid out most of their transocean air routes.

Today, Charles A. Lindbergh is almost unknown. In 1967, when some forty high school students were inspecting his transatlantic plane, Spirit of St. Louis, at the Smithsonian Institution in Washington, few of them had any idea who Charles A. Lindbergh was, or whether he was still alive. Twenty-three thought he was dead—probably killed in the war. Twelve had no idea where he was, and the guard standing nearby could not explain whether the Lone Eagle was dead or alive, nor could several oldsters on the fringe of the student group. At the time he was living on an estate near Darien, Connecticut, and was often mentioned in connection with the national conservation programs.

Early in 1928 the Robertson company, carrying passengers between St. Louis and Chicago, added another segment between St. Louis and Kansas City. For this addition they purchased several Cessna cabin monoplanes, powered with the Wright Whirlwind engines. These aircraft provided 100-mph transportation for four passengers cramped in an uncomfortable, noisy cabin—but over the first year about 2,500 risked this aerial adventure. However, despite the apparent success of the extended route, it proved to be too short to be economically feasible. So on December 31, 1928, the Robertson Aircraft Corporation became associated with the Universal Air Lines System which had additional routes running through Chicago and the Midwest. This combine later became one of the operating divisions of American Airways, known today as American Airlines.

Another early airline venture was founded in May 1927 by the financial syndicate that in 1925 had established the Colonial Air Transport, operating between New York and Boston on a post office "feeder" contract. This was known as Colonial Western Airways, and was organized to fly another "feeder" route between Albany and Cleveland. In order to handle this, new backers were introduced and a separate company incorporated. The intent here, of course, was to be in operation with an airmail contract when Big Business made its anticipated move.

Colonial Western Airways had its base in Albany, and three new passenger-carrying Fairchild FC-2 monoplanes were purchased. These interesting machines were fitted with passenger cabins, accommodating four, sheltered under the high monoplane wing. There was no soundproofing nor cabin heating, but the passengers were made fairly comfortable in wicker seats and a cabin-wide settee. The pilot sat just ahead in the cockpit, close enough, in fact, to shout his spiel about the beauties of the Mohawk Valley below, seen through the large side windows. The Fairchild was powered with a 237-hp Wright Whirlwind, and, in addition to passengers, could carry about two hundred pounds of cargo. Throughout 1928 Colonial Western carried 243 passengers and 45,309 pounds of mail.

Scheduled operations began on December 17, 1927, over the Buffalo–Cleveland leg, and full-scale operations started early in 1928 with six daily roundtrips per week. The westbound flight, for instance, left Albany at 10:00 A.M., and after stops in Schnectady, Utica/Rome, Syracuse, Rochester, and Buffalo, arrived in Cleveland at 4:15 P.M. The one-way fare was $60.

Like the parent company, Colonial Western Airways continued operations until 1930, when they were bought up by American Airways which, as noted above, became American Airlines.

One of the early ventures in the airline business was an organization known as Standard Airlines, formed by Jack Frye, Paul Richter, and W. A. Hamilton—who started out as partners in a Los Angeles flying service registered as the Aero Corporation of California. As a side line they handled the Eaglerock Biplane, and then acquired the sales rights to the American-built Fokker line. All this resulted in the purchase of a six-passenger Super Universal for demonstration purposes, but the Fokker planes were not popular in California.

Having a modern cabin plane on their hands, the three former barnstormers decided to put their unwanted demonstrator to work. They started an airline, which is how Standard Airlines was conceived. In November 1927 they scheduled three trips a week between Los Angeles and Tucson with an intermediate stop at Phoenix. Their Fokker took off from Los Angeles at 10:00 A.M. on Mondays, Wednesdays, and Fridays, arriving in Tucson at 5:00 P.M. After an overnight stop the Super Universal left for Los Angeles at 8:00 A.M. Tuesdays, Thursdays, and Saturdays. Sunday was devoted to base maintenance. The Los Angeles–Tucson fare was $60.

For a time business was rewarding. Many movie people were glad to spend their weekends at vacation retreats in Arizona, and during rush periods an extra passenger could be accommodated in the pilot's compartment, while the baggage was tucked in any available space. At times, the overloads necessitated half-filled tanks, but this was made up by refueling stops at Desert City.

During 1928 Standard Airlines added more Fokkers to its fleet and extended the route to El Paso, Texas, with some success. By 1929 Standard was bought by Western Air Express and subsequently became part of TWA. Two of Standard's founders, Jack Frye and Paul Richter, later became president and executive vice president, respectively, of TWA.

Another airline venture that started with considerable promise but wound up insolvent was Florida Airways Corporation, which in 1926 had been awarded an airmail contract over the Miami–Jacksonville "feeder" run. Operations began on April 1, 1926, and by September 15 of that year the company had extended its mail and passenger schedules to Atlanta, Georgia, a total route of 683 miles. Florida Airways began operations with one Tri-Motor— the Liberty-engined version—two Travel Airs, powered with Curtiss OXX-6 150-hp engines, one Stinson Detroiter, and a Curtiss Lark. The Miami-Atlanta run was made with stops at Ft. Myers, Tampa, Jacksonville, and Macon. Each trip took about ten hours.

Florida Airways earned some prestige and favorable publicity during the hurricane that swept southern Florida in September 1926, for they were one of the few transportation systems operating during, and for some time after, the storm. Their Tri-Motor plane was destroyed when it was torn loose from its tie-down at the Miami Airport during the height of a 120-mph wind. After the big blow, Florida Airways used their remaining aircraft to fly in doctors, nurses, medical supplies, and emergency foods to the devastated area.

Throughout the rest of that year it continued its service, carrying 13,200 pounds of mail and 939 passengers. More than 90 percent of all scheduled flights were completed and only twelve forced landings were logged. For the time being, on paper, the whole operation was a success, but the route did not connect with any of the northbound or western lines out of Atlanta, and the post office suspended their airmail contract, soon putting a halt to the line's scheduled operations.

(There are, as usual, several versions to the Florida Airways story. Floyd D. Hall, while President of Eastern Air Lines, gave a speech in 1965 before the Newcomen Society in which he stated that "despite all the bright auguries: flying talent, adequate finances and good flight equipment: paying traffic eluded them. Passengers were few, express packages even rarer, and the air-mail pouches were light. The back-breaker was the lack of mail from the north and while they waited for Harold Pitcairn to build his own planes and deliver mail into the Forida area, Florida Airways became insolvent.")

While refinancing plans were under way, Pitcairn underbid the grounded Atlanta–Miami route and forged the eastern coastal links into a single line. Shortly after, Juan Trippe's syndicate stepped in and picked up Florida Airways, using it as an initial link into Cuba.

One of the first airlines to use aircraft specifically designed and built to carry paying passengers was the Philadelphia Rapid Transit Air Service, which went into business with two Fokker F-VII three-engined high-wing monoplanes. The PRT Air Service was started to coincide with Philadelphia's Sesquicentennial Exposition—the 150th anniversary of the Declaration of Independence—and to demonstrate the many possibilities of air travel. During the Exposition the service, which flew between Philadelphia and Washington, operated at 70 percent capacity. But it proved to be unprofitable after the Exposition closed, and so it had to be abandoned.

The Fokker transports were powered by three 200-hp radials, believed to be Wright Whirlwinds, but some records show that in a few instances British Armstrong–Siddeley Lynx engines were used. Ten passengers could be accommodated in the cabin which offered "picture windows," upholstered wicker chairs, and spacious footroom.

PRT began operations on July 16, 1925, flying two round-trips daily. The 130-mile flight was usually completed in about 90 minutes, and the roundtrip fare was $25. Passengers were allowed thirty pounds of baggage and charged twenty-five cents per pound for any excess. PRT was also awarded a mail contract between the two cities, and in September 1926 the service was extended to include one trip per day to Norfolk, Virginia. This necessitated a third Fokker F-VII for the fleet. Longer routes, less spacious seating arrangements and greater mail revenue might have saved PRT, but after six months of operation the enterprise had to be closed down although the Fokkers had carried 3,695 passengers, flown 93,770 miles, and made 613 scheduled trips in complete safety.

Another early entry in the commercial field was Aeromarine Airways, founded by Inglis M. Uppercu, who had made a lot of money selling Cadillac cars to wealthy Manhattanites. This seasonal passenger-carrying operation began in the fall of 1920, flying out of Key West to Havana with converted F.5-L Navy flying boats. These aircraft had been designed for U.S. Navy operations, but with imaginative conversion became luxury over-water airliners. Each accommodated eleven passengers and a crew of three. This conversion was made by the Aeromarine Plane and Motor Company of Keyport, New Jersey, and was then listed as the Aeromarine Model 75. Powered by two 420-hp Liberty engines, the Aeromarine cruiser had a top speed of 85 mph and a flight range of 340 miles. In addition to the passenger load it could carry 300 pounds of freight.

After several months of trial-and-error operations out of Key West, the company shifted its base north and offered regular service (during the summer months) between New York, Atlantic City, Southampton, and Newport. It even had a booking office in the old Waldorf Astoria hotel in midtown Gotham. During the winter of 1921–22 there was a return to Florida and service was expanded to Miami, Palm Beach, Bimini, and Nassau, still including Havana in their schedules. This seasonal operation—south in the winter, north in the summer—continued until 1924, and by then Cleveland and Detroit were added to the northern leg.

Officials of the company worked hard, but it was soon obvious that it was too early for scheduled airlines to be financially successful. The hit-and-miss "fly for adventure" trade was not enough to warrant continuing.

However, at its peak, Aeromarine Airways was operating seven 11-passenger Model 75s, and nine 4-passenger flying boats. By 1924 it had carried more than 25,000 passengers, flown well over a million miles, and hauled close to 100,000 pounds of freight. During its four years of operations, it had established many advanced airline procedures, a program of pilot training, and efficient maintenance systems.

9

The Douglas Dynasty

Donald W. Douglas, one of the most important figures in commercial aviation in the United States, was first inspired with flying when he watched the Wright brothers in 1909 put on a sales demonstration of one of their early biplanes before a group of U.S. Army officers at Fort Myer, Virginia. That historic event shaped a sound foundation for a manufacturing empire which has lasted until today.*

Unlike many who had blundered into aviation, Donald Douglas began as a skilled engineer. He had started his studies as a midshipman at the U.S. Naval Academy, but found there was little enthusiasm for flying at Annapolis, so he resigned after three years and enrolled for a four-year course in aeronautical engineering at the Massachusetts Institute of Technology. Four years was too long to waste, so Douglas completed the course in half the time—two years—and stayed on as an assistant in Aeronautical Engineering at the princely salary of $500 a year. Over the

* Source material for this chapter was provided by M. R. Fowler, Public Relations Representative of McDonnell Douglas Corporation, through their history booklet *Flight Plan for Tommorow*.

next year he worked with Jerome C. Hunsaker, an aeronautical genius, and together they brought out advanced ideas which were to lead to the present-day wind tunnel.

After one year as an assistant in Aeronautical Engineering, Douglas left M.I.T. and became a consultant to the Connecticut Aircraft Company. By 1915 he was summoned to Los Angeles by Glenn L. Martin, who had opened a factory in San Diego. They were to meet in the lobby of a Los Angeles hotel, but when the youthful Douglas tapped the busy manufacturer on the arm, Glenn Martin took one look at him and decided this was a typical touch. He snapped, "Go away, boy. I haven't time for you. If you're looking for a job, inquire at my plant. I'm very busy, now." Young Douglas then introduced himself, and from that hour on Martin always called him his boy engineer. It was this young man who was to design a bomber, the predecessor of the famed Martin bomber of the postwar era.

During the latter part of 1916 Douglas was called to Washington and made chief civilian aeronautical engineer for the Aviation Section of the Army's Signal Corps. Finding that the military and civilians can seldom agree on anything, Douglas felt after a few months he would be better off where the company shackles were less bureaucratic, so he returned to the Martin plant that now had been transferred to Cleveland.

On his return he discovered the Martin firm had been given an assignment to design an attack plane for the U.S. Army. Whether it was called an attack plane is debatable since the term was not used until late in the 1920s. However, a military aircraft designed for low-level attacks was built and apparently satisfied Washington. With that, Martin and Douglas turned back to their twin-engined bomber concept. By now the Martin staff consisted of Lawrence D. Bell, production manager; Eric Springer, a recognized test pilot; and Douglas, who was in charge of the design. This redoubtable foursome produced what was first known as the

Martin Twin-engined Bomber, which for all-around efficiency proved to be a formidable aircraft. It was unfortunate it could not be put into production in time to be considered for bombing raids on Berlin.

Powered by two 400-hp Liberty engines, the Martin had
a top speed of 118.5 mph with a full bombing load. Later,
more efficient propellers bettered this mark. In addition, it
could climb to 10,000 feet in fifteen minutes. Its service
ceiling was 17,000 feet. (As an interesting comparison,
the Handley Page 0/400 twin-engined bomber, used in the
latter months of 1918, had a top speed of 97.5 mph,
climbed to 10,000 feet in thirty minutes, and had a service
ceiling of only 8,000 feet. The four-engined V/1500, which
was issued to only one squadron, had a top speed of 99
mph, climbed to 10,000 feet in twenty-one minutes, and
had an endurance of twelve hours.)

Later on, several Martins were modified for cargo and
passenger-carrying. The revised cabin could accommodate
a ton of mail or express, and twelve passengers. It is said
that four of these were built for the Apache Aerial Transportation Company of Phoenix, Arizona.

By March 1920, Douglas decided he would like to open
his own plant and have full control over his designs. He
also liked the idea of living in Southern California where
flying weather was generally good and where his family
could enjoy the salubrious climate. There was only one
drawback—all he had was $600 and a few letters of intro-
duction to well-heeled Californians. Still, he thought the
risk was worth the candle. Once he had his family settled,
he rented desk space at the rear of a downtown Los Angeles
barber shop and from there pounded the pavements in
search of benevolent investors.

His first lucky break occurred when he met a well-to-do
young man, David R. Davis, who agreed to finance the
building of a plane which could fly coast-to-coast nonstop.
Douglas said such a plane could be built, but it might cost

in the neighborhood of $40,000. Davis was willing, and they formed the Davis-Douglas Company and went to work. With money in the cash drawer, Douglas then persuaded six of his former Martin associates to come out and work on a plane already called the *Cloudster*. This memorable aircraft was built in sections on the second floor of a planing mill—the parts lowered to the ground floor through an elevator shaft—and moved piecemeal to a suburban hangar for assembly and test flying. Later on the firm moved to a discarded motion picture studio just off Wilshire Boulevard near the eastern limits of Santa Monica.

The Cloudster, which eventually became a passenger transport carrying eleven paying patrons, added some prestige to the Davis-Douglas firm, although the plane itself never received the acclaim due it. It was a smart-looking, sturdy, single-bay biplane that, though not the first to fly coast-to-coast, was the first airplane in history to carry a load exceeding its own weight. It was Claude Ryan who in 1926 converted a Cloudster into a lavish liner and used it on his early Los Angeles–San Diego Air Line. But the basic aircraft had efficient design, a sturdy undercarriage, clean lines, simple stressing; and a fuselage and cockpit which could be modified for several requirements. The Cloudster first took to the air on February 24, 1921, and in April of the same year the company received its first Navy contract to design and build three torpedo planes, later known as DTs. Douglas and his team of designers drew to a great extent on the basic form of the Cloudster, changing the wheeled undercarriage to a pontoon landing gear, building in a two-place cockpit, and designing the sling and launching gear for a Whitehead torpedo.

In those days a Navy contract did not necessarily mean an advance in cash. Although Douglas and Davis had built a successful Cloudster, it had not brought in an immediate return, so they had to hit the streets again to find someone to back them. One of their best aids was the famous Bill Henry, a noted sports writer who had wide influence in Los

Angeles. Bill helped them to obtain the signatures of ten prominent businessmen, among them Harry Chandler, publisher of the Los Angeles *Times*; an attorney; the vice president of a bank; the president of a drug company; and several others who listed their occupations as "Capitalists."

Needless to state, the new DTs were a service success, and once Navy aviators could be trained to fly torpedo runs and hit a simulated target, more orders were forthcoming. At one time the Davis-Douglas Company had an order backlog of 38 DTs being built at the old studio-factory alongside a cow-pasture airfield in Santa Monica. By 1924 this same dust and turf strip had acquired an importance far beyond its pretensions. On March 17 of that year four wide-winged biplanes stood growling through the exhaust ports of their 400-hp Liberty engines, and as the propellers twirled in idle movement their great blades raised small dust spouts, smothering Douglas workmen and U.S. Army Air Service men who were to fly these ships around the world. The U.S. Army had awarded its first contract to the Davis-Douglas firm, and in return Donald W. Douglas had produced another fantastic aircraft. It was known only as the DWC—Douglas World Cruiser—and seemingly was designed simply to put on an aviation "first" by the U.S. Army Air Service.

The formation flight was commanded by Captain Lowell H. Smith and his pilots were Lieutenants Henry H. Ogden, Leigh Wade, Eric H. Nelson, Leslie P. Arnold, and John Harding, Jr. (who acted as Flight Commander in the air). The circumnavigation of the world, as the flight was known, began at Santa Monica on March 17, 1924, and took in Seattle, crossed Alaska and the Bering Strait to Siberia and Japan, then over China, Malaysia, India, Arabia, the Balkans, Vienna, Paris, London, the Orkneys, Iceland, Greenland, Labrador, Montreal, Washington, and across the continent to their starting point. They had covered a course of 27,553 miles in 15 days, 11 hours, 7 minutes of flying time. More than 200,000 people greeted the world fliers on their return to Santa Monica, and in honor of their flight a square acre on the field at the point of their touch down was covered with a layer of flower petals which rose up and provided a variegated slipstream.

The success of the DWCs placed the company high on the contract list of the U.S. Army. The Navy also kept the firm busy turning out improved versions of the DT. Then the European market was heard from when Norway ordered two modified DTs and later purchased manufacturing rights to produce them under license. By the time the World Flight had been milked of its publicity features, the U.S. Army next ordered a prototype observation plane that was to be known as the O-2. This triggered a frantic search for more skilled workmen. In 1920 Douglas had started with himself and six employees in a 3,600-square-foot planing-mill loft. By late 1924 the work staff had grown to 112, and the annual payroll was $248,867.21. By 1966 Douglas was to employ 75,000 skilled workmen in 1,500,000 square feet of factory property, owned or operated by Douglas, and the backlog would be well over $3,000,000,000.

The O-2 observation aircraft was a very profitable product for the company, and before the initial order was completed the Army Air Corps requested a utility plane that could be used as a cargo or troop transport, one which could handle several types of air-evacuation work. Douglas turned out what became known as the C-1C, a distinct military craft capable of 121 mph, and showing a service ceiling of 16,000 feet.

Douglas was next drawn into the airmail business, and his Wilshire Boulevard plant turned out O-2Ms for the Post Office Department. These planes carried a much larger pay load than the de Havillands and at a much higher speed. For instance, trips between route points were made at a speed averaging 150 mph. One between Chicago and New York, on December 16, 1926, was carried through at 167.5 mph, and the fastest trip on record at the time was flown on January 30, 1927, between Chicago and Cleveland at a speed of 175.1 mph. These Douglas airplanes, with their greater cruising radius, eliminated the stops at Bellefonte, Bryan, and Rawlins on the westbound trips. In addition to these stops, Iowa City, North Platte, and Rock Springs were discontinued eastbound.

It was during this period that the bewildering alphabet-number designations for aircraft were introduced, a system that has driven aviation writers the world over into insane asylums. As an example, ten of the 50 O-2Ms were redesignated M-3s, and forty became M-4s. When the Mexican government purchased 10 O-2s with which to make war on the Yaqui Indians, they were listed as O-2Cs. But this was not all. In 1927 the Army Air Corps ordered sixty-two planes to replace the original O-2s, and they were designated O-2Cs, the same as the Mexican models. Ultimately, 142 of these were ordered and the numerical madness was on. There was no respite from this until World War II when we learned to recognize and love the Mustangs, Lightnings, Fortresses, Liberators, and Devastators.

Production requirements at the Wilshire Boulevard plant demanded a more suitable airfield on which to test the planes as they came off the Douglas production line. Already, partly assembled aircraft were being towed by road to the Clover Field some two miles away, and eventually the firm was able to transfer its factory operations to this area.

It was not until 1928 that the Douglas designers saw the commercial-transport aviation business was something to be reckoned with. True, they had cleared their production line of the airmail O-2Ms, and had noted the publicity concerning the "feeder" lines, but they had not taken the commercial business seriously. But in that year, Douglas, as a change of pace, considered the possibility of building a commercial craft which would employ the roomy hull of the flying boat and provide a new level of convenience for passengers.

This resulted in the design and production of what came to be known as the Douglas Dolphin, a high-winged amphibious monoplane, powered by two 300-hp Wright Whirlwind engines. This luxurious aircraft had a price tag of $45,000, but despite this the operators of a Wilmington–Catalina airline bought one of the first available. The U.S. Navy, the Army, and the Coast Guard also invested in this handsome flying boat, and—according to one booklet of Douglas publicity—another private version of the Dolphin, complete with a bar, lounge, business office, and other refinements, was assembled and sold for $57,000. The purchaser was said to be a French industrialist whose name was kept secret. However, early in 1969 the Douglas Public relations executives explained that in 1934 William E. Boeing of Seattle, who became a business rival of Donald Douglas, bought a Dolphin for use as a tender for his yacht. Much was made of the purchase in the newspapers: "Would Mr. Chrysler buy a car from Mr. Ford? Did Mr. Firestone ever purchase a tire from Mr. Goodyear?" Eventually that Dolphin was sold and used by several subsequent owners, and as a compliment to the Douglas quality of workmanship and materials, is said to be still flying.

The reader may enjoy meditating on whether the $57,000 luxury craft was sold to an unnamed French industrialist or whether the story was a cover-up of a sale to Bill Boeing—who, a year after his purchase of the Douglas flying boat, produced the 314 Clipper, and in 1940 had his XPBB-1 Sea Ranger in the Boeing catalog. But, of course, it may be recalled that in 1920 Boeing built two flying boats, the B-1 and BB-1. In 1925 he produced his PB-1 and PB-2, and between these dates his firm turned out several floatplanes under government contract.

A memorable date in the Douglas saga is August 2, 1932, when the directors decided to risk their profitable association with the military services and make a definite bid for some of the airline business. At the time, it could have been a debatable decision, although the bulk of military orders was swinging to the Boeing concern in Seattle. Between 1930 and 1935 Boeing was taking over the heavy-bomber market with their B-299 Flying Fortress which became the B-17 of World War II fame. Boeing was also active in the service fighter field. Considering the many limitations of the military service in those days, Douglas probably wondered how long he could compete and make money selling aircraft to Uncle Sam.

In mid 1932 the fast expanding Transcontinental and Western Air (TWA) sent out a form letter to Douglas, Curtiss-Wright, Ford, Martin, and the Consolidated Aircraft Company, soliciting bids for ten or more tri-motor transport planes. No price bracket was mentioned, but TWA also wished to know how soon the first would be available for its service test. A simple paragraph stated that an all-metal, three-engined monoplane, accommodating twelve passengers in comfort, was wanted—an airliner which would have a cruising speed of 145 mph, a landing speed not to exceed 65 mph, a service ceiling of 21,000 feet, and a range of 1,080 miles. The airline also demanded radio equipment and "instrumentation" to permit night flying. The gross weight was not to exceed 14,200 pounds and the pay load was to be 2,300 pounds.

The Douglas team decided to venture into the commercial field, which seemingly promised good profits over longer production runs. Within eleven months they had produced an airliner that greatly exceeded all the TWA specifications. In the first place, they ignored the three-engine requirement, knowing that new high-powered radials were becoming available. If properly streamlined with sleek cowlings, two would provide all the power necessary. A retractable landing gear would assure a speed increase of at least 20 percent.

On September 20, 1932, TWA announced the purchase of the Douglas twin-engined transport design, first known as the DC-1. The price per plane was $65,000, which meant about 75 of them would have to be sold to bear the expense of the design, research, and tooling-up for production-line manufacture. The prototype was first flown on July 1, 1933. Before the basic DC-1 model was discarded nearly two hundred were built to various configurations. Much of the contract work was carried out in complete secrecy, but within a few days after TWA had accepted the design Douglas stock went from $7 a share to $16.

(The Davis-Douglas Company, incorporated in South Dakota, was succeeded by the Douglas Company, incorporated in California. The present Douglas Aircraft Company, incorporated in Delaware, was organized in 1928 to purchase the assets of the old Douglas Company with an authorized capital stock of 1,000,000 shares. Only 300,000 shares were issued, of which Donald Douglas received 200,000. The balance was distributed to the public through brokers.)

When the first—and only—DC-1 was rolled out of its shed and onto the Clover Field it looked like a winged monster. The fuselage was 60 feet in length, much longer than the body of the average transcontinental bus. One commercial pilot of that day took one look, let out a low whistle and said, "It will never get off the ground. It's too big!"

There were anxious minutes when those who were permitted to watch the first flight were ready to agree. It was a perfectly clear day with a light west wind blowing in from the ocean. The taxiing tests were completed without a hitch. The project engineer then climbed aboard and joined the chief pilot. The DC-1 was run to the east end of the runway, turned into the wind, and began its take-off at 12:30 P.M. All went well for half a minute, and then the port engine spluttered and quit cold. The pilot managed to clamber for a few hundred feet of altitude, and then the starboard engine coughed out. The pilot nosed down, hoping to find a space to make a forced landing which would not result in too much damage.

The instant he put her nose down, both engines picked up with a breathtaking roar, churned on, and then quit again. It was obvious the pilot was facing engine malfunction with the change in the nose-up position of the plane. Whenever he flew level, or nose-down, the engines would run perfectly, but would conk out when he tried to climb. He nursed this condition until he reached 1,500 feet, and then he turned gingerly and made a safe landing. Investigation disclosed that the carburetor floats were mounted in such a position that the fuel flow was stopped every time the plane's nose was tilted upward. In due course the carburetor mount was reversed, the fuel lines connected in the opposite direction, and both engines gave their power whether climbing or diving.

The overall performance of this remarkable plane far exceeded TWA's exacting specifications. The 145–150 mph cruising speed proved to be nearer 180 mph. When the new Wright Cyclone 710–hp engines were installed, eliminating a bulky third engine, the pay load was raised by 20 percent. Also, passenger space could accommodate 14, instead of 12 people, and variable-pitch propellers improved take-off and landing characteristics.

About a month after the initial test flight, the same DC-1 was sent to Winslow, Arizona, to put on a manufacturer's demonstration. Loaded with 18,000 pounds of ballast, the test crew planned to make a normal take-off, using only one engine. The general idea was to have the plane become airborne at a marker halfway down the runway, reduce power, retract the landing gear and continue the take-off. The idea was sound, but the airport at Winslow is set at an elevation of 4,500 feet and the DC-1 did not get its wheels clear until more than three-quarters of the runway had been used. To the people looking on it seemed the plane would never get off the ground. But at that point the pilot cut the switch of the starboard engine and retracted the undercarriage. The plane continued on and maintained a normal climb up to 8,000 feet, proceeded on to Albuquerque using only one engine, and arrived fifteen minutes ahead of a TWA Ford Tri-Motor, which had taken off from Winslow a short time before the DC-1.

TWA took delivery of this particular plane on September 13, 1933, and used it chiefly for pilot-familiarity flights. The airline had previously ordered twenty more, and another twenty were contracted for by November 1, 1933. By this time the DC-1 had been somewhat improved and was known as the DC-2. In March 1935 one of these models set a new west-east transcontinental record of twelve hours and forty-five minutes, and still later an east-west mark of fifteen hours and thirty-nine minutes. The Douglas DC-2 established nineteen American and world records before it was further improved and known as the DC-3. Before the year 1935 was ended President Roosevelt awarded the Collier Trophy—which had been donated by Robert J. Collier for the "Greatest Aeronautical Achievement of the Year"—to Donald Douglas for his DC-2 airliner.

Until the advent of the Douglas DC series, passenger carrying, generally regarded as a rash venture, was far from a comfortable experience. Those who tried it either as a novelty or for reasons of emergency were subjected to periods of deafness, gastric distress, cold feet, and long hours of teeth-rattling vibration. The aircraft being used prior to 1935 were Ford Tri-Motors, Fairchilds, Boeing 40-As, tri-motor Fokkers, Sikorsky amphibians, and a few single-engined mail planes which had been modified to take four or five passengers. The comparative comfort, luxury, and speed factors of the DC planes raised commercial passenger-carrying to a new level of transport operations. It was obvious other major manufacturers would have to face up to this advance in commercial air progress.

By 1935, too, the big manufacturers were also aware of the increasing political tension in Europe, and it was plain that another European war was in the making. There was quiet talk of bombers and bomb raids on capital cities, and wise executives, looking for a continuation of their production lines, came to the conclusion that a basic bomber design could be easily modified into a commercial aircraft . . . and vice versa. This pattern was obvious in Germany where the Hitler regime was seemingly engrossed in building numerous commercial aircraft for as yet uncharted airline operations. Only a few sage historians, who remembered the remodeling of World War I bombers into postwar commercial carriers, realized the opposite modifications were grimly logical. As an example, it may be recalled that in 1935 the Boeing Aircraft Company had produced the 314 Clipper flying boat, but had also turned out the basic B-299 that was to become the B-17 Flying Fortress. A variation of the Fort, using the same wings and tail assembly, was to appear first as the 307 Prototype and then the 307 Stratoliner. By 1940 the B-29 Superfortress was magically fleshed out and became the XYC-97, flying later as airliner 377 Stratocruiser. The 314 Clipper flying boat of 1935 turned up again in 1940 as the XPBB-1 Sea Ranger, a naval craft. Several other basic designs of all manufacturers were, of course, inspired by the development and perfection of the jet engine.

In 1934 commercial aviation learned through a bitter and pointless political controversy that it could no longer rely on the subsidy from flying the mail, and realized all the investments and airline structure would have to be revised to fit the passenger-carrying trade, with airline fares carrying the full expense of running the schedules.

But before Hitler put the torch to Western Europe, the Douglas plant produced the greatest contribution to the airline industry. The popular DC-2 was enlarged to carry more passengers, and became the renowned DC-3. It provided the same style, convenience, and safety the public had experienced since TWA's jackpot strike in 1933, and it was the first airplane which could make money by just carrying passengers. This airliner completely revolutionized the world of commercial aviation. It was first flown on December 17, 1935, from the Clover Field strip but, strange to relate, aroused no startling reactions from the VIP onlookers. It simply was a clean-lined cabin plane, powered at first with two Wright or Pratt & Whitney engines, but to the experienced eye it was the logical and evolutionary development of the DC-1 and DC-2. As has usually happened in aircraft development, what had produced the remarkable improvement was the availability of new power plants. Both Wright and Pratt & Whitney had perfected new radials that could produce 1,000 hp, and permitted the DC-3 to carry twenty-one passengers at a cruising speed of 195 mph over a range of 1,380 miles. This extended performance made possible a coast-to-coast flight in fifteen hours, as against nineteen hours for the speediest airliner produced by the opposition.

More than 10,000 Gooney Birds, as the DC-3 was affectionately known to servicemen, supported the Allied forces during World War II, and more than earned their place among the outstanding contributions to the ultimate victory. General Dwight D. Eisenhower declared the DC-3 to be one of the single pieces of equipment that did most to win the war. Many historians have written paeans of praise to the DC-3 which in military circles was also known as the C-47, the R4D, and the Dakota—as the British knew it. But air travelers will long remember the comfort, safety and work-horse characteristics of the DC-3, and today many people still yearn for the sense of security they enjoyed while being initiated into America's legions of air commuters.

The advent of Walter Folger Brown as President Hoover's Postmaster General came at a time—1929—when the airlines needed more than casual interest from Washington officialdom. After a memorable consultation with half a dozen leading airline operators, the McNary-Watres Act, which was simply an amendment of the Kelly Air Mail bill, established a new "base mile rate,"—with extra pay for planes flying at night when they were equipped with two-way radio and passenger accommodations, and were capable of crossing high-altitude mountain areas. This indicated that the post office was willing to pay for available cargo space in an aircraft whether it was loaded with mail or not.

This resulted in a frantic demand for bigger and costlier planes such as Fokkers, Curtiss Condors, and Fords. Boeing Air Transport immediately dropped its famed single-engined Monomail, only recently introduced, and developed the Boeing 80, which carried twelve passengers and a fair load of cargo. It was obvious that using a plane designed expressly for carrying mail was no longer sound business. It soon became apparent that the bigger the aircraft—within aerodynamic limitations—the greater chance for higher profits. With a nudge from the accountant's office Clair Egtvedt was soon roughing out a new low-wing, twin-engined, cabin monoplane, using the basic lines of the Monomail. This new model was first listed as the 247 and later became the prototype of a long catalog of Boeing air-liners. It was designed to take the new Pratt & Whitney Hornet radial engine, higher powered than the Wasp, and although most BAT pilots were delighted with the Wasp, Egtvedt wanted to build a 16,000-pound plane that would require the extra power output of the Hornet. However, in this instance the views of the pilots were respected and Egtvedt scaled down his plans to a 12,000-pound transport which would carry ten passengers in comparative luxury and still provide ample space for mail. It would cost $68,000 as compared to $50,000 for the Ford Tri-Motor, but the 247's top speed of 160 mph was much faster than anything on the market.

The 247s were first introduced in 1933. United Aircraft

& Transport appropriated $4,000,000 to order sixty of these new Boeings and planned to standardize their coast-to-coast service.

In placing such an order, United Aircraft tied up Boeing's output and made certain no competitor would match their equipment for some time. This domestic arrangement, however, did not prevent Boeing's selling two 247s to the German Lufthansa. The two new passenger craft were shipped over, along with a test pilot to teach Lufthansa pilots to fly them. After a short period of instruction, the Boeing man was dismissed and sent home, somewhat puzzled by the strange, unfriendly behavior of his hosts.

It turned out later that the Germans had not purchased the 247s for their airline operations; higher Nazi officials took over the Boeings and made a very complete study of the airframe, the engines, and the know-how that had gone into their design. It was no wonder that, as a result, several German bombers of World War II—particularly the Focke-Wulf 200C, the Heinkel He 111, and in many respects the Junkers Ju 88—showed the earlier Boeing influence.

Back home, in order to compete with the 247, the Douglas plant was to beef up the DC-3 until it produced 180 mph. The new model was snapped up by TWA and American Airlines. Other operators found themselves outside the Boeing-Douglas market and were glad to appeal to the Lockheed concern in Burbank, snatching at their Lodestar. This aircraft became a World War II utility plane, serving as a paratrooper carrier, a troop transport, a cargo plane, a hospital plane, and in a few instances as a light bomber. In the early 1930s the Lodestar at one time was the fastest passenger-carrier in commercial aviation.

10

The Army Airmail Blunder

From 1920 until 1928 the growth of commercial aviation was dependent on a number of short-haul, or feeder, lines which had come into being through the support of the post office contracts. By 1928 the airmail rate was ten cents per ounce, and on most routes the average load flown was two hundred pounds. Passenger-carrying was a side line, often forced on most of the smaller operators and, until the availability of the Douglas DC-2, far from profitable. As previously explained, the first air passenger service was scheduled by Western Air Express, which had been financed by the Daniel Guggenheim Fund when the line was operated as something of an experimental laboratory.

Farsighted executives soon realized the small feeder lines would eventually have to be absorbed by a few well-financed transcontinental lines and, once this general merger was carried out, the transcontinental lines would have to assume the obligations of private enterprise. But it was also obvious that these major operators would require a constantly increasing volume of mail or cargo if they were to pay skilled pilots, buy larger aircraft, and erect substantial base hangars and maintenance shops. To cope with this approaching situation, Representative Kelly sponsored an amendment to his original act of 1925, and it was passed on May 17, 1928. This set the airmail postage rate at five cents an ounce which at first decreased revenue but increased the volume of airmail handled by the airlines.

The operators were being paid on a pound-per-mile basis, a figure governed by their original bids. The new amendment increased the airmail traffic loads by 95 percent, about doubling the income of the lines without appreciably increasing their operating overhead. For instance, during the fiscal year of 1928 the post office paid out $11,000,000 for hauling airmail, and collected only $4,250,000 in postage. Still, Postmaster General Harry S. New refrained from reducing the payments to the airlines although he had full authority to do so.

It should be explained that Postmaster General New was facing a two-way problem. He wanted the airmail to become a profitable undertaking, and like all hard-headed businessmen, he applied the principle of reducing the unit price to attract volume business. He also had to encourage the carriers to expand and purchase new equipment. A loss had to be taken somewhere, and he was willing to leave that problem to the Post Office Department. He decided to let the five-cents-an-ounce experiment run for six months. By that time another election would be coming up and Postmaster New felt it would be wiser to let the airmail situation simmer while the electorate debated the issues of the two parties.

In November 1928 Herbert Hoover was elected President to replace Calvin Coolidge. Postmaster New's successor was Walter Folger Brown, who had been active in Republican politics. For his devotion, Brown not only gained the Postmaster General's Cabinet post, but also inherited the problem of the airmail. He was a sound business man, and after studying the situation he decided the airlines should be able to operate profitably without relying on airmail support. He argued that the best way to stimulate growth was sound competition. He also felt that only big, well-financed companies with first-class management, heading a few transcontinental airlines, were worth supporting in the network planning. Whether he was responsible for the overall airline system as it operates today or whether it would have worked out its own destiny has long been debated.

In February of 1930 Postmaster Brown recommended a third amendment to the Kelly Bill which became known as the McNary-Watres Act. This gave the Postmaster General unquestioned power over all commercial aviation in the country. As an example, certain provisions of the bill were:

1. The method of computing payments to the airlines for hauling the mail was changed to pay for available cargo space of not more than $1.25 a mile, whether or not there was any mail to be carried.

2. Contracts were to be awarded only to the lowest bidder, if the line had completed a daily schedule over a route of at least 250 miles for a period of six months.

3. The Postmaster might extend or consolidate routes when in his judgment the public interest was thereby promoted.

4. Any airline with two years of operation behind it could exchange its mail contract for a route certificate, good for ten years, unless revoked by the Postmaster General for willful neglect of postal regulations.

When queried on these points, Postmaster Brown stated that most of the airmail lines did not carry passengers and depended entirely on revenue from airmail. If they were to become self-supporting they had to be encouraged to carry passengers, and in that way compete with each other. He also argued that paying for space instead of weight would encourage the operators to use larger planes, which would develop a passenger service. He agreed that certain terms of the bill favored the bigger, well-financed lines, but pointed out that the post office was buying a service that was highly specialized and hazardous, a field in which the small businessman had little hope of competing. In closing, Brown also explained that if the post office were to encourage passenger carrying, it would become responsible for the safety of the passengers. This was why he had inserted the clause that gave the Postmaster General the right to revoke route certificates.

Later in 1930 in a meeting with a number of airline executives—a gathering that became known as the "Spoils Conference"—Brown made it clear that he believed no transcontinental route could be successful unless it came under the management of one company. Furthermore, he did not believe airmail contracts should be the subject of competitive bidding, because under the new bill the safety of passengers was involved. This meant the small, independent airline could not make a low bid without showing it could provide for the safety of its passengers. Naturally, owners of the small airlines realized they were being pushed out of the business. They complained so loudly that John R. McCarl, the Comptroller General, had to step in and limit Brown's powers by ruling that an extension could never be longer than the basic or original route.

To counteract this, and forestall any "wildcat" bidding, Brown specified that bidders on airmail contracts must have six months of night-flying experience over a route of at least 250 miles. Again, he was arguing for the safety of future passengers. Since only veteran mail carriers had operated at night, most of the small, independent airlines were kept out of the bidding.

An example of Brown's views and decision was to be noted on August 25, 1930, when bids were called for on the two main transcontinental lines. American Airlines had no trouble in gaining the southern route, but the Postmaster General insisted on the merger of Western Air Express and Transcontinental Air Transport into Transcontinental and Western Air Line, Inc. before he would award the contract for the northern route. He continued his autocratic control until the spring of 1931, but it must be admitted he did have a network of airways spreading over the whole country. United Air Lines flew a route across the northern section of the country from Chicago to Seattle. Eastern Air Transport covered most of the East Coast, operating over the three chief north-south routes. United also flew two north-south routes, one between Chicago and Texas, and the other along the Pacific coast.

On the surface it would appear that Brown's drastic control of these air operations was setting up a most satisfactory continental airline system, but a number of small operators were burrowing and tunneling beneath the network to bring his autocratic regime to an end. In one instance, E. L. Cord, manufacturer of the Cord and Auburn automobiles of that day, had been working his way into the airline business. His pilots were flying his Century Air Lines planes out of Chicago, and his Century Pacific Air Lines was flying a West Coast route. Neither operation was making money, but he hoped to obtain mail contracts to make one or the other of these twin ventures pay. To draw attention to his efforts, Cord argued that most rival airlines were too extravagant and luxurious, and stated he could carry airmail anywhere in the country for thirty cents a mile—about half of what the successful airlines were earning.

He may have had a point since at the time he was using Stinson aircraft powered with low-output Lycoming engines quite suitable for airmail operations, but, of course, they would not accommodate paying passengers. Cord also claimed it was ridiculous to pay pilots an average of $7,000 a year in those depression days when hundreds of hungry pilots were willing to work for less. It was apparent the automobile man hoped to break into the airline business with inexperienced fliers and modest-priced aircraft unable to meet Brown's high standards. It was learned later that Cord had gone so far as to force his pilots to sign their resignations at one desk, and sign up for a guaranteed $150-a-month base pay, plus $3 an hour for daytime flying, and $5 an hour for night flights.

A short time previously, David L. Behncke, formerly a pilot for the Boeing company, had organized the Air Line Pilots' Association in cooperation with the American Federation of Labor. As soon as Cord's moves were known, Behncke's union called a strike against Century Air Lines. In retaliation, Cord hired nonunion pilots, and the ensuing quarrel aroused the interest of Congressmen A. J. Sabath and Fiorello La Guardia, who demanded an official investigation.

Alderman John Wilson, Chairman of Chicago's Aviation Committee, persuaded the Chicago Aero Commission to inquire into the dispute. Captain Lipsner was appointed chairman of the hearing. Lipsner later submitted a report to the commission as a whole, and it turned out that the wage-scale point was relatively unimportant—it was a question of whether Century Air Lines should be allowed to operate out of Chicago.

During this pilots' strike post office officials had been considering Cord's bid of thirty cents for carrying airmail, but to Postmaster General Brown, Cord was staging a mutiny in order to get a contract that would ignore passenger carrying and limit operations to the remunerative airmail returns. This would undo all Brown had built up over the past three years. Brown finally induced the post office to deny Cord and his Century Air Lines any contract in the airmail operation, and with that Cord sold his interests to the Aviation Corporation of California, the parent company of American Airways. This ended the strike, but left Century's pilots without jobs.

Postmaster Brown had worked tirelessly to put over his ideas, and eventually he could see a clear picture of commercial aviation's future. He had increased the airline routes by some 9,000 miles, but had driven most of the small, independent operators out of business. Airmail that had cost the government $1.10 a mile in 1929 had been reduced to 54¢ a mile in 1933, but this impressive record had left many a wound, and those affected sought a weapon of retaliation.

In November 1932, Franklin D. Roosevelt was elected President by an overwhelming majority. The long months of financial depression that had begun with the stock market debacle—Black Friday in 1929—had to be brought to a halt, and a series of bold government strokes were required to bring some semblance of relief to the American public. Everything the Hoover administration had done, or attempted to do, was declared to be at variance with the good of the commonweal. As with every change of administration in Washington, there was a hurried program of investigations, exposures, and bitter blanket charges. The new broom must always prove it will sweep clean.

In February 1933, a month before the Roosevelt administration was to take over Washington, Senator Hugo Black of Alabama convened his Special Committee for Investigation of the Air Mail and Ocean Mail Contracts, a body formed to halt a long-time dispute over ocean-mail contracts. But Senator Black managed to switch its chief interest to the airmail situation.

One morning investigators for the Interstate Commerce Commission made a concerted raid on all airline offices and seized their files for examination. President Roosevelt then named James Aloysius Farley Poastmaster General, and Walter Folger Brown closed his desk and left the field to a Democrat.

The Black committee went into high gear, and its airmail "disclosures" became headlined features day after day. The new Postmaster General summed up the charges as follows:

1. That airmail appropriations had been used to favor a few corporations which employed the money "as the basis of wild stock promotions."

2. That the five original contracts which had been due to expire on November 7, 1929, had been illegally extended so these favored corporations could avoid competitive bidding until the Postmaster General could provide for them after passage of the McNary-Watres act.

3. That those favored operators had been invited to a spoils conference during May and June of 1930, at which conference the airway network of the United States was laid out.

4. That the Postmaster General had avoided open bidding and had given out nearly 13,000 miles of airway by extension. Nine thousand of these miles had no bidding at all.

5. That airline and post office officials had destroyed certain incriminating evidence.

6. That American Airways had received the contract for the southern transcontinental route as the lone bidder after a pre-arranged deal with a rival.

7. That the central transcontinental route had gone to the highest bidder, and as a result the government had lost $2,500,000.

8. That from July of 1930 through December of 1933 airmail contractors had received more than $78,000,000 from the government, although actual service rendered amounted to only 40 percent of that amount.

9. That the airmail contracts were held illegally because they had been obtained by collusion.

10. That it was the duty of the administrative officers to disqualify such contractors for a period of five years.

It will be seen from the above that the main contentions were that Brown had shown undue favoritism to certain airlines from which they had profited unfairly, and that there had been collusion in several instances—although some of the charges were proved groundless. Still, when all the Black Committee's claims were illuminated under the national spotlight, widespread suspicion justified drastic action. Postmaster Farley and the Roosevelt administration felt there was sufficient conclusive evidence to cancel all airmail contracts.

Authority for this drastic stroke was to be found in the Postal Laws and Regulations which gave the Postmaster General punitive powers when conspiracy was apparent, and on February 9, 1934, General Benjamin D. Foulois, Chief of the Army Air Corps, was called to the White House and asked if the Army could take over the airmail. In the first glow of importance the general pointed out that Army fliers and military planes had done just that in 1918. Whether the reference justified the inference that in 1934 his Air Corps could, and was ready to, fly the mail again, would be long debated. But it is understandable that General Foulois considered his service able to take on any national emergency, and hoped Congress would see that the Air Corps was worthy of more realistic financial backing. Actually, General Foulois was in a difficult position, and he had little choice but to accept the unenviable situation.

As a result of the general's decision, an order was issued from the White House over the President's signature canceling all airmail contracts and commanding the Army to fly the postal loads. Thus, with a stroke of the pen, United States commercial aviation suffered a blow from which it would not completely recover until the outbreak of World War II.

The airline operators were ordered to complete their final airmail runs on February 19, just ten days after the President had first considered cancelation of the contracts. The order involved 27,062 miles of airways flown by ten commercial airlines, and it was doubtful whether any of them could have continued on their passenger-carrying revenue for any length of time.

General Foulois and his staff looked over the combined routes and realized that much of the airmail mileage would have to be cut to something nearer 11,000 instead of 27,062 miles. The Air Corps had few airplanes suitable for cargo-carrying among the 800 planes distributed all over the

country. The observation planes appeared to be most suited
for temporary modification, although there were about 140
single-seat pursuits and a few bombers that might serve as
mail carriers. Before the military effort was called off, almost every type of aircraft on the Air Corps list, except
primary trainers, participated in one way or another.

To clearly understand the impact of General Foulois's
decision to take over even a small portion of the airmail
network, one should have some idea of the overall standards of the Air Corps in the early 1930s. At the top, com-
placency and a general attitude of country-club indolence
stifled much of the program. There was little international
unrest to justify stiff service discipline. That Nazism in
Europe would soon be laughed off the front pages, and what
did Germany have that could cause concern? Hitler was a
stuffed martinet, a comic paperhanger who was operating
on the dues extracted from a lot of goosestepping goons
who liked to dress up in black or brown shirts and stage
their antics outside German beer saloons. It took real money
to run an army—or an air force. Where would der Führer
get it? Here in the United States there wasn't enough in
the treasury to furnish gasoline for primary trainers—or so
the politicians in Washington claimed.

This peacetime ennui was not confined to the Air Corps.
The Army and Navy also had come under the corrosive spell
in the years that followed the Armistice, for the serviceman
no longer was the saviour of the nation, the defender of
democracy, the warrior who had gone "Over There" to win
the war. Now the situation was reversed. Men in uniform
were looked on as slackers who were dodging the responsibilities of the country's peacetime problems. Is it any wonder that the services were far from the parade-ground
standards of West Point or Annapolis?

There was none of the old-time Regular Army tradition
in the flying service—in any country. Guest nights were a

On June 11, 1918 pilot Torrey Webb flew the first New York–Boston mail run. Mayor William F. Murray of Boston is shown turning over the first bag of mail. (Post Office Photo)

The first Air Mail insignia was copied from a Mail Pouch Tobacco package of the day. Max Miller accepts an American flag from Mrs. Rose Lipsner. The plane is a Curtiss JN–4H. (Benjamin Lipsner Photo)

Earle Ovington made the first air-mail flight in America September 14, 1911, carrying a pouch from Sheepshead Bay to Jamaica, Long Island: a distance of about six miles. (Post Office Photo)

This Boeing Model 40 was designed to fill a definite need for the Chicago–San Francisco air mail run in 1925. It carried 1000 pounds of mail at 135 mph. (Boeing Aircraft Photo)

In 1915 William E. Boeing built his first airplane, then known as the B & W flying boat. Today Boeing's 747 is in great demand by the world's greatest airlines. (Boeing Aircraft Photo)

The Boeing Model 80, brought out in 1929 to carry not only mail, but passengers as well. With this aircraft United Air Lines established a 27-hour coast-to-coast service. (Boeing Aircraft Photo)

Captain Benjamin B. Lipsner who started and directed the early operations of the air mail service.

James H. Doolittle, best-remembered for his raid on Tokyo in WW II, made a great contribution to the science of instrument flying through the Daniel Guggenheim Fund. (U.S. Air Force Photo)

The legendary Ford Tri-Motor transport designed around a cantilever wing and all-metal construction by William B. Stout. (United Air Lines Photo)

The final version of the Douglas mail plane designed expressly for the U.S. Post Office. It was known as the O–M3. Later models were sold to Mexico as military planes. (Douglas Aircraft Photo)

National Airlines began operations in 1934 with a 142-mile route between St. Petersburg and Daytona Beach, Florida. The Stinson Trimotor was one of their first planes. (National Airlines Photo)

Donald Douglas was awarded the Collier Trophy for his DC airliners. This is the second version, known as the DC–2, which carried fourteen passengers and set a new west-east transcontinental record of 12 hours, 45 minutes. (Douglas Aircraft Photo)

Following their great success with Lindbergh's trans-Atlantic plane, the Ryan Company went into the mail-passenger business and produced this 4-passenger monoplane. (National Airlines Photo)

This is the 1938 DC–3 fleet of TWA, when
it was proved that airlines could make
money simply by hauling passengers.
(Douglas Aircraft Photo)

The Douglas DC–4 was the
first four-engine transport
designed for larger and faster equipment. More than
forty were ordered by the
airlines for delivery in 1942,
but the U.S. Army Air Force
commandeered the whole
production. (United Air
Lines Photo)

The first modern cabin interior to grace the skyways in the mid-1930s.
(United Air Lines Photo)

This five-passenger Lockheed Vega for small air lines and private owners, established 43 flight records and became the mount of racing pilots including Amelia Earhart. (Lockheed Aircraft Photo)

The 1933 Boeing 247 was America's first all-metal monoplane transport and was one of the first planes that used supercharged engines of the type formerly limited to military planes. (Boeing Aircraft Photo)

The Lockheed Model 14 was a twin-engine commercial airliner that introduced the single-spar, all-metal wing and the Lockheed-Fowler flaps that reduced landing speed and improved the takeoff performance. (Lockheed Aircraft Photo)

The first Constellation became a flying laboratory for further development of the famous "Connie." It also became a testbed for aerodynamics, engines, and other components. (Lockheed Aircraft Photo)

With the advent of the jet airliner only a few months away, Douglas produced its last piston-engined DC-7B and DC-7C, and 230 were built before the first of the Douglas DC-8s came off the assembly line. (Douglas Aircraft Photo)

In 1920 Donald W. Douglas began building airplanes with a staff of six workers. Today he employs 75,000, building military and commercial planes and boosters for space vehicles. (McDonnell Douglas Photo)

William A. Patterson, president of United Air Lines, whose business methods were a revelation to a floundering industry. (United Air Lines Photo)

Northeast's Fairchild-Hiller F-27 turboprop airliner was a short-range aircraft designed to carry 45 passengers. (Northeast Airlines Photo)

Juan T. Trippe whose bold and inspired moves built Pan American Airlines up from one plane on a mud flat off Key West to a world leader in air transportation. (Pan American Photo)

The dynamic C. R. Smith, by masterful selection of vital population centers for his line's routes, made American Airlines the country's leading carrier. (American Airlines Photo)

Airline stewardesses were introduced by United Air Lines in May 1930. They were paid $125 a month for 100 hours of flying. All were registered nurses. The uniform was designed by Helen Church who stands with her back to the open door. (United Air Lines Photo)

In time the fashion designers took over the airline uniforms and the progress is shown from left to right. (United Air Lines Photo)

Lockheed moved into the jet era in 1957 with its prop-jet Electra, which was to serve fourteen airlines on four continents. (Lockheed Aircraft Photo)

Douglas's DC–8 Jetliner is capable of speeds of up to 600 mph. It was introduced in 1958. (Douglas Aircraft Photo)

In 1958 Pan American got the jump on the jet age with the delivery on its first Boeing 707 and began a new series of commercial records. Cruising speed shot up to 575 mph and operating altitudes to 25,000– 35,000 feet. (Pan American Photo)

On September 30, 1968 the first Boeing 747 airliner was rolled out at Everett, Washington to give the aviation world some idea of the size of this unusual air transport. (Boeing Aircraft Photo)

To compete in the short-range field, Boeing produced its 727 tri-jet and adopted the rear-mounted formula to provide a quiet cabin and higher lift in the wings. (Pan American Photo)

Designed for tomorrow's air-travel requirements, the Lockheed L–1011 Tri-Star is scheduled to enter airline service in 1971. (Lockheed Aircraft Photo)

This mockup of the main coach section of the Tri-Star promises unusual roominess for future air travelers. Center aisle seats are divided by coat-rack modules to afford privacy.

Airports must also improve to fit the new "jumbo" jet planes. This is a model of the proposed Dallas–Fort Worth Regional Airport that should be ready in the mid-1970s. (Dallas–Fort Worth Photo)

far cry from the ceremonial affairs staged by the Army or Navy, and what formalities were attempted usually were short, colorful formation-flying displays, or concerts by the squadron band. There was no money for flashy dress uniforms or luxurious clubs which contribute to the all-important esprit de corps.

Serving with the Air Corps, when a young pilot was paid only $187.50 a month—even when he qualified for flying pay—was better than bucking the problems of a civilian in the years of the Depression. In 1930 some 25,000,000 people had lost $150,000,000 almost overnight, and by June 1935, 4,700,000 were on relief. Against these figures the Army Air Corps looked like a sinecure. During the Christmas holidays of 1933, a few weeks before the Air Corps was handed the airmail assignment, most service posts had only skeleton groups kept on hand to police the hangars and sit beside the telephones. Everyone had gone home, gussied up in well-pressed uniforms to enjoy Christmas with their families.

Air Corps personnel who had their families nearby desired no part of civilian life. They could shop at the Post Exchange where a pound of coffee cost but nine cents, and $15 would purchase enough staples, vegetables, canned goods, and milk to supply an average family for a month. Liquor was available at the commissioned and noncommissioned officers' clubs for less than $2 a quart, and nourishment at the bar was only fifteen cents a drink.

It was into this aviation situation that Foulois's airmail bombshell was dropped. The tranquillity of the Air Corps was rudely shattered. Individual post and squadron commanders made frantic moves to prepare for—they knew not what. Over the week end of February 10–11, aircraft were washed down and fuel tanks filled from the limited stocks. Pilots renewed their interest in navigation and meteorology. All leave was canceled. Mechanics, with justified anticipation, drew extra equipment and spare parts from the Air Corps Supply, and another alphabetical jawbreaker was introduced—AACMO (Army Air Corps Mail Operations). Brigadier General Oscar Westover was named to command the operation.

His first task was to decide upon a network of routes, covering three main portions of the country. Major Byron Q. Jones, 8th Pursuit Group at Langley Field, was to take over the Eastern Mail Zone comprising all of the United States from the Atlantic to the Mississippi River. Lieutenant Colonel Horace M. Hickam of Fort Crockett was placed in charge of the Central Zone, which spread west from the Eastern Zone as far as a north-south line through Cheyenne, Wyoming. Colonel Henry H. Arnold of March Field took over the Western Zone which extended from the Central Zone west to the Pacific Ocean.*

Second Assistant Postmaster General Harllee Branch pointed out the service to the country's banks, particularly in the transfer of drafts, checks, and similar important documents, and he considered it essential that the selected mail routes provide interconnecting service between cities where the twelve banks of the Federal Reserve System are located. As a result, the final plan called for 41,000 miles to be flown every day, linking up 68 airmail stops. Thus, by far the greatest amount of flying would be over the Eastern Zone where 36 stops would be made in a total of 20,164 miles of daily flying. The Western Zone was set up for 20 stops over 11,922 miles, and in the Central Zone, where traffic was lightest, 12 stops would link up 8,744 miles of route flights.

There was some Gilbert & Sullivan business about financing the cost of fuel and salaries for reserve officers who might be called back to active duty. Post office funds could be drawn for contract service only, and for a time it looked

---

* The source of much of this detailed information is found in *Air Mail Emergency*, by Norman E. Borden, Jr., published by Bond Wheelwright Company, 1968.

as though General Foulois would have to finance out of his own pocket the takeover by the Army. A temporary loan of $300,000 was made from impounded War Department funds, and to conserve this money everything bought in the field had to be purchased locally, using procurement Form 15. But this ignored the $5 per diem allowance made to authorized military personnel living off the base, and any Air Corps man serving on airmail duty would have to bear that expense out of his own pocket until other money could be siphoned from the public funds.

To further appreciate what the Air Corps had assumed: this was a temporary assignment to fly 41,000 miles daily, which meant 310 hours of actual time in the air, with equipment that was not suited to the task. Another 140 hours of flying each day would be needed for added training, test-flying, and administrative duty. At best only fifty percent of the planes could be kept in serviceable condition if they were to fly an average of six hours every day. A total of 148 airplanes were drawn from service squadrons, and to maintain and fly them 550 officers and men were assigned to AACMO. There were 216 officer pilots, only a few of whom were supervisory personnel. There were 324 mechanics, riggers, radio technicians and clerks, all of whom were based at control centers around the three zones.

On paper this might seem a reasonable inventory to fly a limited segment of the airlines' mail-carrying operation, but the aircraft figures are misleading. Few new types of the Air Corps were even remotely suitable for long-distance airmail flying. Few had the speed or instrumentation for all-weather—and certainly not for night—flying. For instance, a Curtiss A-12 attack type was modified somewhat for carrying mail. A box was temporarily built into the rear gunner's cockpit, and additional space was found in what was known as the aircraft's baggage compartment. The A-12 was used in the Central Mail Zone. The Keystone B-4A and B-6A bombers were also used. They were twin-engined aircraft that could carry 1,100 pounds of mail in spaces usually used for bombs or in the gunners' cockpits. The Keystones flew in both the Western and Eastern zones, but were replaced gradually by new Martin YB-10s.

A few Douglas Y1B-7 bombers were used on the Western Zone routes, as well as a number of Boeing Y1B-9A twin-engined bombers, but there is no record of their actual mail capacity. The Curtiss O-1G Falcon observation plane was used extensively in the Eastern Zone, carrying the mail in the baggage compartment and in a box built into the rear gunner's cockpit—though even with this modification the Falcon carried only 150 pounds of mail. The Curtiss O-39, another observation type, was detailed for the Allegheny Mountain route of the Eastern Zone and hauled about 250 pounds of mail sacks.

The Thomas Morse observation planes of the O-19C category were assigned to routes west of the Mississippi, but they carried only 150 pounds of postal cargo. The Douglas O-25C, a contemporary observation aircraft, was pressed into the emergency service, but again the space problem limited the cargo to 160 pounds.

Among the pursuit planes employed was the Boeing P-12E which was used from the beginning of the Army's effort to fill in. They were flown chiefly in the Eastern Zone, but proved unsatisfactory for all-weather flying and could carry only a 50-pound load of mail sacks in the so-called baggage compartment. The Boeing P-26A, then the most advanced single-seat fighter in the Air Corps, was tried out in the Western Mail Zone, but proved to be unsatisfactory for the mail routes.

Ironically, on the day before the Army took over the mail routes, the new Douglas DC-2, previously mentioned, with Jack Frye of TWA at the controls and Eddie Rickenbacker acting as co-pilot, took off from San Francisco, picked up a tail wind and headed for Newark on a speed-demonstration run. Refueling stops were made at Kansas City and Columbus, but still the transcontinental run was completed in 13 hours, 4 minutes. The immediate publicity given this flight was a shocker for the men of the Air Corps who were expected to take over the airmail runs from such professionals, using advanced equipment.

Penuriousness, political disinterest, and the Hoover Administration's honest attempt to cut expenditures had hit the Air Corps hard. Its equipment was far below that available to the commercial airlines. Few military planes of the day carried "blind flying" instruments. Only 20 out of the 80 pilots assigned to the Eastern Zone were qualified to fly on instruments, and only 35 had had training in the use of any aircraft radio. In other words, it was assumed that future military air action would be carried out only during the hours of daylight. Fighters, or pursuits as they were known then, could attack an enemy plane only when it could be seen. Bomber pilots would never think of using night cover to strike at enemy targets, a doctrine that was carried into World War II. Aerial photography by the observation squadrons could be attempted only in natural daylight.

To sharpen the precision of the pilots and revive service discipline in the mechanics, a week of "training" was carried out before a bag of mail was carried. Some "under the hood" blind flying was made, and a primary course of instrument flying was carried out. Pilots who were to be entrusted with the mail had to be sworn in as·official mail carriers by local postmasters, and all were ordered to wear side arms and, when possible, drop their military rank and wear civilian clothes. Probably in compassion, some of the airlines offered their help and advice. At Atlanta and Miami Eastern Air Transport, men briefed the Air Corps pilots on the routes they were to fly, and Eastern also offered to provide airliners and pilots to fly Army men to their assigned control points gratis. United Air Lines offered much the same aid at the Kylertown mail stop just west of Belle-fonte. All this helped the Air Corps to get through its week of training and preparation without bursting a tire. Then on Friday, February 16, 1934, two fatal accidents within a few hours of each other occurred in the Western Zone. Lieutenant Jean D. Grenier of the 3rd Attack Group at Fort Crockett and Edwin D. White, who were flying together from March Field, crashed in a blinding snowstorm at Webster Canyon, Utah. Later the same day Lieutenant James Eastham, flying a Y1B-7 twin-engined monoplane, was burned to death when his plane went into a stall during a landing at Jerome, Idaho. All three died before one bag of mail had been carried over any route.

Over the first week of flying the mail, five more pilots were killed and six more critically injured. Eight aircraft were washed out, representing a cost of $300,000. On February 22 two pilots lost their lives and another was severely injured. Lieutenant Durnward O. Lowry of the 1st Pursuit Group crashed near Dashler, Ohio, while flying the Chicago-Cleveland run. He was 50 miles off course at the time. On this same day Lieutenant Fred J. Patrick was killed while en route to take command of an airmail post. The following day Lieutenant J. H. Rothrock, flying a Douglas Dolphin amphibian out of Floyd Bennett Field, was carrying two ferry pilots, Lieutenants W. S. Peacock and George F. McDermott, to Langley Field, Virginia. On the first leg of the flight the Dolphin's two engines quit cold and Rothrock had to ditch in heavy weather off Rockaway Point, Long Island. All three men climbed out and hung on to the wing, awaiting rescue, but due to high winds and rough water no rescue craft could get near them. Soaked to the skin, cold and numb, they next clung to the engine mounts for more than five hours. Finally, a destroyer, *Bernadou*, came up and as it maneuvered to move in, McDermott lost his grip and slipped into the near-freezing water. He drowned before a boat could be lowered to rescue him.

Lieutenant H. L. Dietz, flying a Curtiss Falcon, became lost between Camden and Newark, and while looking for guidance ran out of gas. Fortunately, he made a safe dead-stick landing on a farm not far from Dover, New Jersey. On February 22 Dietz crashed again, piling into a tree in Maryland. He was in a hospital for a long spell.

Lieutenant J. H. Gibson, en route from Middletown to Columbus, Ohio, was more fortunate. He became lost, the engine of his O-39 ran out of gas, and he had to abandon his plane in flight. He landed unhurt near Mansfield, Ohio.

Still, Army authorities were determined to prove the Air Corps was capable of carrying out General Foulois's agreement to fly the mail, and were positive that as soon as all control points were in efficient operation the work would go ahead as planned. In Chicago, Captain Lipsner—who had organized the first Army Aerial Mail Service sixteen years before—could no longer stand reading of the terrible slaughter and made a call to President Roosevelt on March 8. The President agreed to talk to him, and over the next few minutes Lipsner made an impassioned plea to halt this dreadful experiment.

The President acted a few days later and ordered a cut in the airmail service to which the Postmaster General responded. President Roosevelt also sent a sharp note to Secretary of War George H. Dern, stating that the carnage must stop. "I was given definite assurance that the Army Air Corps could fly the mail." Secretary Dern responded, and blamed the high death toll of this senseless experiment on his military chiefs.

By mid-March the airmail schedules were drastically curtailed in the hope of retrieving some sanity from the chaos. Flights were limited to daylight hours with cross-country flying only when the weather warranted, but despite these cautionary measures the crashes and fatalities continued.

On March 8 Sergeant Edward C. Sell, a crew chief flying with Lieutenant William N. Reid aboard a B-6A Keystone bomber, died of injuries suffered when their aircraft lost both engines and the pilot tried to land on Daytona Beach. They crashed, instead, in a wooded area and Sell received a skull injury from which he died.

The next day Lieutenant Otto Wienecke of the Regular Army took off from Newark with a load of mail destined for Cleveland. He was flying an O-39 and ran into a snowstorm. He apparently lost control, went into a spin, crashed in a field near Burton, Ohio, and was killed. Two hours after Wienecke died, an O-38E, flown by Lieutenant F. L. Howard with Lieutenant A. R. Kerwin as a passenger, burst into flames while landing on the Cheyenne airport. Both airmen were killed. It was learned later that they had been on a night-familiarization flight when their engine began to lose power. Howard tried to get back to the field, and was actually making a dead-stick landing when his wheels struck an electric power line bordering the airport. The ruptured cable set fire to the doped fabric of the fuselage and by the time the plane was touching down the cockpits were enveloped in flames. No one could get near the aircraft to rescue the airmen.

These fatalities brought an immediate response. President Roosevelt announced the airmail would be returned to the airlines as soon as possible. All Air Corps planes were grounded for eight days while "better equipment" was installed. Only the most experienced pilots were to attempt any mail flights.

Then on March 15 the eleventh Air Corps pilot was killed. Lieutenant H. C. Richardson—who previously had been an airline pilot and had taken active duty with the Air Corps to help tote the mail—was flying an O-38E near Cheyenne on a refresher course, carrying no mail. He, too, had engine trouble, but apparently lost flying speed and spun in.

Mail flying was resumed on March 19, and for a few days some success was enjoyed over the daylight hours. But then on March 31 the twelfth Air Corps flier was killed. He was Lieutenant Thurman A. Wood, who had taken off from Chicago in a Curtiss A-12 with twenty-three bags of mail for Omaha. He encountered a thunderstorm over Iowa, lost control of the airplane in the eye of the turbulence, and crashed near the town of Dewitt. His death was charged to "complete pilot failure," meaning that Lieutenant Wood had through ignorance, carelessness, or a false sense of bravado, made no attempt to fly around the storm.

It is perhaps unfair to charge all these fatalities to Air Corps incompetence. Lieutenants Grenier, White, and Eastham were killed before any mail had been carried. Lowry *was* on a mail flight, but because of inclement weather in which he should not have been aloft, he became lost and eventually crashed about fifty miles off course. Patrick was killed while en route to take over an airmail post. McDermott was lost from a ditched amphibian while it was being flown to Langley Field. Wienecke died needlessly in a snowstorm. Howard and Kerwin were burned to death in the Cheyenne airport tragedy, and Sergeant Sell died as the result of a crash in which he was the only fatality. Richardson was on a training flight, chiefly to become acquainted with a military aircraft, and Wood, while on a mail run, crashed in a thunderstorm. It will be seen that only Lowry, Wienecke, and Wood were lost while actually flying the mail. However, the others were lost on flights that were set up by the Army's decision to take over the operations.

Considering everything, the Air Corps pilots had made a gallant stand, and resented the unfavorable publicity given their efforts by the press. In those days there was no determined public relations staff to defend them or to attract favorable public opinion, but during their short span of emergency mail duty between February 19 and May 7, 1934, Air Corps pilots delivered 786,215 pounds of mail and flew 14,745 hours, covering 1,707,559 miles over the national airways system. Training flights, administration, and engineering required an additional 32,641 hours. The Post Office Department had paid out $3,767,355 to the Army to carry the mail, so the cost per mile was $2.21, compared to the average of 54¢ per mile which had been paid to the airlines in 1933. However, by the time the airlines were commanded to take over the airmail, the Air Corps had developed a cargo-carrying team they believed to be the equal of any that the commercial airlines had taken several years to build.

One feature of the Air Corps' effort has long been forgotten, but it was to have a lasting effect on military aviation. Early in March a series of experiments in blind flying were carried out under the direction of Captain Alfred F. Hegenberger. In 1927 Captain Hegenberger, along with Lieutenant Lester J. Maitland, had completed a nonstop flight between Oakland, California, and Hawaii. They covered this 2,400-mile course while using only a radio beam and a sextant. It was one of the greatest feats of aerial navigation of the day.

Hegenberger had set up a blind-landing school at Wright Field in Dayton, Ohio, to teach a new instrument-landing system he had developed. As many AACMO pilots as it was possible to accommodate were given this training aboard the Martin YB-10s—as fast as these new bombers could be flown from the factory. From all accounts the Hegenberger system was simple and most successful, and had the Air Corps been allowed to fly the mail a few weeks longer, blind-landing facilities would have been set up from coast to coast, making it possible to fly mail-loaded Martins from New York to San Francisco in any weather.

Complete tests of the system were started at Newark, New Jersey, on May 3, and on May 8 nine successful blind landings were made there by military pilots, all of which was to justify continued research in blind landing at all major airports. Captain Hegenberger was awarded a cluster to his Distinguished Flying Cross for his contribution, and a year later the same system was adopted for commercial flying under the supervision of the Bureau of Air Commerce and the Department of Commerce.

Whatever its worth, it was appreciated later that the general shakeup had given a new impetus to Air Corps training, growth, equipment, and public interest. Had it not been for the dauntless attempt to fly the mail, America's air arm might have deteriorated into that of a fourth-class power. World War II was only a short five years away, a breathing spell in which to re-form and spread stronger wings for the global conflict that was to come. Whatever the government paid the Air Corps to take over the airmail was money well spent.

11

Back to Business

The airmail emergency, brought about by the investigations of the Black Committee in 1933, had struck the airlines a severe financial blow. But by June 1934 the government and the public realized that the operators had not been exaggerating when they had reported high overhead costs and low profits. It was not until July 14, 1941, however, that Commissioner Richard H. Akers of the U.S. Court of Claims had reached an official conclusion that the charges brought against Postmaster Brown were untrue and that there had been no fraud during his administration, proving again that it takes but a minute to make a charge which is widely publicized, but years to prove innocence—by which time the original accusation has often been completely forgotten.

On March 30, 1934, the Post Office Department advertised for new bids for 90-day contracts over 21 airmail routes. The successful bidders would be required to resume flying the mail within 30 days after being awarded new contracts. Again, the rate of pay was to be based on a definite weight-per-space available per airplane mile; one cubic foot of space being computed as the equivalent of nine pounds of mail. Postmaster General Farley had little trouble bringing the operators back into the fold, although it was realized later they might have demanded exorbitant rates to compensate for what they had lost while the Air Corps was trying to fly the mail routes. But Farley was a shrewd lawmaker, and he insisted that no airline could have a new contract if it in any way had been represented at the so-called "spoils conference," held by Postmaster General Walter Folger Brown. And added to this, President Roosevelt issued a decree that blackballed for five years all airline executives who had even attended the conference.

Heads rolled, reorganization plans were rushed into type and for a few days the airline industry was again stunned. Executives of many of the important companies were banished, including Philip G. Johnson, United's president. On the other hand, William A. Patterson, who was presiding over NAT, BAT, PAT, and Varney of the United chain, was immune, since in 1930 he was only a junior officer and did not attend the Washington meeting. He thus became head of United which suddenly was an operating, as well as a management, company. Philip Johnson emigrated to Canada where he organized the Trans Canada (now Air Canada) Airlines for the government north of the border, and ran it during his five years of exile. Just before the outbreak of World War II he returned to Boeing Aircraft to take over the production of Flying Fortresses and B-29s.

Other airlines, involved in the "spoils conference," made some tricky transformations—switching executives, electing new officers, and even changing their corporate names. Western Air Express became General Airlines for a short time. Overnight, American Airways became American Airlines. At the suggestion of Eddie Rickenbacker, Eastern Air Transport resumed business as Eastern Air Lines.

In the confusion of reorganization and bidding for the reassignment of airmail routes, it was feared that many of the smaller operators would make low bids simply to get the contracts, hoping for adjustments later on. W. A. Patterson, who had become president of the new United Air Lines, decided to figure costs closely and bid on that basis. Consequently, United regained all its previous airmail routes except the Chicago–Dallas run, which it lost to Braniff Air Lines. Patterson was awarded the other routes with bids from 38 to 39.5 cents per airplane mile, or less than one-fifth the Air Corps' cost. This was not the Braniff Airways we know today. Thomas E. Braniff founded the airline in Oklahoma in June 1928 with a five-passenger Stinson-Detroiter, and flew the 116-mile route between Tulsa and Oklahoma City. The present Braniff Airways was incorporated in November 1930. It established no sensational records or financial standing until 1934, when it was awarded its first mail contract to fly the Chicago-to-Dallas run, taking in Kansas City, Wichita, and Oklahoma City.

The re-awarding of the airmail contracts did not mark the end of the airlines' problems. There still were too many companies angling for the choicest routes, the best aircraft, and the cream of the business. While the pilots were giving up their seat-of-the-pants technique and taking modern instruction from the indubitable Link Trainer, the executives and their banker backers were staging guerrilla warfare in the narrow canyons of Wall Street and the emplacements of the Stock Exchange. Directives from Washington and the Air Mail Act of 1934 hit the big airlines hard. Already, a corps of executives had been dismissed and their positions taken by second-stringers. New legislation turned over the airmail business to the Interstate Commerce Commission, entirely eliminating the Post Office Department. This prevented financial or interlocking directorate connections between the airlines and the manufacturers of planes, engines, propellers, and other equipment. No longer could the executive of an airline hold the presidency of an aircraft or engine-manufacturing company. The act also limited the salaries of executives holding mail contracts to $17,500 per annum.

For instance, United Aircraft & Transport had now grown into a corporate giant, and was given just over five months to break up the involved merger. This meant ousting Rentschler of Pratt & Whitney, and Bill Boeing of Boeing Aircraft. Patterson had to call in Joseph E. Ripley, a Wall Street wizard, to unravel the tangle. He devised a reorganization force that brought in Joseph F. McCarthy, secretary and comptroller of United Aircraft & Transport. To this executive group was added a stockholders' protective association of some 23,000 shareholders. With this overall backing, Ripley went to work unscrambling, dividing, and redistributing a $30,000,000 aviation monster.

The operation required approximately a month. The original holding company was reshuffled into three operating companies. Fifty-one percent of the assets were poured into a new United Aircraft Company, made up of the Pratt & Whitney engine company, the Vought and Sikorsky airplane factories, and several eastern propeller companies. The Boeing Airplane Company was given 14.5 percent of the holding company's assets to continue operations in Seattle and Wichita. The United Air Lines Transportation Corporation was now made up of four established airlines (National Air Transport, Boeing Air Transport, Pacific Air Transport, and Varney Air Lines) and the United airport at Burbank—all amounting to 34.5 percent of the holding company's resources. Each owner of a share of the holding company stock now received one share of the new United Aircraft stock, one-half share of United Air Lines Transportation Corporation, and one-quarter share of Boeing Airplane Company. In this manner Ripley started the new United Air Lines off with about $4,000,000 of working capital—which was most fortunate, as there were four "black years" ahead for all air transport companies. Regular users of the United Air Lines Transportation Corporation, as it was now incorporated, refused to gulp that mouthful and persisted in calling the company United Air Lines. After nine years, the company capitulated and accepted it as the official and corporate name (1943).

From this hectic beginning United became the country's oldest airline, if we consider that among its corporate organizations was the Varney Air Lines, started in 1926. Since those days United has racked up many "firsts," notable innovations, and scores of technical and service features. United Air Lines was the first to fly fare-paying passengers coast-to-coast (1927). They were the first to develop and adopt two-way plane-to-ground voice radio (1929). Stewardess service was first provided by United (1930). Six years later they established the first flight kitchen. They were the first to offer air coach service as well as all-cargo flights (1940). It was the first domestic airline to set up systematic training of flight crews, using electronic flight simulators (1954). It was the first to place an order for a jet transport (1955), and the first to install weather radar as standard equipment on every aircraft. For the reader with an eye for revenue figures, United Air Lines was the first to reach and exceed $1,000,000,000 in annual revenue (1967).

To pursue further the early history of the present major airlines, we learn that American Airlines, as it is known today, began when the first airmail contracts were awarded. One contract went to the Robertson Aircraft Corporation to fly the Chicago–St. Louis route, in which Charles A. Lindbergh flew the inaugural flight. In 1928 the Robertson company was absorbed by Universal Aviation Corporation along with the stock acquisition of five other airlines. By 1930 a new syndicate known as the Aviation Corporation, one of the big three holding corporations— actually a $35,000,000 firm—bought control of Universal Aviation Corporation, five other airlines, and three aviation companies. These were Braniff, Continental Air Lines, Northern Air Lines, Inc., Universal Air Lines, Inc., Air Transportation, Inc., Northrop Air Lines, Inc., Mid-Plane Sales and Transit Company, and Universal Air Lines System Terminal Company.

Order out of this chaos was necessary, and on January 25, 1930, the Aviation Corporation consolidated the subsidiary lines into what they called American Airways. In 1932 an operations group was established to manage the whole system, and this became American's first centralized Operations Department. C. R. Smith, who had been managing the southern division operations, took over this job and, being a dynamic and persuasive Texan, soon put the whole airline network on a working basis. Within two years he became president of American Airlines, a post he held until the late 1960s when he became Secretary of Commerce for Air.

The original American Airways had two nonstop flights between St. Louis and Chicago, advertised as the "Skyline Limited," using Fokker Super-Universal six-passenger monoplanes. The mail sacks were carried in a separate cargo compartment, eliminating the earlier necessity of accommodating passengers on the mail bags. The "Skyline Limited" flights cost an extra $3 for the status of sitting in wicker chairs. Another new feature was added when Harold Otto, who had joined the company in 1930 as a pilot, now assumed the duty of "courier"—and served coffee, sandwiches, and doughnuts. Hostesses were not known until about 1930 when United introduced uniformed girls to add a homey touch to the industry. It should be noted here that there seems to be considerable discrepancy as to when *uniformed* hostesses were included in the flight crews. Dates running from 1930 to 1934 are offered by several airlines. Early hostesses first appeared in white smocks, or the uniforms worn by nurses, over which they wore the capes and caps of the registered nurses of the day.

Pilots of passenger planes did not immediately wear distinctive uniforms since there remained an abhorrence of anything smacking of the military—or the inference that they were aerial chauffeurs. But from all accounts, it remained for Bud Gurney, who was in charge of personnel at Lambert Field, to begin a trend. One day he turned up in a blue, brass-buttoned coat, white flannel trousers, and a peaked cap bearing the initials of the airline. Uniforms for flight crews probably marked the beginning of a new era, for by 1935–36 passenger-carrying had become as important as toting the mail, and all lines searched for any outward and visible sign that would identify their operations. By this time the planes, paced by the earlier DC-2, had been stepped up to the DC-3s, Lockheed Vegas, Stinson trimotors, Fokker F-10s, newer versions of the Ford Tri-Motor, Boeing 80s, Consolidated Fleetsters, Northrop Deltas, Lockheed Orions, and Vultee V-1s.

As C. R. Smith explained to a gathering of the Newcomen Society,* "The aircraft of the 'thirties' had dispensed with external struts, wires and fabric, and gave the airlines all-metal craft. The power plants had reached the levels of high efficiency, particularly the air-cooled radials which returned greater horsepower per pound of engine. All this provided bigger and faster aircraft and speeds of more than 100 mph were expected in every quarter."

It was also evident that the airliner was taking on a distinctive and more efficient form, a configuration that has not changed greatly, even with the advent of the jet engine. Compared to the development of the plane, professional skills of pilots, and ground maintenance, the development of instruments, radio, and meteorological equipment was still far from adequate, and more years were required to bring these important factors up to date. Op-

---

* The Newcomen Society is a British-American group which aims to increase an appreciation of traditions and ideals in the Arts and Sciences.

eration costs were high, for passenger-carrying was far from a paying business as was proven when the mail contracts were canceled. Over the next few years, or until the outbreak of World War II, commercial aviation in the United States still depended on mail contracts—or the same financial aids that were keeping European airliners aloft.

Once the airmail contracts were restored, the air transportation system was switched into high gear. American Airways, flying the southern transcontinental route with good weather over most of the year, felt encouraged to introduce a new company image and changed its name to American Airlines. It offered the industry's first Curtiss Condor sleeper service, and registered nurses, acting as stewardesses, flitted up and down the aisles serving first-class meals and providing assurance that flying was safe.

American Airlines made the most of their DC-3 fleet, which, for its day, was the perfect passenger transport. It struck the balance in speed, gross weight, power, pay-load space, and wing area, permitting economies never before obtained. American Airlines named its craft "Flagship," and purchased 94 of these planes shortly after putting the first in service in June 1936. Next, full-feathering propellers were fitted to their DC-3s, which improved take-off and landing characteristics. High-octane gasoline was developed, and considerable money and time were spent in the further investigation of the instrument-landing system. The company was working out a high-speed network of flight-and-reservation information when World War II created a new crisis for the airlines.

Another modern giant, Eastern Air Lines, emerged from Harold Pitcairn's lucky gamble to obtain an airmail contract. Its first passenger-carrying flight was on April 1, 1926, over what was claimed to be the first service for passengers and cargo over a contract airmail route in the United States. At the time twelve airmail contracts had been awarded, but only one outfit was eager to get into the air, and how the basic organization was established adds another chapter to the story of commercial aviation.

Major Reed Chambers, who had been a senior flight commander in Captain Eddie Rickenbacker's 94th Squadron in World War I, shared his squadron leader's dream of putting the airplane to work when their wartime patrols had ended. Both men believed the public would support some form of commercial aviation, whether to fly goods and passengers, or simply to move quickly to vacationlands.

On looking over the available territory, it was obvious that manufacturers of the industrial East would see the opportunities of a line through the south to Florida, on to Cuba, and then gradually into the available markets of South America. An initial link with Florida was the key to this possible network. There was a chain of Bowman-Biltmore hotels in New York, Atlanta, Miami, and Havana, which in themselves would set up a paying flow of traffic. In addition, the Post Office Department was ready to pay $3 a pound for all the mail an airplane could carry. The weather was always ideal in Florida, and there were no mountains hiding in the clouds, such as were to be found in the Alleghenies and the Rocky Mountains.

Major Chambers first took this plan to a number of wealthy New Yorkers, including Percy Rockefeller, Miss Anne Morgan, Charles Stone, and one or two others who were looking for a fairly sound investment. With some substantial encouragement, Chambers next headed for Detroit where Eddie Rickenbacker was working with General Motors. Ford was dabbling with Mr. Stout's all-metal monoplanes, and amid all this Motor City interest in flying, Chambers eventually raised $300,000 and started Florida Airways, mentioned previously. At first he used four Ford-Stout single-engined monoplanes, powered with the Liberty-12 engines, but he switched later to Boeing Monomails. All the equipment had been flown east with planes to fly a Tampa-

to-Jacksonville run. But it was discovered that Harold Pitcairn had, by a twist of fortune, gathered in the complete
New York–to–Atlanta airmail contract and was planning to
fly the route with planes he was building in his own factory.

Undaunted, Florida Airways began to fly its route, extended by now between Atlanta and Miami, and made a
memorable showing during the Florida hurricane of 1926.
But in doing so it spent itself into insolvency. It was while
the company was being refinanced that Pitcairn underbid
the Atlanta-Miami route, and with that forged the eastern
coastal runs into a single line. The Florida Airways' new
money was put into the link to Cuba, which was to become known as Pan American Airways, and Major Chambers went on to found U.S. Aviation Underwriters.

As explained previously, Harold Pitcairn sold his New
York-to-Miami airmail route to North American Aviation,
Inc., an aeronautical complex headed by C. M. Keys, and
the corporate name was changed to Eastern Air Transport.
In this setup were the Curtiss, Wright, and Sperry manufacturing companies, American Airways, Transcontinental
Air Transport, Western Air Express, and some twenty-nine
subsidiaries and eighteen other aviation companies. This
fortunate connection with the Sperry interests gave Eastern pilots every chance to become familiar with all new
types of flight instruments. They were among the first to
use the automatic pilot on a transport plane, and with this
technical familiarity Eastern's pilots soon added the instrument rating to their licenses, all being able to cope with
limited visibility and carry passengers at night.

With the passing of the McNary-Watres Act in 1928, and
the change from poundage carried to miles flown, it was
clear the highest rates would go to multi-engined planes
suitable for passengers. To cope with this, Eastern brought
all of its Ford Tri-Motors up from the Florida area to
make regular passenger runs out of New York. There
was no city airport in those days, so a shed was moved to

a cinder runway on what was known then as North Beach, and became Eastern's New York terminal. (Today the area is La Guardia airport.) A speedboat was chartered to bring passengers from the city, and on August 18, 1930, eleven paying patrons were brought to the "airport." The twelfth seat was taken up by a spare tail wheel. Only five pounds of mail was carried on this inaugural flight between New York and Washington, but it was hardly a triumph of speed and efficiency. The pilot became lost while crossing the lower bay between New York and Newark, the first stop. On taking off from the field at Newark, motorists chugging along Route 1 in their four-wheeled Fords seemingly kept up with and waved at the passengers in the Tri-Motor, which was encountering head winds.

Eastern soon stretched its new service all the way to Miami, and to become familiar with the air-tourist business, bought Pan American Airways' route between New York and Atlantic City. By 1931, Eastern was flying passengers in the Curtiss Condor, a giant biplane that was fitted out as a sleeper and, incidentally, the first commercial plane to use soundproofing. With this aircraft the New York–Miami run could be completed in 13 hours, 15 minutes—with 11 stops!

The Condor showpiece, publicized by pretty models in filmy lingerie, was Eastern's big selling point. But on the routine flights there were plenty of headaches—keeping many types of planes in the air over a tangled network of unprofitable routes, and being burdened with equipment supplied by various corporate cousins. A serious deficit was the natural result, but some relief was forthcoming in 1933 when General Motors bought up the whole North American Aviation, Inc., complex to fill out its own aeronautical ventures. This move kept Eastern out of bankruptcy long enough to get a breather before James Aloysius Farley canceled all the airmail contracts.

When temporary routes were restored, Eastern won back

its original New York-to-Florida and the New Orleans link, plus one more—Chicago–Florida. But with passage of the Black-McKellar law, manufacturers with airline subsidiaries came under fire. North American Aviation, Inc., Transcontinental Air Transport, and Western Air Express now combined as a coast-to-coast carrier, and other airline properties were sold. General Motors might have sold Eastern, too, if anyone had offered even one million dollars, but the Depression was still a major factor and G.M. had to hold on.

Eddie Rickenbacker was assigned to salvage what he could of the General Motors investment, and at first he had no idea of hanging on to the airline when he took over as Eastern Division General Manager. He moved in on January 1, 1935, and immediately began flying up and down the line, studying the situation and rallying everyone to his support. To cut down on heating bills, he moved the maintenance base to Miami. His executive family was transferred to the General Motors building to save rent. Ignoring corporate ties, he sold off all obsolescent Condors, Kingbirds, Stinsons, and Mailwings and bought a few Douglas DC-2s. Only two Stinsons were kept, and these were fitted with covered cockpits to keep pilots up on their instrument flying. The maintenance crews worked twenty-four hours a day to keep the airplanes in first-class condition.

All this brought encouraging returns. Flying time between Miami and New York was cut to eight hours. Chicago from Miami was now within a nine-hour flight. A meteorological service supplied accurate weather forecasts around the clock, and by the end of 1935 Eastern could show its first net profit. This justified the purchase of more new planes and moves for additional routes. At the time, the Houston–Corpus Christi–Brownsville run attracted several operators, and there followed a typical rough-and-tumble battle for the mail contract. Braniff opened the bid with a figure of one ten-thousandth of a cent per mile. In other words, they were willing to fly the mail for one full year for one dollar! Eastern replied with the low bid of zero cents per mile, and thereby won the Brownsville contract, which gave it a link into Mexico.

But during the half decade before World War II the American airline industry was far from robust. The network was little more than a hodge-podge of routes established on shoestrings by over-ambitious operators with delusions of wealth, which resulted in an unhealthy, weedy growth. There was unnecessary duplication and the acceptance of contracts that promised no future, and many airlines were heading for the same fault of over-extension that the railroads had created for themselves at a comparable stage of development.

Again, Congress had to step in and draw up the Civil Aeronautics Act of 1938 which decreed that public interest, not price, would determine the issuance of franchises. Next, a Civil Aeronautics Board would develop and maintain an independent system of air transportation, and manufacturers would have to renounce their airlines. Under Rickenbacker's continued drive, Eastern had three years of unprecedented profit, attracting the attention of a powerful Wall Street group which was offering $3,500,000 for Eastern Air Lines. Alfred P. Sloan, chief executive of General Motors, gave Rickenbacker a personal option in the hope he could raise the money and meet the syndicate's price.*

Rickenbacker went off again, scouring the country for money, and, in a frantic eleventh-hour spurt, succeeded. On April 22, 1938, he not only saved Eastern from the Wall Street group, but became president of the line, and in the next quarter century Eastern Air Lines forged ahead at an amazing pace. New routes were studied and then estab-

* *My Years with General Motors*, by Alfred P. Sloan, Jr., Doubleday & Co., Inc., 1963.

lished, particularly in the East where principal cities were linked into the main network. Next, new flights were carried into Canada and Bermuda, while Puerto Rico and Mexico paralleled the southern border west to California, linking up any area that considered itself a vacationland. This remarkable growth continued until all the airlines had to drop their commercial ventures and join the colors when the attack on Pearl Harbor shocked the whole country.

Eastern teamed up with America's armed forces, not only contributing its aircraft but its entire personnel, who served with distinction on many wide-flung fronts. Among these assignments, its Military Air Transport Division operated over the 7,000 miles of supply routes which crossed the South Atlantic.

12

Juan Trippe's Triumph

Probably the most fascinating chronicle of United States' commercial aviation will be found in the pages of Pan American World Airways' history, which began back in the early days of postwar flying. From the point of view of earnings, miles flown, and mail-cargo poundage, it was not an important aviation operation, but Pan American was the first line to operate a permanent international air service and the first to operate regular foreign airmail service. As an aside, Pan American was the first airline operation to attract the attention of *Fortune* magazine—which presented in its April 1931 issue a three-page review of Mr. Juan Trippe's illogical venture that paid off. Exactly five years later *Fortune* offered a complete résumé of Pan American's activities and financial figures, showing that by then Pan Am had grown into a 40,000-mile transportation system, operating in thirty-nine countries and returning a revenue of $13,000,000.

When the flare-up torched by Postmaster General James Farley in 1934 put America's airlines out of the airmail business, it was not immediately noticed that he had apparently overlooked Pan American, although Mr. Trippe's bid for the mail run between Key West and Havana was the highest tendered. Mr. Farley probably intended to put Mr. Trippe out of business, but before he could unsheath his machete, Cordell Hull, then Secretary of State, wagged a negative finger, and Pan American continued to pick up and deliver the mail.

There had to be a reason, of course, and eventually the situation was explained. By 1934 Pan American had become linked with half the nations of the world and any cancellation of its airmail contracts would have resulted in complete disruption of service to more than thirty countries beyond America's shores. This would, in turn, fracture hundreds of international trade agreements. There would have been unpleasant repercussions the world over.

A close look at Pan American of that day will show that it was backed by a formidable group of United States capitalists, much like any other corporation. More important, it represented the rights of United States citizens along the airways of the whole world. Pan American alone had acquired those rights and it was holding them in the name of the American people. It did not compete with other American airlines but with foreign lines which the State Department felt had been set up to seize the trade routes as the official representatives of their own governments. At the time, the lines concerned were France's Air France, Germany's Lufthansa, Britain's Imperial Airways, and Holland's KLM. Russia was also building up its Aeroflot, but keeping its activities and route mileage a government secret. Most of the European airlines were openly operating under a government subsidy in one form or another. The United States abhorred the word subsidy, and rightly so, since it means financial aid directly by a government to an individual or a private enterprise, deemed beneficial to the public.

Before World War I, South America enjoyed a foreign trade involving some $2,000,000,000 a year, of which about

16 percent was with the United States. Great Britain, because of her mercantile supremacy, had absorbed the bulk of trade with Argentina, Brazil, Peru, and Uruguay, and was the dominant power in South America, holding about 30 percent of the total commerce. Germany and France also were important factors in this market, but during 1914–18 these European powers were occupied with the war and had to let their overseas commercial markets dwindle. American businessmen saw this wide-open opportunity, seized it, and by 1921 were holding about 26 percent of the South American trade.

Once the Great War was over, Europeans began to move in again, trying to salvage something of what was left. Because of their shipping routes and cheaper labor it was not long before they were making great inroads into the American beachhead. Many months later some economists claimed that it was this come-back of European foreign trade that first greased the skids for the Depression. Be that as it may, the United States' State Department saw that Pan American had linked America with dozens of foreign markets. For instance, Juan Trippe had girdled the West Indies, linked Los Angeles and Brownsville with Mexico City, tied in Mexico City with Colombia and Venezuela. Pan American had flown down the east coast of South America, faced up to French and German opposition in the Argentine, and bought a half-interest in the only trunk line that covered South America's west coast, touching in at the Argentine, Chile, Peru, Ecuador, Colombia, and Cristobal, Panama. As we know, Trippe had also bought up the major Alaskan airlines and acquired 45 percent interest in the national airline of China before the Europeans could get their breaths. He next turned to a number of little-heard-of islands in the Pacific, and by 1936 Pan American was flying Clipper ships out of San Francisco all the way across the Pacific to Manila, P.I., taking in Honolulu, Midway, Wake, and Guam over routes that originally had been explored by Charles A. Lindbergh.

But hooking up this linkage of thirty-nine countries was not just a matter of obtaining equipment which could cover the distances, or pilots and navigators skilled in long-distance transocean flying. Emergency landing areas, airports, and radio service had to be set up, and suitable maps and charts prepared. There were only four weather stations on the routes—Havana, Puerto Rico, the Canal Zone, and a station in Mexico City. Across the United States the Department of Commerce would spend about $54,000,000 to set up the same ground facilities for the domestic airlines. But Pan American had to do all this itself, and ended up owning or leasing 202 airfields, 129 radio stations and the required real estate, necessitating a total investment of more than $5,000,000, and annual rent for leases on operating properties amounting to $300,000.

Even a cursory consideration will reveal that all this represented an enormous economic market, particularly for American automobile manufacturers, oil companies, international communications companies, and even the motion picture producers in Hollywood. It had become the blood system and nerve network of America's foreign trade. In fact, Pan American now represented a world economic philosophy and became our industrial ambassador, going to any reasonable lengths to promote United States overseas trade. If an American manufacturer wanted to sell shoes in any South American country, Pan Am would collect data on prices, competitors, politics, and the depth of the market. It offered suggestions as to the best way to exploit the market and took all necessary steps when an American salesman got into trouble.

It can be seen that Pan American's airline operation was a long hop from the Jenny-D.H.4 gropings of the early 1920s, and explains why Postmaster General Farley seemingly looked the other way when the airmail contracts were canceled. There was nothing he could do about Juan Trippe's amazing operation, for it had become linked to the territory it served, not only commercially, but politically and diplomatically. It had come to represent the North American continent, had created new inter-American relationships, and its prestige was bound up inextricably with U.S. trade in a manner comparable to that of the United Fruit Company and the Grace Line.

This brings up another interesting point. These two shipping lines, while completely American, were to a great extent under foreign influence. Their business was entirely foreign, and they faced operating problems while working their routes on the principles of the sea. But for airlines there was no cardinal rule of freedom of the air—except well out over the ocean. All governments own all the ground below and the air above their geographical boundaries. Therefore, a foreign aircraft cannot fly through that air without committing illegal trespass. The pilot must land somewhere to have his papers and manifest examined, and he cannot continue on his course without official permission. It will be seen that no international airline can become operational without being linked politically and diplomatically to the territory it wishes to serve.

When in 1936 Pan American set up a schedule of transatlantic crossings, beginning with several exploratory flights, Great Britain, France and Germany were also making the same preparations. Italy, Russia and Norway showed keen interest in the project. But the gamble had to be taken, knowing that whatever franchise was granted would be retained forever.

A situation of this kind arose when the first international cables were laid and United States diplomats were outsmarted by the Europeans. It took fifty years for American interests to get a cable into Venezuela. They succeeded only by making a deal with the French. The British had held the rights into Brazil for more than sixty years, and up until 1936 a cable sent from the United States by way of All America Cables to Rio de Janeiro had to be rerouted all around the South American continent, looping over the

Andes to the Argentine. At that time, too, Western Union tied up with Rio only by courtesy of a British cable out of Barbados.

A similar fiasco was prevented only when Pan American planned their transoceanic routes, for then it was not only a question of who could fly over an ocean—any ocean—but who was in possession of the rights to fly it and land on some foreign airport.

In an effort to regain their South American markets after the war of 1914–18, the major European powers decided to gamble on the fleet wings of the airplane, although aircraft of those days could not support a rigid schedule. But their appearance on foreign soil would eventually justify a formal application for landing rights in the near future. As early as 1919, Dr. Peter Paul von Bauer, advertised as an Austrian war ace (though no reliable air-war history mentions him), was already in Colombia organizing an airline—with German capital—which was known as SCADTA (Sociedad Colombo-Alemana de Transportes Aéreos). It became an organization to be reckoned with. In 1925 the Germans were in Bolivia and the next year saw them at work in Argentina. Then in 1927 a company, known as Sindicato Condor, working under the aegis of Lufthansa, acquired the first license issued by Brazil.

Not to be left out of the picture, France inaugurated in 1927 a service between Natal, Brazil, and Buenos Aires, Argentina. The following year it took the big gamble and established a Paris–Buenos Aires mail route, using fast naval cruisers across the South Atlantic which connected with their airlines at Dakar, Senegal, and Natal. This connection put Buenos Aires closer to France than to the United States, since it took eighteen days to reach New York but only nine to Paris. With that, American businessmen in South America pointed out that they could lose their newly acquired markets while their own government made no competitive response. The same howls were heard echoing out of Washington and along the Wall Street canyon, but few people took the complaint seriously. After all, what had aviation to do with international commerce? Colonial Air Lines was clambering from New York to Boston on fabric wings and Brahmin prayers. National Air Transport was attempting to maintain scheduled flights over its 770-mile route between New York and Chicago. Who in his right mind would consider financing an airline across South American jungles, one that would have to fly its planes over 18,000-foot mountains, cross a country for which there were no maps and where the cities were often battered by hurricanes? No American with any brains would consider such an enterprise.

But, of course, there was Aeromarine Airways which in the 1930s had linked up Florida, Havana, Nassau, and Bimini. By 1925 the Austrian, Dr. von Bauer, was using two flying boats over the jungles of Central America, and in fact had gone so far as to apply for landing rights in Florida and the Canal Zone. General Billy Mitchell put a stopper to that, pointing out that the administration had already allowed Germany to establish SCADTA at a base only three hours away from the Panama Canal. Dr. von Bauer was politely turned down by the State Department.

But within a year the air was cluttered with rumors concerning the establishment of all sorts of airlines interlacing the islands of the Caribbean, but these rumors eventually simmered down to the fact that Juan Trippe had, within three hurried years and by an amazing series of quiet deals, taken bits and pieces of these projects and welded them into the armature that was to become the support of the present-day Pan Am air transport system.

In as few words as possible, since the organization of Pan American simply illuminates the general tactics of all airline corporations of the day—except for its importance in the fields of foreign trade and international diplomacy—

Trippe's network resulted from a series of mergers, fast action, and the idealistic guile of the young man who was to become its president. Early in 1927 there were three outstanding groups planning to take over the Caribbean market. The first was headed by Captain John K. Montgomery, a U.S. Army man, who with G. Grant Mason, Jr. and Richard B. Bevier organized something called Pan American Airways, Inc. A second group was headed by Reed Chambers, by now Vice President of U. S. Aviation Underwriters. He teamed up with Eddie Rickenbacker and they formed Florida Airways, which flew the Atlanta–Jacksonville–Miami run while waiting for the government to award airmail contracts so Cuba could be added. (In the delay, Florida Airways, financed by Percy A. Rockefeller, Charles A. Stone, Charles Hayden, George Mixter, Richard F. Hoyt, and Anne Morgan, had to go into bankruptcy. It was taken over by a holding company, known then as Atlantic, Gulf & Caribbean Airways, to be held until conditions improved.) The third group introduced Juan Trippe, son of Charles Walter Trippe, a Manhattan banker. After a spell in the Trippe counting house, Juan took a whirl at aviation and launched the Long Island Airways, which was little more than a charter operation. The mild-mannered Mr. Trippe had persuaded John A. Hambleton, a Baltimore banker reputed to be a war ace, and Cornelius Vanderbilt Whitney to join this questionable venture. The Long Island Airways eventually became the New York Airways to compete with Colonial Air Transport for the New York–Boston airmail contract. The deal, of course, was awarded to Colonial, so the New York Airways group apparently bought in. But they soon discovered the New York–to–Boston run was much too short to make any money, so they hoped to take over other routes reaching as far south as Florida. After all, the airplane was more suited to long-distance operations.

At about the same time, Tony Fokker, the Dutch plane

manufacturer, had moved to the United States with one of his new tri-motored transports. Juan Trippe asked Tony Fokker to take him and John Hambleton on an exploratory flight from New York to Havana and return. The trip was a great success, and Trippe suggested buying several Fokkers and trying for the run into the Caribbean, but the directors of Colonial couldn't see much farther than Hartford from their Boston office, so Trippe severed his connections with Colonial and took Hambleton and Whitney with him.

They persuaded Robert Thatch, another war ace who was a lawyer in Alabama, to draw up papers organizing the Aviation Corporation of America. Grover C. Loening, W. Averell Harriman, William H. Vanderbilt, Edward O. McDonnell, Sherman F. Fairchild, John Hay Whitney, William A. Rockefeller, and Seymour H. Knox all contributed and brought the total paid-in capital up to $300,000. The original idea was for this group to invest in several aviation organizations, chiefly to obtain information on the business from various angles. They bid on a few airmail contracts and hired André Priester to act as their operations man in case an airmail contract came through the letter box. To while away the time, Priester operated the New York Airways, which was flying a vacation service between New York and Atlantic City.

All this took time, although Big Business knew that the group was holding $300,000, awaiting an opportunity to buy some of Tony Fokker's tri-motors. Then, too, the word got around that the other two groups were trying to get the right to fly mail in and out of Cuba. Trippe suggested that they put their $300,000 into Pan American Airways, and offered to chip in 45 percent if the Chambers-Hoyt-Bevier group would raise the rest. Bevier had no money, and Chambers and Hoyt were not inclined to open their wallets, so the matter hung fire all through the summer of 1927 with both sides chivvying each other to put up or shut up.

It should be remembered at this point that Imperial Airways of Great Britain, Air France, KLM Royal Dutch Airlines and Lufthansa of Germany had been operating international transport services for several years. In the early 1920s the United States had no international air policy—and had no idea any such policy was needed.

During the time it took to organize Trippe's Aviation Corporation of America, the Montgomery-Mason-Bevier Pan American Airways, Inc. had been awarded the contract to carry airmail to Havana and had also negotiated a deal to haul Cuban mail to Key West. These agreements were reached on October 3, and the inaugural flights were to be carried out on October 19, which left only about two weeks to put a mail-carrier into the air. During this impasse, Cornelius Vanderbilt Whitney of the Trippe team quickly organized a holding company, known as the Atlantic, Gulf and Caribbean Line. This was absorbed into the Aviation Corporation of America complex, and Whitney finally rearranged the tangle, from which emerged a Pan American Airways Corporation. The original Pan American Airways, Inc. was held as an operating company with a nominal capitalization. The original Florida Airways, which had gone into bankruptcy, was also taken over by the Atlantic, Gulf and Caribbean Line.

So now the nucleus of the Pan American Airways Corporation found itself faced with a mail-contract run, connecting the United States with Havana, but having no basic airline with which to carry out the operation. Fortunately, Mr. Trippe was gifted with remarkable foresight, a factor that was to mark his management for many years to come. While his banker and lawyer friends had been carrying out the intricate manipulations that eventually were to bring all these companies under one management, Trippe, aided by Priester, had organized a skeleton airline that included pilots, mechanics, and three new Fokker F-7 trimotor planes. Their base was a drained mud flat and there was some faint hope of an immediate operation until it was learned that Key West would have to be designated as an official airport of entry, and a new set of maritime clearance regulations drawn up before any international business could be conducted. Next, passenger convenience—and hangar accommodations where the planes could be stored and serviced—had to be provided. All this had to be completed, or the Post Office Department would cancel the airmail contract—and possibly levy a fine of $25,000!

Trippe faced problem after problem of this nature, but it was sound training for the Pan American management, for over the next few years they had to cope with such crises with each expansion of their international operations. Had they not been able to fan out in double-quick time, the United States might have been eliminated from many airtrade routes.

It must not be presumed that Juan Trippe succeeded in setting up a practical airline in sixteen days. But by the October 19 deadline a Fairchild FC-2, bearing Pan American's name and an early form of the company trademark, was chartered by Trippe to fulfill the original airmail contract, carrying 30,000 pieces of mail from Key West to Havana. This flight was flown by Cy Caldwell, a former Royal Flying Corps pilot who later became a well-known aviation journalist. Fully scheduled operations did not begin until October 28 when one of the Fokker F-7s, piloted by Hugh Wells, made Pan Am's first official flight from Key West to Cuba. Another flight was made by Edwin C. Musick, who eight years later was to fly the first China Clipper across the Pacific to Manila.

Hugh Wells' inaugural flight to Havana marked the end of Pan American's preface to its remarkable history of airline operations. The original project began with the carrying of mail only, but by January 16, 1928, regular passenger-carrying schedules were started. Then, on March 8, Congress passed the Foreign Air Mail Act and by the end of that month the Postmaster General advertised for bids on a network of mail routes linking up Latin America. In this, Trippe held the key card—Cuban operating rights, personally presented to him by President Machado. In the face of this, Pan American (the Montgomery-Mason-Bevier combine) could fly their contract run only with the cooperation of Trippe's Aviation Corporation of America, and as a result the three original groups merged on June 3, 1928, forming Aviation Corporation of the Americas, with Pan American Airways as the operating organization. This company fitted exactly the United States' concept of a chosen instrument for an overseas airmail service.*

Pan American obtained every foreign airmail route for which bids were invited—at the maximum rate of $2 per mile. Any lower or competitive bids were meaningless without the backing of foreign operation rights, which Trippe usually had obtained by shrewd purchases of stock in foreign airlines. In 1928 he had bought in with West Indian Express, Peruvian Airways, and Chilean Airways. The following year he had obtained stock in Compania Mexicana de Aviacion and Pan American–Grace Airways. In 1930 he purchased stock in SCADTA and the New York, Rio, and Buenos Aires Line and its subsidiary, Panair do Brasil. This last deal eliminated a threat set up by Montgomery and Bevier, who previously had secured rights down the South American east coast by establishing the above New York, Rio, and Buenos do Brasil route. However, Trippe soon overcame that obstacle since he held U.S. Post Office mail contracts for the long and costly route, whereas Montgomery and Bevier did not.

This marked Pan American's remarkable expansion through Latin America. Mail and passenger service was opened to San Juan on January 9, 1929; to Cristobal (Canal Zone) February 4; to Mexico City on March 10;

---

* Much of this early history of Pan American World Airways was kindly provided by the publishers of FORTUNE, who allowed two articles, published in 1931 and 1936, to be used as source material.

Santiago, Chile, July 12; to Paramaribo on September 23; to Montevideo, via Santiago and Buenos Aires, on October 12, 1929. The east coast service reached Santos on November 27, 1930, and completed the circuit to Buenos Aires November 23, 1931.

This pioneering period required aircraft of more suitable characteristics, and the inventory soon included the Sikorsky S-38 amphibian to link Central and South American west coast cities. A number of Ford Tri-Motor and Consolidated Commodore planes were taken over from the Montgomery-Mason-Bevier combine, and by November 19, 1931, the company had adopted the Sikorsky S-40, first of the four-engined flying boats to initiate the "Clipper" trademark of all Pan American equipment. This remarkable aircraft was in regular service within four years after the Fairchild FC-2's charter flight.

With the acquisition of the long-range S-40, Trippe could now plan a true transoceanic route. As early as 1929 he had held preliminary talks with Imperial Airways and with France's Aéropostale concerning a transatlantic route that would link the United States and Europe through the Portuguese-owned Azores, then held by the French. Before this North Atlantic run could be set up, Pan American busied itself with the prospects of flying the Pacific from San Francisco to Manila. At that time nonstop flights between Newfoundland and Ireland, and between California and Hawaii, were considered impractical. So any route into east Asia would have to be flown via Alaska and Siberia, while an airline into Europe would have to be flown via Greenland and Iceland. In fact, on August 1, 1931, Sikorsky S-41 boats were flown between Boston and Halifax, Nova Scotia, chiefly to gain experience with climatic and marine conditions totally unlike those of the Caribbean. There Commodores were regularly flying the 600-mile nonstop jump between Kingston, Jamaica, and Cristobal, a run being used as a training school for advanced direction-finding and precise aerial navigation.

In 1928 Trippe had engaged Charles A. Lindbergh as Pan Am's technical adviser, a post Lindbergh holds to this day. In 1931 Trippe dispatched Colonel and Mrs. Lindbergh on their famed survey flight over the Great Circle Route to the Orient. On the other side of the globe Trippe induced Vilhjalmur Stefansson to explore and investigate the meteorological problems of Arctic flight. Two years later he sent the Lindberghs off to survey the Great Circle Route across the North Atlantic. The couple conducted an expedition to Scandinavia via Greenland and Iceland. They used the supply ship SS *Jelling* to further check meteorology and sites for airport bases and harbors. Their findings indicated that the difficulties of operating air services via the northern latitudes had been grossly exaggerated.

An interesting point came up on December 12, 1935, when the U.S. State Department announced that understandings had been reached with several countries to facilitate transatlantic air transport. The Director-General of Civil Aviation of Great Britain advised the Secretary of Commerce that he would grant Pan American's request for a permit, subject to the U.S. government's approval of that airline. Needless to state, this was given immediately.

At about the same time Trippe was carrying out discussions with DNL, a Norwegian airline. These talks resulted in a mutual assistance program, including landing and traffic rights, and studies were made for a Sikorsky S-43 route from Reykjavik, Iceland, to Stavanger, Norway, via the Faroe and Shetland islands.

The European negotiations were long and protracted, whereas setting up a transpacific run was comparatively easy—for Juan Trippe. In this instance, all he had to do was to get the Lindberghs to make a survey flight to the Orient in a Lockheed Sirius. Next, in June 1932, he arranged an internal corporate reorganization in which Pan American created a Pacific-Alaska Airways, and purchased two minor Alaskan airlines. A year or so later China National Aviation Corporation was brought into this setup, simply because CNAC held the franchise for the Chinese coastal route between Shanghai and Hong Kong. November 13, 1934, Trippe acquired the Alaskan Southern Airways and thereby picked up another missing link—that between Seattle and the southernmost point in Alaska territory.

There was one stumbling block—the failure to reach an agreement with the USSR to link up with the Chinese coastal route. But again Trippe had taken the precaution to plan for equipment that would fly direct from California to Hawaii. He had commissioned both Martin and Boeing to produce long-range flying boats which could cover distances of more than 2,500 miles. Martin came up with their M-130, while Boeing took a little more time, finally producing their famous 314 Clipper. Somewhere in between Sikorsky came out with their S-42.

The Pacific route began to fall into place like a magic jigsaw puzzle because in that area there were fewer political problems. Hawaii, Midway Island, Guam, and the Philippines were U.S. territories, and at that time China was under American influence. But other than Honolulu, there were no facilities for flying boats along the proposed route, and Pan Am had to build its own. On March 27, 1935, the SS *North Haven*, a 15,000-ton freighter, left San Francisco, carrying two complete villages, five air bases, 250,000 gallons of fuel, 44 airline technicians, 74 construction men, provisions, motor launches, landing barges, generators, windmills, water storage and fuel tanks. During the following summer complete flying-boat bases were constructed at Midway, Wake, and Guam, and the Honolulu and Manila bases improved and enlarged.

In mid-April of 1935 a number of survey flights were begun between San Francisco and Manila with stops at Honolulu. Each sector of the route was covered carefully, and by November 1935 a Martin M-130, christened the China Clipper, was flown out of San Francisco on a simulated run to the Philippines. Six days later the flight was successfully completed without a hitch, but survey flights were still continued under the eye of André Priester who had become Pan Am's safety director.

Eleven months were to pass before Pan American decided to risk a transpacific passenger run. On October 21, 1936, with Captain Edwin C. Musick at the controls and Harold E. Gray (now Pan Am's president) as First Officer, the Hawaii Clipper NC-14714 Martin M-130 took off from San Francisco and arrived safely at the Cavite Base, Manila, on October 27. The passengers on this historic flight were R. F. Bradley, Aviation Manager of Standard Oil; Wilbur May, Los Angeles department store executive; T. F. Ryan III, San Francisco capitalist; Col. Charles Bartley, Chicago grocer; Alfred Bennett, aviation executive; Mrs. Clara Adams and Mrs. Zetta Averill, reputed world travelers. Mr. Bennett disembarked at Honolulu and six more passengers boarded for the trip to Manila. They were Dr. Hilario Moncado, G. R. Carter, Louis Weinzheimer, Edward Brier, and Herbert Shipman. The westbound trip—San Francisco, Honolulu, Midway, Wake, Guam, Manila—7,309 miles—was completed in 56 hours, 22 minutes flying time. The eastbound run over the same route, but reduced to 7,056 miles for navigational purposes, was covered in 63 hours, 13 minutes flying time.

Once this transpacific route was securely established, Trippe next worked with the government of China and created the China National Aviation Company. CNAS, setting up a supply route over what was to become known as "the hump," provided China's only lifeline to the outside world during the Japanese invasion. After the attack on Pearl Harbor the U.S. Air Transport Command took over this memorable task.

With the Pacific business well in hand, Pan American turned back to the problems of the North Atlantic. There had been many long, tedious discussions, debating reciprocal operating rights with the United Kingdom, but by February 1937 these were finally brought to a satisfactory close. Again, Trippe and Priester scheduled a new series of survey flights, and attempted the first of a program of passenger flights from New York to Bermuda. The first of these was flown on June 18, 1937; the fare, one-way, was $100, and the flying boat was a Martin M-130.

Now Trippe was determined to carry Pan Am's insignia all the way to the major cities of Europe, but mounting experience warned that larger aircraft of greater range would be needed, and on July 21, 1936, he ordered six Boeing 314 flying boats at a cost of $4,000,000, an investment that staggered the treasurers of other airlines. The 314 had a remarkable performance in pay load and range and was capable of carrying thirty passengers from New York to Southampton, England. This Boeing flying boat was years ahead of any aircraft in that category, European or American. But this astounding financial venture was not enough. On March 15, 1937, Pan Am ordered three Boeing 307 pressurized landplanes which were at first intended only for mail and express transatlantic services.

The Boeing 314 put Pan Am months ahead of any company in Europe. Britain had worked hard and spent a considerable sum of money on its Short and Supermarine flying boats, but they lacked the load-carrying factor at the required ranges. The French were nowhere in the picture, and the Germans had placed too much faith in their lighter-than-air dirigibles and not enough in an airplane that could compete on the North Atlantic routes. It will be seen once more that the homogeneous contributions of a continental nation could always produce a better product than anything a multi-nationed area, such as Europe, was capable of.

Pan American made only one survey flight over the North Atlantic route, a 10,000-mile inspection trip piloted by Harold E. Gray with a crew of 11. In addition, there were 9 passengers, 6 of whom were technical observers representing the Federal government, Boeing Airplane Company, Wright Aeronautical Corporation, and Pan American Airways. This flight schedule was carried out as follows: Baltimore to Horta in the Azores, on to Lisbon, Biscarosse (a large lake in western France), Marseilles, Southampton, Foynes, back to Lisbon, Horta, Bermuda, and Baltimore.

On May 20, 1939, Pan Am inaugurated its scheduled airmail service *eastbound* over the southern route to the Azores, Portugal, and France. Captain Arthur E. Laporte commanded NC-18603 on this trip and carried a crew of 11, with 3 technical observers. The total mail load was 1,804 pounds.

On June 24 the line began its transatlantic airmail service *eastbound* over the northern route, taking in Shediac, New Brunswick; Botwood, Newfoundland; Foynes, Ireland; and into Southampton, England. About 20 VIP passengers were carried as well.

The first actual passenger-carrying transatlantic flight was flown on June 28, 1939, with Captain R. O. D. Sullivan piloting the Dixie Clipper NC-18605. They left Port Washington, New York, stopped at Horta and Lisbon, and disembarked at Marseilles. The total flying time was 29 hours, 20 minutes, but the elapsed time, including an overnight stop in Lisbon, was 42 hours, 10 minutes. Besides a crew of 12 the Dixie Clipper carried 19 paying passengers. The initial passenger-carrying flight over the northern route (Port Washington–Shediac–Botwood–Foynes–Southampton) was flown on July 8, 1939, and piloted by Captain A. E. Laporte, with a crew of 12 and 17 passengers.

World War II loomed just over the horizon and its eventual outbreak curtailed Pan Am's further expansion over the North Atlantic, so Trippe turned back to his Pacific operations. Shortly after, the Pan Am dynamo was called upon by the U.S. government to sit in on some important planning that eventually would bolster the country's national defense. At first he was requested to set up at Pan Am's Miami base a school to train Allied military flight crews in long-range flying—a skill which had been highly developed by his flying-boat pilots. At Miami thousands of service airmen were carefully trained, and during the three years following the attack on Pearl Harbor, 325 American pilot graduates of this school were decorated for their gallantry and extraordinary service.

At the prompting of the United States, the governments of several South American countries displaced all German interests in their airlines. With that, on United States bidding, Pan American moved in to take over these operations, all of which might have threatened the Panama Canal. Then, too, the War Department needed vital bases throughout South America to protect further the Panama Canal and the important South Atlantic supply routes. At the time the United States was neutral, and in that role could not make formal requests for such bases, so Trippe was asked to enlarge his existing bases and build new ones at specified points. By the time of the attack on Pearl Harbor, Pan Am had constructed a network of bases and air routes throughout the hemisphere. Later on it was widely agreed that the importance of these PAA bases, established before the war, contributed greatly to the success of the South Atlantic ferrying and transport routes.

In 1941 President Roosevelt summoned Trippe to the White House and asked him to establish and operate an airline across Africa from the Atlantic to the Nile, chiefly to support the British Army fighting to drive General Rommel out of Egypt. Scheduled operations began in sixty-one days and the route was later expanded to stretch from Miami across the South Atlantic, across Africa and the Arabian Sea, to India.

Both before and after America's entry into the war, Pan Am was carrying cargo and personnel on missions critical to national defense, and was ferrying government aircraft to overseas destinations. With the attack on Pearl Harbor, Trippe immediately put Pan Am on a wartime footing, at the complete service of the United States government and its Allies. Pan Am stations automatically became U.S. air bases.

With the return of peace, Trippe assumed commercial operations and devoted his attention to new route development.

13

Trials of United Air Lines

The Air Mail Act of 1934, which had followed the breakup of several corporate bodies, had gone even further than the original F.D.R. edict. It banished for five years most of the men who had been responsible for setting up the major airlines. But in many instances the breakups and reorganizations gave the executives a certain sense of emancipation, for the airline presidents no longer had to check with the aircraft builders or the engine manufacturers before they made new decisions.

For instance, the heads of United Air Lines no longer had to consult Boeing or Pratt & Whitney when they wished to consider the purchase of new flying equipment. Their main office was moved from Park Avenue, New York City, to Chicago, a more centrally located headquarters where the directors of traffic, advertising, and public relations had their offices in the La Salle–Wacker building. In a short time a two-room suite spread out to a complex covering two floors and, as explained previously, NAT, BAT, PAT and Varney; the Boeing School at Oakland; and the United Airport at Burbank were incorporated into a new

Delaware company to keep them from contaminating the airline corporation.

The legal and financial structure was comparatively easy for Joseph Ripley to set up, but to make the airline a paying proposition was another matter. Almost immediately United lost the remunerative Pacific Coast route as the Air Mail Act prohibited any one carrier from retaining airmail contracts for more than one primary route and two secondary routes. At the time the four transcontinental airways were considered primary routes, as were the Pacific Coast and Atlantic seaboard lines. This left President Patterson with the problem of making Pacific Air Transport completely free and independent of United Air Lines.

Congress had to be told the facts of life, and after considerable protest and explanation droning on until January 1935, a Federal Aviation Commission finally recommended that the Air Mail Act be amended to eliminate that unreasonable clause. It designated the San Diego–Seattle linkage as a secondary route. With that, United reorganized and transferred dozens of young men from the various corporate ownerships to important executive and technical positions in the airline. These transfers were soon reflected in the management operations and were to give United a youthful, but most dependable, organization.

On the other hand, the Air Mail Act had created other problems, for the airlines now were badgered by the whims of three Federal bureaus instead of the single control of the Post Office Department: the Interstate Commerce Commission took over the routes and rates, the Post Office Department assigned the mail loads and paid the tariff, and the Department of Commerce maintained airway beacons, ran the meteorological service, laid down and enforced the safety rules. In addition to this three-way authority, both the Senate and the House presumed to set up their own committees to check on the airline industry.

The Interstate Commerce Commission proved to be a

real stumbling block to the operators, who were slaving to recover from the effects of the earlier mail contract cancelations. Whatever rate increases any airline suggested so as to show a fair and reasonable return on its investment, the I.C.C. usually reduced, explaining, "The costs of service are, of course, important to those rendering it, but we are not here fixing the rates for the operators; we are fixing rates for the routes irrespective of the contractors operating them."

To show clearly what they meant, the Commission rejected a United proposal that airmail carriers be paid on a simple pound-mile basis, and instead established a highly complicated system which cut United's average return on the coast-to-coast route from 38 cents to 31 cents per plane mile, with corresponding reductions on the Pacific Coast and Salt Lake–Seattle runs. The Commission also set a 300-pound revenue limit on the amount any one plane could carry, and as a result stacks of mail piled up at many mainline airports. United had to fly them to their destinations but could receive carrier pay for only 300 pounds of mail per flight.*

This high-handed ruling cut United's mail revenue for 1934 to well below their 1932 income, and to counter with suitable economies the Chicago–Kansas City passenger-cargo run had to be canceled. This was a route NAT had pioneered some eight years before. It was two years before the Interstate Commerce Commission would listen to reason and make a suitable adjustment.

Years later Patterson reflected, "It was tough, but in some respects a blessing in disguise. The decisions certainly put a halt to the financial manipulations of the development days and saved the airlines from the long period of specula-

* Source material for much of this chapter is from Frank J. Taylor's *High Horizons* (1955). Permission for its use was given by Marjorie Mitchell, Manager Copyrights and Permissions, McGraw-Hill Book Company.

tion and consequent receivership that the railroads went through."

Unquestionably, this was true. In every area served by United the traffic men worked like beavers to fly passengers and cargo, and it must be admitted that they succeeded— particularly over the New York–Chicago run. In 1933, for instance, United's passenger revenue, $3,955,622 for 68,984,770 passenger miles flown, constituted 40 percent of the airline's income. By 1935 it was $4,933,376 for 83,473,000 passenger miles, and in 1936 the company's aircraft topped the 100,000,000 passenger-mile mark which resulted in an income of $5,844,331 from passenger fares. This was almost 58 percent of United's total earnings.

It was much the same in the cargo business, although frieight brought in only one-tenth as many dollars as the mail or passenger operations. They were quietly gleaning in a seldom tilled field. This cargo business demanded some ground assistance, and in 1934 United made a deal for the Railway Express Agency to pick up and deliver express handled by the airline for 12.5 percent of the revenue. The basic rate was four cents per mile per hundred pounds.

On paper this looked like a fair deal, but in a short time United was at odds with American, TWA, Eastern, and several other airlines which refused to go along with the idea. They presumed that the Railway Express would live up to its name and favor the railroads, delivering little business to the airlines. These other operators undertook to establish their own pickup and delivery service, organizing a General Air Express to operate in the larger cities. This turned out to be a pointless venture. General Air Express soon went out of business, and the airlines concerned had to draw up a new general contract with the Railway Express Agency. The new agreement stipulated that the air operators were to pay the Agency fifteen cents of every express dollar taken in.

United's cargo figures for this period, while relatively

small, began to show an impressive gain, and the improvement can probably be applied to contemporary airlines. For instance, in 1933 United's planes brought in $133,153 for hauling 184,285 ton-miles of air express. By 1936, under Railway Express cooperation, they took in $431,653 while handling 760,000 ton-miles of air express—which that year was 4.27 percent of the airline's income.

At this point—1934–35—United Air Lines, operating over an area of heavy population, was handling more traffic than any airline in the world, but the business was considerably off-balance as most of the traffic was in the West. It was obvious that United required more productive outlets in the East. By 1937 American Airlines, under the management of C. R. Smith, had doubled the number of population centers served by its system and American had become the United States' Number 1 airline. It embraced sixty major traffic centers, and covered a territory in which one-third of the country's population lived.

United had concentrated on developing its Main Line territory, the overland route from coast to coast. When requests for extensions were submitted to Washington, they were delayed or ignored. But at the same time American and TWA were granted extensions over United's route between Chicago and New York. (Further details on this situation will be explained in later pages.)

There was nothing Patterson could do but try to increase his line's revenue by organizing or buying up key feeder lines. In one case, in a proposed deal to buy the Pennsylvania Airlines and Transport Company which was flying an airmail route between Milwaukee and Detroit and a passenger service between Washington and Detroit, the I.C.C. stepped in, and Pennsylvania eventually merged with Central Air Lines to form what became Capital Airlines— another competitor over United's eastern leg of its Main Line.

In a similar situation Patterson negotiated for the

Cheyenne–Denver leg of the Wyoming Air Services, Ltd. Denver businessmen had long complained that their capital of the Rocky Mountain country had been cut off from any major air route, just as it had been denied contact with the major railways. They felt it was time that Denver was recognized as an important city. Perhaps because of this Patterson was able to buy the Cheyenne–Denver run, along with its airmail contract, and place Denver on a first-class airway. A few years later the capital of Colorado became the vital junction of the entire United system.

United Air Lines was unable to make the equipment switch from Boeings to Douglas DC-3s until late in 1936, when Patterson turned over most of his Boeing 247s to the feeder lines which connected with the United system—a policy he employed to develop United in areas that were becoming air-travel conscious.

Now began a country-wide battle for air-passenger revenue, one of the most dangerous periods in American airline history. In this bitter competition several of the rapidly extending lines almost competed themselves into bankruptcy. The number of passengers carried made no difference. In 1934, for example, when United carried more passengers than any airline in the world, the company lost more than $2,000,000. In 1935 United broke just about even, and the following year made $371,000 and paid a dividend of twenty cents per share—the last the stockholders were to receive for several years.

One feature in this competition to attract more passengers was the introduction of an overnight sleeper service by American, TWA, and United; an aircraft which provided boudoir and cheesecake-promotion layouts but attracted few passengers. Also, these Pullman-type planes were limited to night operations and had to stand idle during most of the daylight hours. Later, a "Skylounge"—a fourteen-passenger extra-fare plane—was introduced by

United, and though its cabin provided club-car swivel chairs and plenty of leg room, not many patrons relished paying $2 extra for the convenience. Eventually, the Skylounge cabins were converted back to normal twenty-one-passenger accommodations, and in several cases to sleepers flown over the San Francisco–Chicago route. Aboard these 150-mph luxury liners, the hostesses had to double as chambermaids and be alert to rouse their charges out of bed, get them properly dressed, packed, and provided with a breakfast in time to disembark. Needless to state, these overnight schedules usually caused considerable confusion.

American Airlines introduced the idea of air-travel scrip coupons that offered a discount of fifteen percent on the price of a fare. United adopted the idea and persuaded other airlines to make travel-scrip interchangeable. The coupons lured a few more passengers up the ramps, but the discount prices canceled any slim margin of profit. These, and other temporary inducements, did attract more passengers, but eventually the law of averages took its toll, and in 1936 a new gloom blanked out the faint glow of prosperity. That year saw the unprecedented number of eight accidents, all of which provided sanguinary headlines. Five more crashes were recorded in 1937, and the newspapers told in "shocker" detail the full stories of these disasters. This panicked the regular flying public, and cancellations poured in. United Air Lines, which lost two planes during this frightening period, in one day saw its passenger revenues drop from $25,000 to $5,000. Many airliners took off empty—to maintain their schedules—and thus contributed to the company losses. Amid all this the Post Office Department arbitrarily canceled one of United's daily mail flights between Chicago and New York.

President Patterson knew some drastic step had to be taken, and he gave Major R. W. Schroeder, a veteran war and test pilot, carte blanche to set up new standards of airline safety. To a certain extent, Schroeder's name and careful publicizing of his safety code brought renewed confidence in commercial flying. He not only improved the safety factor, but pointed out that the airline would have to give its passengers much the same comfort as the railroads, and he persuaded the directors to increase the company's shares from 1,200,000 to 2,000,000. Regardless of the shock of the crashes, the added shares were eagerly taken up by the stockholders and the general public. This refinancing gave Patterson $4,000,000 to follow Schroeder's suggestions.

The rejuvenated United management with its Main Line of populous cities believed it had a high potential of passenger traffic. It had developed a fantastic system of handling planes, and put up a remarkable record of maintaining schedules. With its extra financing United made plans to capture the bulk of the business, not only between New York and Chicago, but over their whole 6,000-mile system. What followed illustrates the government and corporate double-shuffling with which Big Business had to contend. While Patterson was studying Schroeder's safety code and in-flight conveniences, TWA was awarded a certificate to fly the Chicago–Pittsburgh–Newark route, and before the ink was dry on that decision, American Airlines was awarded the Chicago–Detroit–Newark run. These two routes were slightly longer than United's direct Main Line via Cleveland, but they attracted much of the passenger business in that profitable area. In those years the Chicago–New York run was a reliable segment of revenue, for it not only drew from the vital cities of the northeast, but Chicago was the key point for most transcontinental passengers to or from the West. Obviously, United Air Lines was in for terrific competition.

TWA opened its new route with a fleet of Douglas DC-2 transports which were twenty-five mph faster than United's Boeing 247s. American Airlines held much the same advantage, and overnight both lines were providing 5-hour, nonstop flights between Chicago and New York. The best Patterson could offer was a 5½-hour, one-stop flight. (Actually, both American and TWA usually stopped en route for reserve fuel if their loads so demanded, but this was adroitly kept out of the timetables.) The Douglas ships were quieter and roomier and the seats luxurious compared to the conveniences in the Boeing. It was clear that the air traveler was no longer the wealthy adventurer who flew for the thrill and status symbol. The airlines were now being patronized by businessmen—executives who felt their time was precious—and by many women who enjoyed the care and comfort of a modern airline system. Time was of the essence to most air travelers, but in-flight convenience was also a factor, and the passengers were getting both if they flew with the lines using the Douglas planes.

It must be said that United tried every trick in the aviation book. Patterson spent $1,000,000 to soup-up the Boeings with improved engines, and three-bladed constant-speed propellers increased their speed from 160 mph to 170 mph, but this was not quite enough. Donald Douglas countered with a larger, faster DC-3 which cut down American's and TWA's Chicago–New York run to 4½ hours. The Boeings still had to stop for fuel at Cleveland, and even worse required seven hops to cross the country. They could carry only ten passengers, whereas the DC-2 hauled fourteen with plenty of seat space, and the DC-3 accommodated twenty-one.

Balked in the equipment field, United tried to improve the on-board service. Trim stewardesses served hot meals in thermal trays that kept the food warm, providing a sky-high dining-room aspect that pleased the patrons for a time, particularly the elderly, but businessmen were more concerned with their arrival time than in compartmented dinners served in cramped quarters. Despite hot meals and glamorous hostesses, TWA and American were still skim-

ming the cream from the segments of the New York–
Chicago run, and the DC-3s were taking in the money that
United was losing every day of the year. In late 1935 Patterson had to appropriate another $1,000,000 to purchase
ten DC-3s from Douglas, but he tried a new idea. His contract demanded that the DC-3s be powered with Pratt &
Whitney 14-cylindered Hornet engines. These radials cost
more and weighed more than the Wright Whirlwinds, but
produced faster climb, and either engine could keep the
DC-3 aloft with a full load at 11,000 feet. This was a margin of safety that was to put United back in the race for
patronage.

The new Douglas planes were not delivered until 1936,
but almost immediately triggered a new battle for the blue-
chip run. Although the Hornet-powered DC-3s returned
some financial reward, Patterson soon realized this aircraft was providing only a stopgap and that the opposition
would waste no time with counter strokes. This still obtains
to this day, for any "latest" airliner is just an interim plane
while the opposition searches for a better air transport.

While staring out of his office window one day, the president of United conceived a four-engined aircraft, one of
great pay-load capacity with good performance, but above
all one with a wide margin of safety—a quality that would
overcome the passengers' dread of crashes such as those
that besmirched the schedules in 1936. Whether Patterson
thought he alone had this concept of a four-engined aircraft would be hard to determine, but it certainly was not
original with him. A small crew of designers who worked
with the earlier United Aircraft and Transport Company
had roughed-in the details of such an aircraft, but when
that aviation empire was broken up, the general design
went to the Boeing Airplane Company. It might have gone
into immediate production except that Boeing was concentrating on a four-engined flying boat for Juan Trippe of Pan
Am. This aircraft was first known as the Flying Clipper,

and then renamed the Pan American Clipper. At the time it appeared to be a promising product, but only Pan Am was striving to develop transoceanic routes, and Boeing found itself devoting every production-line facility to building these very dependable flying boats. When it was too late, Boeing realized that Pan Am could use only a certain number—they had contracted themselves out of the more remunerative landplane airline field.

Patterson revived his four-engined transport idea in 1936, and queried Frederick B. Rentschler of Pratt & Whitney whether such an airliner was feasible. Rentschler had long wanted to see his engines in a four-engine plane, and he called in George J. Mead, his chief engineer and Commander Jerome C. Hunsaker, an aerodynamics expert at Massachusetts Institute of Technology. Together the three men roughed out a general idea of a 54,000-pound gross-load luxury airliner which they guaranteed would show a speed of 175 mph.

Patterson took a preliminary blueprint of this project to several aircraft factories. Boeing felt they couldn't take it on, as things stood. Consolidated Aircraft thought that any plane designed or conceived by an airline wouldn't get off the ground. Sikorsky, then a subsidiary of United Aircraft, submitted a bid so low that Patterson was advised to ignore it. At the Douglas works Patterson received little encouragement, but their Chief Engineer, a Mr. Raymond, pointed out that a four-engined airplane would take a lot of engineering time—and money. Raymond felt that Patterson was simply picking up some free advice. However, to prove he meant business, the United man offered to underwrite half the engineering cost—about $300,000—if Douglas would foot the rest of the bill.

News of this advanced project soon swept through the industry, and TWA, Pan Am, Eastern, and American offered to assume a portion of the underwriting cost. After studying the new Mead-Hunsaker drawings again, it was clear it would take an initial $1,000,000 to deliver a flying prototype. Douglas was still willing to pay half, and the rest was picked up by the heads of the five interested airlines. United, which had initiated the project, paid forty percent of the half in order to have first call on the first lot to come off the Douglas production line. TWA paid twenty-four percent, American chipped in sixteen percent, Pan American eleven percent, and Eastern eight percent.

The first model, known as the DC-4E, created something of a false start. The prototype embodied many new advances in commercial design, including under-wing fueling, a retractable tricycle landing gear, complete cabin-climate control, and several other novelties which, as it turned out, required longer periods of development to reach everyday operations. The Douglas firm claims it invested $3,000,000 and months of flight testing in the DC-4E, and then realized the program should be further undertaken by "orderly evolution of sound, well-developed principles." From that point on, Douglas concentrated on what was to become the DC-4.

The first DC-4, as it was to be known in the commercial field, was not ready for its test flight until June 1938. And it was almost another year before the Douglas firm allowed a United Air Lines pilot to fly a demonstration flight—when Benny Howard, a well-known flight engineer, took one over the complete United system to initiate the publicity program. Millions of interested people were shown this fabulous airliner, and United gleaned a million dollars' worth of prestige, for the new Douglas did all that any of the demonstration pilots asked of it.

So far, so good, but the development of the DC-4 had taken more time than had been anticipated, and $600,000 was spent in building the experimental model. Production-line planes were to range from $450,000 each in orders of five, and $182,000 apiece for fleets of sixty. The five airlines had agreed among themselves not to purchase another airliner in the 50,000-pound class, but during the two-year delay Boeing had seen the light and had produced a prototype of the 307 Stratoliner.

The Stratoliner had been conceived while Boeing was busily engaged in developing a long-range bomber for the Air Corps. The prototype was to utilize the wings and tail assembly of the B-17, which was encountering some opposition in Washington. When it was learned that some of the airlines were becoming dissatisfied with the progress of the Douglas DC-4, Boeing executives decided to speed up their 307 transport venture. Fred Collins, Boeing's sales manager, showed a set of Stratoliner drawings around and explained that his transport could be produced quickly since his firm had had considerable experience with their four-engined military aircraft. Both TWA and American jumped at the chance and ordered five Stratoliners, which were designed to weigh 1,000 pounds under the 50,000-pound limit. In the Boeing project, too, Pan American agreed to underwrite part of the development cost, for Juan Trippe was already planning to fly his transocean routes "over the weather" with landplanes! This move broke up the DC-4 cooperative plan and left Douglas, United, and American bearing the brunt. Eastern had given up all hope long before and pulled out of the deal.

During the DC-4 demonstration flight around the country both United and American engineers devised several modifications that were designed to improve passenger comfort—including a pressurized cabin that would allow high-altitude flying and evade bad weather. In fact, these demonstrations proved to be fortunate shake-down flights which resulted in the design of a novel galley from which two stewardesses could serve hot meals to fifty or more passengers in the short time it would take to fly between two major cities. As early as 1937–38 it was evident that success in commercial flying did not wholly rely on a comfortable plane powered with four engines, providing 200-mph speed and greater seating capacity. Air travelers were losing their fear of flying and were bringing their appetites aboard with them to enjoy first-class meals—"on the airlines"—a feature that has been thoroughly established to this day.

But before any completed DC-4s could be delivered to United Air Lines, Robert A. Lovett, Assistant Secretary of War, talked to Patterson, pointing out that a second World War was building up in Europe and the Pacific, and that the DC-4 was exactly what the Army Air Force needed for global transport. Patterson agreed to cancel United's order, allowing the Douglas plant to concentrate on producing a military version. American Airlines also agreed to the arrangement, and in this manner the DC-4 became the Douglas Skymaster. In Army khaki it was known as the C-54, and in the Navy as the R-5D.

14

The Building of Braniff

Braniff International Airways, probably the largest airline based in the Southwest, began with modest planning. After seven years of sound business effort it started its climb and expansion with its first airmail contract, enabling it to spread over ten Texas communities. Today, Braniff operates more than 18,000 miles of domestic and international routes through the United States and ten Latin American countries. Over more than three decades Braniff has developed into a major airline serving the Midwest, and flying key routes into the Midsouth, Washington, D.C. and New York. In 1948 the line expanded into Latin America, providing international service to Havana, Panama, and Guayaquil, Ecuador. By June of that same year Braniff moved into Lima, Peru, flying DC-4 and DC-6 air transports.

The Braniff corporation was founded in Oklahoma on June 20, 1928, by Thomas E. Braniff, and on that date the line flew its first commercial run with a five-passenger Stinson Detroiter over the 116 miles between Tulsa and Oklahoma City. Only one trip daily was attempted since the company owned but one airplane. Two years later business had picked up to the point where it was deemed necessary to incorporate, and on November 3, 1930, the present Braniff Airways was organized with T. E. Braniff, president; E. E. Westervelt, vice president; and Paul Braniff, secretary-treasurer. Ten days later Braniff carried out its first scheduled passenger flight, linking Tulsa, Oklahoma City, and Wichita Falls. Its equipment was two six-passenger Lockheed Vegas. Early in December of the same year the service was extended from Tulsa to Kansas City.

This memorable Lockheed was actually designed and built in 1927 for small airline operations, and it subsequently established thirty-four flight records when flown by such aviation greats as Wiley Post, James Mattern, Amelia Earhart, and Sir Hubert Wilkins. Amelia Earhart was the first woman to fly the Atlantic when in 1932 she piloted her Vega from Newfoundland to Ireland in 15 hours, 18 minutes. Wiley Post's Vega, the Winnie Mae, made the first solo flight around the world in 1933, covering 15,596 miles in 7 days, 18 hours, and 49.5 minutes. In 1931 Post and Harold Gatty, together, flew a Vega around the world for a speed record of 8 days, 15 hours, 51 minutes. Sir Hubert Wilkins made the first flight over Antarctica in 1928 in one of the maiden Vegas to come off the production line.

In the next few years Braniff spread its transport tentacles in a startling manner, considering that so far they had no post office airmail contracts over any segment of their area. In February 1931 service was extended to Chicago with one round trip daily, taking in Chicago–Kansas City–Tulsa–Oklahoma City–Wichita Falls. Another round trip included Tulsa–Oklahoma City–Wichita Falls, and two round trips were carried out between Tulsa and Oklahoma City. Four months later St. Louis was brought into the Braniff schedules with stops at Tulsa–St. Louis–Kansas City–Chicago. In June of 1932 the summer passenger traffic increased considerably, and more Vegas were added to the fleet. The schedules also picked up Bartlesville, Oklahoma; Coffeyville, and Chanute, Kansas; and Springfield, Missouri.

Further expansion was made possible when Braniff was granted a post office contract on May 7, 1934, to link Dallas and Chicago. This was the route lost by United Air Lines during the reorganization period. This contract gave the line stops at Dallas, Kansas City, Wichita, Ponce City, Oklahoma City, and Fort Worth. Their first official mail flights were made on May 17, 1934, when the line had grown to forty-seven employees. Passenger and express service became routine by the end of that month, and before the year was out operations and maintenance sheds had to be moved from Oklahoma City to Dallas, although the administrative offices were retained in Oklahoma City.

In January of 1935 Braniff bought up the Long and Harmon Air Service which held post office contracts to serve ten Texas cities. This addition to the system prompted Braniff to call itself the "Great Lakes to the Gulf" airline, over which it was operating more than 3,000 route miles, and logging 13,000 miles daily. A few weeks later Chief Pilot Ray Shrader flew in the first of a new fleet of seven Lockheed Electra, 10-passenger transports. The first Electra was assigned to the Dallas–Corpus Christi run, and aboard these new planes Braniff inaugurated its first inflight meals—cold sandwiches, coffee, or milk. By 1937 the Braniff fleet included a number of Douglas DC-2s and later on, by 1940, the company was able to purchase a number of 21-passenger DC-3s.

During World War II Braniff turned over more than half of its transport fleet to the U.S. government. It also flew a number of contract routes to the Panama Canal Zone, domestic military routes for the Air Transport Command, and operated a number of training schools where Army pilots, radio operators, and mechanics were instructed in modern air transport operations.

In 1942 Braniff began a new series of expansions to match the construction of a new operations base at Love Field in Dallas. Over the months following the ground-breaking for this complex, the treasury and legal departments moved to Dallas, and by mid-1942 the traffic and advertising offices left Oklahoma City, completing the airline's transfer to the Dallas base.

In April 1942 Braniff began operation of a new system of foreign air-cargo routes for the Air Force which connected Army depots and bases. One of these, operated wholly by company personnel, flew between San Antonio and the Canal Zone. Later, similar service was set up between Dallas and the West Coast, and from Dallas to Dayton, Ohio. Nine DC-3s and DC-2s were converted from standard airliners to service-cargo carriers in an effort to facilitate a suitable transport system. In 1943 a new service extended a route from Amarillo to Pueblo, Colorado Springs, and Denver. A month later another route was flown from San Antonio to Laredo, Texas, bringing Braniff's route mileage to 3,108 miles and increasing the payroll to 1,300 employees. Through the rest of the war Braniff continued its Army contract, flying 4,840,517 miles, carrying 6,494,181 pounds of cargo and 16,890 service passengers. A total of 2,300 trips was made without a fatality or the loss of any cargo. Meantime, domestic service between Dallas, the West Coast, and Ohio continued until September 25, 1944, when a final flight from Sacramento to Dallas was completed.

Gradual extensions were made with a limited number of aircraft until early in 1946, when the company picked up a few DC-4 four-engined planes and began daily round-trip service between San Antonio, Dallas, Kansas City, and Chicago. In May 1946 the Civil Aeronautics Board awarded

Braniff 7,700 miles of routes in Latin America including service to Cuba, Panama, Colombia, Ecuador, Peru, Bolivia, Paraguay, Brazil, Argentina, and Mexico. But before any of these routes could be flown Braniff had to finance and build its own system of navigation and communications facilities, spanning oceans, mountains, and jungles. More than half a million dollars were involved in a powerful radio network. Six 52-passenger DC-6 sleeper planes had to be purchased, and by 1951 three more were added to the luxury fleet. In 1947 Braniff became the first American commercial airline to use the ILS (Instrument Landing System) with its 300-foot minimum ceiling. Meanwhile, DC-6s were placed in service on daily round-trip schedules between Chicago, Kansas City, Dallas, San Antonio, and Houston.

In June 1948 international service was established to Havana, Panama, and Guyaquil, Ecuador. This was soon extended to Lima, Peru with DC-6 and DC-4 equipment. That year, too, Braniff completed the one billionth passenger mile of safe operation.

Between 1951 and 1967 the Braniff combine continued its progress and expansion, first by million-dollar purchases of new equipment (twenty-five Convair-340 airliners), and second, by selecting Miami as its international gateway into Latin America—which in turn led to service into São Paulo, Brazil. On August 16, 1952, Braniff merged with Mid-Continent Airlines, which introduces the interesting details of a little-known corporation.

Mid-Continent Airlines had begun business in 1928 as Hanford's Tri-State Airlines, which had originated as a small flying school, headed by Arthur Hanford, Jr. Hanford soon branched out into the charter service and offered intermittent scheduled flights from Omaha to Sioux City, Minneapolis/St. Paul, and Bismarck, North Dakota. In 1934 Hanford's was awarded a sheaf of airmail contracts by the post office, and began a passenger and mail service from Minneapolis to Kansas City via Sioux Falls, Sioux City, and Omaha; from Sioux Falls to Bismarck via Huron and Aberdeen, S.D.; and from Chicago to Winnipeg via Minneapolis.

Young Hanford died in 1935, and his father, A. S. Hanford, took over the business. In July 1936 Thomas Fortune Ryan III acquired the controlling interest and was named vice president. J. W. Miller, became vice president and general manager. The administrative offices were moved to Kansas City that same year. At this time Hanford's was flying routes between Kansas City, Minneapolis, and into the Dakotas with four 4-passenger Lockheed Vegas and three Ford Tri-Motors. In July 1936 a number of 10-passenger Lockheed Electras were obtained, and the airline's routes were extended southward toward Tulsa. In August 1938 the company name was changed to Mid-Continent Airlines. Mr. Ryan moved up to president, and A. S. Hanford was named chairman of the board of directors.

Mid-Continent purchased a number of Lockheed Lodestars in 1940, chiefly to fly two new routes from Minneapolis/St. Paul to St. Louis via Rochester, Minn., Des Moines and Ottumwa, Iowa, and from Des Moines to Kansas City. Another extension was added between Bismarck and Minot, N. D. In 1942, T. F. Ryan resigned to enter the armed forces and J. W. Miller was made president and general manager. Mr. Ryan did not return until 1946.

The Lodestar proved to be a most versatile aircraft. Introduced in 1939 for varied commercial purposes, it normally carried fourteen passengers, a crew of three, plus baggage and cargo. It was powered with two Pratt & Whitney engines which produced a top speed of 263 mph. It was equipped with Fowler flaps, built-in, fixed wingtip slots, full-feathering hydromatic propellers, and it could fly or climb on one engine while carrying a full load. Drafted for duty in World War II, the Lodestar became a glider tower, hospital plane, cargo plane, troop transport, and paratrooper carrier. In some conversions it carried a two-gun turret set just forward of the tail assembly.

After the war, Mid-Continent moved into another period of expansion and the Lodestars were replaced with Douglas DC-3s. The company service was extended from Tulsa to Shreveport and New Orleans, Louisiana. In 1947 another major route extension was granted from Tulsa to Houston via Tyler, Longview, Kilgore, and Gladewater, Texas. By 1950 the Civil Aeronautics Board had awarded Mid-Continent the North Central routes which consisted mainly of Route 106 between Sioux City and Chicago. That same year the company acquired a number of 40-passenger Convair 240s.

At the time of the merger with Braniff in 1952, Mid-Continent was operating a fleet of twenty-three Douglas DC-3s and four Convair 240s over its 6,241 miles of routes, serving thirty-five cities from Minneapolis/St. Paul and the Dakotas in the north, to the southern termini of Houston and New Orleans. All this was, of course, added to the Braniff combine. Interestingly enough, Braniff Airways, though by then twenty-five years old, was the only major scheduled airline to retain one management during its entire history, and to bear the name of its founder and president. Unfortunately, the airline's president, T. E. Braniff, was killed in a private-plane crash near Shreveport, Louisiana, on January 10, 1954.

In the early spring of 1969 Braniff signed an agreement to acquire additional jet aircraft and dispose of its turbo-prop Electras. A number of Boeing 747s are scheduled for delivery early in 1971, and Harding L. Lawrence, Braniff's president, is said to be "closely evaluating" the wide-bodied Lockheed 1011 and the McDonnell-Douglas DC-10 jets reputed to be ready for airline service in 1971.

National Airlines, which has its headquarters in Miami, Florida, is the only Florida-born, Florida-based and Florida-chartered trunk carrier, and was founded in 1934 following the award of a 142-mile airmail route between St. Petersburg and Daytona Beach, linking Tampa, Lakeland, and Orlando. The first flight originated in St. Petersburg on October 15, 1934 with a four-passenger Ryan monoplane. The line actually began operating with two of these early Ryans and four employees.

Today, National is the sixth largest domestic air carrier serving forty-one cities in fifteen states, and the District of Columbia, over 6,185 unduplicated route miles. It links most major cities in the East, the Gulf, and Pacific coasts. It has nearly 7,000 employees, and its total payroll is well over $60,000,000 a year. Its president and chief executive officer is L. B. Maytag, who was elected to this post and became a member of the board of directors in 1962. Dudley Swim joined the board that same year and was elected chairman on September 12, 1962.

National's all pure-jet fleet includes thirteen Douglas DC-8s, two Douglas Super DC-8-61 jets, thirteen Boeing 727-35 jets and twenty-five Boeing 727-235 airliners. In 1968 National ordered two Boeing 747 jumbo jets with cabins that will seat 380 passengers.

The company was chartered under Florida law on July 8, 1937, and three years later its headquarters were moved from St. Petersburg to Jacksonville, then from Jacksonville to Miami in 1946. During the 1930s routes were extended to Miami, Jacksonville, and New Orleans. In 1944 National was awarded the route from Key West to New York City. Service to Havana was authorized in 1946 but was suspended in 1960. In 1956 the National system was extended to Houston, and to Boston in 1957.

National became a truly national airline in 1961 with the award of the southern transcontinental route between Florida and California. Service was extended from Houston to Los Angeles and San Diego, and to Las Vegas and San Francisco. National is the only airline with authority to operate nonstop flights between Florida and California. The airline also operates daily interchange service between East Coast cities and points in South America with Pan American and Braniff.

This airline has a distinguished record of "firsts" in United States' aviation, which include the first scheduled nonstop flight between Miami and New York in 1944, the first low-cost coach service, the first Florida-package vacations along the East Coast (1950) and the first jet service in the nation (1958). In 1963 National became the first all jet-powered airline using pure jets and Electra propjets. The Electras were retired about five years later.

This airline is an applicant in numerous cases now before the Civil Aeronautics Board asking for extension of its southern transcontinental route from San Francisco, Los Angeles, and San Diego to Hilo and Honolulu, Hawaii. Application has also been filed by National to provide a Miami–London service. At the same time it is requesting extension of routes beyond Key West to Havana, Nassau, Jamaica, Caracas, Aruba, Maracaibo, Barranquilla, Balboa/Panama City, and beyond Miami to San Juan. In addition National has proposed service in a seven-state area from the Gulf of Mexico to the Great Lakes, and also seeks to extend its southern transcontinental service to Dallas/Fort Worth, to Atlanta from Los Angeles, and between San Francisco and Dallas/Fort Worth.

Construction has been completed on a new $16,000,000 National Airlines terminal at New York's Kennedy airport, and in Miami a $5,500,000 expansion program is under way. Further expansions are in progress in other cities throughout National's complete system.

Northwest Orient Airlines has written an interesting chapter in U.S. commercial aviation history. It is outstanding in its early pioneering over rugged mountains and vast oceans, developing into an international airline from a small, regional airmail carrier. Northwest started commercial operations in 1926 with two rented planes, an OX-5 Curtiss Oriole and an OX-5 Thomas Morse, both open cockpit aircraft. Its first real fleet consisted of three 85-mph Stinson Detroiters, so named because they were designed by Eddie Stinson and built in the Motor City. They carried three passengers and were probably the first closed-cabin planes used by a commercial airline.

The Detroiters were replaced by the all-metal Hamilton high-wing monoplane, the Ford Tri-Motor, the Waco J-6, the Travel Air 6000, the Lockheed Orion, the Lockheed (Electra) 10A, the Lockheed (Zephyr) 14H, and a Sikorsky amphibian which shuttled passengers between the Twin Cities and the Duluth boat harbor. In turn came the Douglas DC-3, Douglas DC-4, Martin 202, Boeing B-377, Douglas DC-6B, Lockheed 1049G Super-Constellation, Douglas DC-7c, Lockheed L-188 prop-jet, Douglas DC-8 jet, Boeing 720B fan-jet, long-range Boeing 707-320B and 707-320C fan-jets, and a number of short- to medium-range Boeing 727 fan-jets.

Northwest claims to be the second oldest carrier in the United States with a continuous identification, for it began operating on October 1, 1926, flying an airmail route between Minneapolis/St. Paul and Chicago. The company had been incorporated on August 1 of that year under the name of Northwest Airways, a Michigan corporation backed by businessmen in Detroit and Minneapolis/St. Paul, but its control later shifted to a Twin Cities group of financiers.

Passenger service was inaugurated in July 1927, a service that continued for three months before it was suspended for the winter. Over that period of operation the company carried 106 passengers. The next year—1928—Northwest Airways began a route expansion that in twenty years developed into what we know today as Northwest Orient Airlines, one of the world's largest domestic and international airlines, carrying nearly 5,000,000 passengers a year.

From 1928 through 1933 Northwest expanded westward, city by city, through the Dakotas, Montana, and Washington State. It expanded to the East Coast and overseas across the Pacific in the 1940s until it was serving a 20,000-mile route system stretching from New York/Newark and Washington across the northern tier of states to Portland and Seattle/Tacoma. It also flies a domestic route between the upper Midwest and the southeastern cities of Atlanta, Tampa, St. Petersburg, Clearwater, Fort Lauderdale, and Miami.

Northwest's overseas and international routes serve Honolulu, Hawaii; Anchorage, Alaska; and Winnipeg, Canada. It operates over the North Pacific "Great Circle" route from Anchorage to Tokyo, Seoul, Okinawa, Taipei, and Manila. It also operates a Polar Imperial route from New York and Chicago via Anchorage to the Orient, as well as a nonstop fan-jet service between Seattle/Tacoma and Tokyo.

The company's route expansion through the northern areas—Canada, Alaska, and the Aleutian Islands—was begun after World War II, although Croil Hunter, long-time pioneering president of the line, had visualized a "Northwest Passage" to the Orient in the early 1930s. Hunter is now chairman emeritus on the board of directors.

The Great Circle route across the Pacific, as flown by Northwest, is considerably shorter than the mid-Pacific route because it is far north of the earth's equatorial bulge. New York City via the Great Circle is 9,245 miles from Hong Kong, but 11,154 miles via the mid-Pacific course.

Because of Northwest's experience in flying northern transcontinental routes, the United States government called on the line's executives at the onset of World War II to set up and operate a military cargo route to Canada, Alaska, and the Aleutians. Employing military C-46s and C-47s, Northwest's pilots flew more than 21,000,000 miles with a performance factor better than that of many airlines operating domestically at the same time. Four Northwest pilots were awarded Air Medals by President Roosevelt for their contributions to the war effort and to aviation while flying these northern operations. There is no question that the recipients performed with rare devotion to duty, but the Air Medal was originally given for "meritorious achievement while participating in aerial flight, not warranting award of the Distinguished Flying Cross." It was also awarded to military airmen who had completed five offensive missions over enemy territory. However, Northwest's experience in the Canada-Alaska-Aleutians area during the war was taken into account by the Civil Aeronautics Board when the Orient routes were authorized and the vision of an aerial "Northwest Passage" became a reality.

Northwest made other notable contributions to the war effort. The line set up and operated a bomber modification plant in St. Paul and another at Vandalia, Ohio. Thousands of B-25 and B-26 bombers were flown directly from manufacturing plants to these modification centers and equipped for cold weather operations in northern areas. Bombers, modified at Northwest's bases, were among the first American planes to bomb Kiel and other important enemy targets, and many took part in the bridge-busting operations that marked the preparations for the invasion of Normandy. Northwest also cooperated with the Air Corps in several vital projects, among them research into wing and carburetor icing, communications static, and high-altitude flying.

Because of its experience flying the Great Circle route across the Pacific, the Air Corps called on the company in 1950 to act as a prime contractor in the operation of the Korean Airlift, which began shortly after the Korean "police action" in June of that year. Flying DC-4 aircraft, Northwest completed 1,380 Korean Airlift round-trip trans-Pacific crossings, covering a total of more than 13,000,000 miles. During this period Northwest flew 40,000 servicemen and 12,000,000 pounds of high-priority military cargo, ranging from bomber engines to medical supplies, to the Korean bases. All this was completed with no interruption of its regular commercial schedule of trans-Pacific flights.

Northwest crews, based in Tokyo, also operated "UN-99" a United Nations DC-3 which carried a UN observer team to Allied positions in South Korea during the fighting.

Croil Hunter held the presidency of Northwest Orient Airlines for about fifteen years. In 1954 Donald W. Nyrop was named president, replacing General Harold R. Harris who had handled the position but briefly. Donald Nyrop is a native of Elgin, Nebraska, and was graduated from Doane College in 1934. He taught in the High School of Humboldt between 1934–35 and then went to George Washington University to study law. He received his LL.B degree there in 1939 and while attending law school worked as an auditor in the government's General Accounting office.

In October 1939 Nyrop became an attorney in the General Counsel's office of the Civil Aeronautics Authority, and following that, in 1942, was named special assistant to the chairman of the Civil Aeronautics Board. He served with the Army Air Force from August 1942 until January 1946, and was stationed in Washington as executive officer for operations of the Air Transport Command. He left the service with the rank of lieutenant colonel.

In 1946 Nyrop joined the Air Transport Association of America, and represented the carriers of this organization as a member of the official United States delegations at the International Civil Aviation Organization operations conferences in 1946 and 1947. In July 1948 he returned to government service as a deputy administrator of the Civil Aeronautics Administration. By Presidential appointment he served as Administrator of the Civil Aeronautics Administration in 1950 and 1951. In April of 1951 he became chairman of the CAB and remained in that office until October 1952. The following year he joined the law firm of Klagsbrunn, Hanes and Irwin as a partner, and it was from this private practice of law that he went to Northwest Orient Airlines.

15

Two Great Airlines

On the morning of April 15, 1926, Charles A. Lindbergh, then a little-known barnstormer, stowed a small bag of mail aboard a reconditioned wartime D.H.4 and took off from Chicago for St. Louis. Later that same day, Lindy and two other pilots carried three more planeloads of mail from St. Louis to Chicago. At the time Lindbergh was considered the chief pilot for the Robertson Aircraft Corporation of Missouri, the small concern that had obtained the second airmail contract awarded to private operators. A little more than a year later, in May of 1927, Robertson's chief pilot made aviation history by flying alone across the Atlantic in a special Ryan monoplane.

The runs Lindbergh had flown for Robertson in April 1926 turned out to be the first regularly scheduled flights for what was to become American Airlines. From these hops, carrying a few hundred pounds of airmail, grew the present company that in 1968 carried 14,400,000 passengers and flew 55,460,000 ton-miles of mail.

As explained in an earlier chapter, Robertson Aircraft was one of eighty-five companies eventually absorbed by American. The nucleus of the mass consolidation began in Cincinnati with another small airmail carrier known as Embry-Riddle that had picked up the contract to fly mail between its home base and Chicago, and like many of the other early lines, also operated flying schools, sightseeing tours, and assumed the sales and service of contemporary aircraft.

Embry-Riddle handled Fairchilds, but to buy more planes to fulfill its airmail contract, it needed more money, and another manufacturer offered to put up the necessary cash if Embry-Riddle would handle its planes and drop the Fairchild franchise. When Fairchild executives learned of the proposed deal, they got in touch with a group of Wall Street bankers and proposed that they refinance Embry-Riddle, protecting their particular interests. By mid-1929 a holding company with $33,000,000 capital had been formed to finance not only Embry-Riddle, but several other small aviation concerns. This, of course, was the Aviation Corporation which immediately bought control of the aforementioned Universal Aviation Corporation and two other holding companies—and with some of these widely scattered airlines came bus lines, radio stations, and airport construction companies. The Colonial system operated between New York and Boston, New York and Montreal, Buffalo and Toronto, and Albany and Cleveland, while Embry-Riddle continued its Cincinnati to Chicago schedule. Universal, the successor to Robertson, operated extensively in the Midwest—Chicago to St. Louis, St. Louis to Kansas City, St. Louis to Dallas, Cleveland to Louisville. Interstate flew between Chicago and Atlanta. Southern Air Transport ran from Dallas/Fort Worth to south Texas, and connected Atlanta with Houston. With the addition of a couple of other companies, SAT began operation in October 1930 of a southern transcontinental route between Atlanta and Los Angeles.

These varied acquisitions gave the Aviation Corporation

a tangle of routes that set up many duplications and brought together a mixed bag of transport planes which were difficult to service and produced serious maintenance problems. But in many instances the local managements were loath to give them up. In an effort to knit a workable airline system together, all subsidiaries were incorporated by 1930 into what was known at first as American Airways, Inc. They set out to rearrange the routes and reduce the managements to a workable unit, and high on the priority list was the obvious need for new, standard equipment, aircraft specifically designed for passenger operation.

After an expensive and extensive survey, American ordered a Pilgrim 10A, the first plane ever built to an airline's specifications. It was introduced in 1931. Two years later American put in orders for the Curtiss Condor, the first U.S. sleeper plane, and with the introduction of this doubtful convenience, stewardesses made their first appearance in American uniforms.

This early progressive climb was brought to a halt in February 1934 with the cancelation of the airmail contracts. A new effort was attempted a few months later when the post office contract was restored, and in the revision of corporate managements American Airways became American Airlines. The new company went to work with a more integrated and efficient system of routes.

C. R. Smith was elected president in October of that hectic year and remained chief executive officer until World War II, when he served as deputy commander of the Air Transport Command. In February 1964, he became chairman of the company and Marion Sadler was elected president and chief operating officer.

Although dependent on airmail income, Smith and his early colleagues realized that the future of air transport lay in the development of regular passenger business. In 1934 American introduced the Air Travel Plan, the company's first sales promotion idea. Three years later a series of institutional advertisements were run, promoting air travel—and an ad headlined "Afraid to Fly?" flouted the taboo subject of airline safety and faced up to the situation in a manner that won the public's respect.

American Airlines is also credited with another important contribution to commercial aviation of the mid-1930s. C. R. Smith had purchased a few DC-2s which were satisfactory in a general way, but did not fully fill the industry's need for a transport which could make money in the passenger field. American's engineers decided that if they increased the DC-2's capacity from fourteen to twenty-one seats they would have an economical plane that might turn in a profit, so suitable changes were submitted to the Douglas firm and several modifications were worked out. As usual, they proved to be more extensive than anticipated. When this Douglas-American project was completed the DC-2 had become an entirely new plane, the DC-3—a workhorse that proved to be the most famous air carrier in commercial transport history.

American Airlines inaugurated a DC-3 service between New York and Chicago on June 25, 1936. This airliner, backed by American's aggressive salesmanship, soon put Smith's airline on a profitable basis, and by the end of that decade American was solidly entrenched as the nation's No. 1 domestic air carrier.

The heavy national demands of World War II called upon American to make the same contributions and sacrifices borne by its competitors, and within six months after Pearl Harbor more than half of the industry's fleet of less than 400 planes had been sold or leased to the government. Still, while serving with the armed forces, Smith was able to extend his route into Toronto, Canada, and then push southward into Monterey and Mexico City.

Development of new commercial planes came to a halt with the attack on Pearl Harbor, but at the end of the war American refurbished the DC-3s and reconverted wartime

DC-4s for use as interim transports, while awaiting a new fleet of 75 twin-engined Convair 240s and four-engined DC-6s. Not until 1949 could they retire the last of their 94 DC-3s, but this made them the first airline to be equipped with an all-postwar fleet.

In 1944 American pioneered air freight. On October 15 a DC-3, loaded with fresh spinach, flowers, airplane parts, and wearing apparel, took off from Los Angeles and headed for New York. Another DC-3 flew westward from Manhattan with high-priority material and ladies' apparel. This new feature of the industry was extended over the years and, according to American public relations, was responsible for many innovations in freight equipment, merchandising, and handling. In 1966 the company flew a record 351,000,000 ton-miles of freight, an increase of 38.2 percent over the previous year, and in addition carried another 75,000,000 tons of mail and express.

In January 1964 American Airlines put into service four giant Boeing 707-323C jet freighters, each capable of carrying 90,000 pounds of freight over a range of 3,000 miles. They also introduced the Astro-Loader, an automatic ground-handling system which allows crews to load or unload freighters in forty minutes. Previously, it took three hours to load or unload the 707's largest piston-powered predecessor, the DC-7F.

Since 1964 American's jet freighter fleet has increased from twelve to nearly forty. Four of these jet-cargo aircraft operate two daily round trips between California, Okinawa, and Vietnam, hauling high-priority material under contract to the Military Airlift Command.

Although World War II had provided many people with the opportunity or necessity to fly, considering the population of the United States and the number who could afford to use the airlines, there still were thousands who had never thought of taking to the air—and there still are. With this potential patronage in mind, American Airlines con-

ceived the Family Fare plan in 1948, and a year later became the first airline to offer "coach" service aboard the
most modern aircraft at convenient hours.

During the 1930s American had introduced the "sell
and record" reservation system, which was fine for its day
but as business increased became outmoded. In the early
1950s a new electronic reservation system was devised
and set up, known as Magnetronic Reservisor. In 1964
American took another leading step in their reservations
system with their SABRE complex, the largest electronic
data processing designed for business use. In the forty
years since the first post office airmail flights, commercial
aviation had become a highly technical industry and relied as much on ground and office facilities as it did on
aeronautics and pilot skills.

In 1953 American continued its remarkable progress by
scheduling and flying the first nonstop transcontinental
service in both directions with the DC-7. Two years later
they placed the first order for the Lockheed Electra, the
first U.S.-designed turboprop airplane powered with a jet
engine that not only provided thermal thrust but twirled
a variable-pitch propeller at the same time. The Electra
was flown over American's short- and medium-range routes
in January 1959.

In late 1955 Smith's line ordered its first pure jet planes,
meaning an aircraft that derived its power from a high-
thrust gas-turbine alone. Such power plants produced up
to 10,000 pounds of propulsive thrust. These new planes
were Boeing 707s, and by 1959 these high-performance
engines were cutting transcontinental flying time by 40
percent. By the end of 1960 American was flying forty-
nine long-range Boeing 707-123s, and the shorter range
Boeing 720s, over its far-flung system.

While the configuration of the planes was changing almost weekly, the jet engines were also going through a
period of rapid modification. In gas turbines, air is sucked

in from the outside, compressed, heated by igniting the fuel, and then expended in a turbine area. This compressed air is expelled from the turbine—sometimes referred to as the jet—at a very high velocity, and it is this thermal thrust that provides the propulsion. All this is based on the fundamental law of physics in which the action is equal to reaction. The compressed energy developed in the combustion chamber of the engine is converted into a high degree of impulse and this thrust results from the impulse of the air and combustion gases escaping from the rear of the engine—not from any action against the air in the rear of the engine.

Another example illustrating the principle of action and reaction will be found in a toy balloon. When the balloon is inflated and the narrow nozzle is suddenly released, the compressed air inside the balloon rushes out at high velocity and the balloon zips about under this propulsive thrust—in the opposite direction. Thus, the performance of a jet engine depends on the density of the intake air which in turn diminishes with altitude. But as the drag on the bulk of the aircraft also diminishes, there is an increase in speed at higher levels, obtained with a lower rate of fuel consumption.

The earliest type of jet engine was the ramjet with no moving parts. In this system, air entering the body of the engine is slowed down because of the design of the tube which increases the air pressure. When fuel is injected into the center of the tube and ignited, the hot combustion gases flow out at high velocity from the rear—the nozzle of the jet. At this point the velocity of the nozzle is higher than the rate of flight, so a thrust is created. The ramjet, of course, produces no thrust when the aircraft is standing on the ground, and is efficient only at very high speeds.

The turbojet, a jet turbine engine, was the first improvement on the ramjet. It is provided with a compressor driven by a turbine which draws in the air and compresses it. Again, fuel is injected into the combustion chamber and the rise in temperature produces an increased volume of the gases, and these are expelled through the exhaust tube in the rear. In a turbojet the turbine absorbs only enough energy from the gases to drive the compressor. Performance of the turbojet is often increased for short periods by means of an afterburner which actually is a second combustion chamber set between the turbine and the propulsion nozzle.

The turboprop engine is very similar to the turbojet— except that most of the created energy is used to drive the turbine, which not only drives the compressor but its excess power is used to turn a propeller through a series of reduction gears. The turboprop is much lighter than a piston engine of the same power, and much easier to design and build up to a certain output, but it is a very complex mechanism and soon was limited to certain range and speed requirements.

A modified form of the turboprop employs two concentric shafts revolving at different speeds; one drives the compressor, the other the propeller. This advanced version is particularly suitable for speed ranges that are too high for the standard propeller-driven aircraft and too low for the turbojet. In the low-pressure compressor stage a percentage of the compressed air is bypassed and delivered to the propulsion nozzle where, because of the high power requirement of the turbine, the exit velocity of the gases is reduced, creating an increased propulsion efficiency. The low-pressure stage of the compressor is driven by the second turbine stage, and the high-pressure system is powered by the fired turbine stage.

From this point on, the jet engine has moved through a series of improvements, all marked by technical names taking them wide of the general interest of the paying passenger. As an instance, American Airline's first-generation 707 jets soon became second-generation jets with the introduction of what was to become known as the turbofan engine, the first of which, the 707 Astrojet No. 1, went into service on March 12, 1961. Then straight jet 707s were repowered with the turbofan and by January 1962 the old Astrojets were phased out. Later that year American introduced the first of twenty intermediate-range Convair 990s, a transport powered by fanjets (aftfans), which became known as the 990 Astrojet.

Commercial aviation took something of a backward step when in April 1964 American put into service the first of forty-seven Boeing 727 Astrojets, the first three-engined airplane since the 1930s. This was the distinctive type with a high T-tail and three jet engines grouped in the aft section of the fuselage, cutting down much of the engine noise in the passenger cabins. The following year thirty twin-turbofan 400 Astrojets were added to the fleet and these two short- to medium-range aircraft enabled American to bring jet service to smaller cities.

As more jets were added, American's piston-powered equipment was retired, and in November 1963 their last DC-7 was presented to the National Museum of Transport in St. Louis, where it is on permanent display. The flight deck and forward fuselage section of another DC-7 is on view at the Smithsonian Institution's National Air and Space Museum in Washington, D.C.

Fleet expansion continues at American. Since 1967 they have taken delivery on an order for eighty-eight three- and four-engined subsonic Astrojets costing $725,000,000. Plans include ten 340-plus passenger Boeing 747s, the first of which will be flown on its inaugural between New York and Los Angeles on July 1, 1970. The next step will probably be into the sphere of supersonics. The French-British Concorde, designed to carry 136 passengers at 1,450 mph, has already made its maiden flight. American Airlines has ordered six Concordes and expects to put them into service in the early 1970s. Following that, bigger, faster United

States' supersonic aircraft are scheduled to join the world's fleets in the mid-1970s, if federal funds are available for the continued development. The 350-passenger Boeing 2707 should cruise at nearly three times the speed of sound —1,800 mph. This particular Boeing will actually beat the sun across the United States; the passengers will arrive in Los Angeles before they left New York. This SST, as it is known in the trade, will shrink the Pacific, as the subsonic jet has narrowed the Atlantic. In fact, Tokyo will be less than five hours from New York.

Whether the airports, ground facilities, customs, and immigration schedules will be able to cope with the speed, range, and passenger loads of these fantastic aircraft remains to be seen.

Looking back, it is interesting to recall that Colonial Air Transport, an American Airlines' predecessor, flew its first load of passengers from Boston to New York on April 4, 1927. It took American ten years to carry the first 1,000,-000 passengers, but by 1955 they had flown 50,000,000 passengers. Six years later, December 28, 1961, American became the first airline in the world to carry 100,000,000 passengers. In September 1966 it passed the 150,000,000 mark.

The whole nature of airline technology is changing rapidly, and so is the market for airline services. As personal income and leisure time have increased, more and more people are taking advantage of the airplane for pleasure trips. To make air travel more convenient and less expensive for vacationers, American Airlines in 1964 pioneered their Autojet program that made available low-cost installment credit, low-cost auto rental, reduced family fare, and excursion flights. They also introduced two other special fare plans—their half-fare military and half-fare American Youth Plan. Both offered qualifying travelers half-fair travel anywhere on American's system, on a standby basis. The Youth Plan launched in January 1966 was an instant success—during that year nearly 450,000 young people between the ages of twelve and twenty-one took advantage of the arrangement. They traveled 325,-000,000 miles while saving themselves or their parents some $10,000,000.

While businessmen still predominate among American's passengers, these new services for pleasure are producing a new look on most airlines. For the first time in history the increase in pleasure travel is outstripping the increase in business travel. As the world's economies continue to expand, the air-pleasure travel trend should increase with it.

It is believed that the next big expansion in global air services will be across the Pacific. As a result of the trans-pacific route case, which at this writing is before the Civil Aeronautics Board, American Airlines hopes to break out of its continental limitations and into the fastest growing international market extending its services from various United States cities to Hawaii, Japan, Korea, Taiwan, Hong Kong, Vietnam, Singapore, Guam, American Samoa, Fiji, Australia, and Indonesia.

Trans World Airlines, second-largest airline in the United States in terms of passenger miles flown, was, prior to the transpacific route shuffle, the only carrier with both do-mestic and transatlantic routes. TWA serves thirty-nine major American cities from coast to coast and links them with key centers in Europe, Asia, and Africa. Its system, which measures 50,568 unduplicated miles, stretches from California eastward two-thirds of the way around the world to Hong Kong. Recent adjustments in the transpacific routes allowed TWA to close the round-the-world gap with linkage into Hawaii, Guam, Taiwan, and Okinawa.

Trans World Airlines' history dates back to April 1926 when Western Air Express started the first continuing U.S. scheduled airline service, operating between Los Angeles and Salt Lake City. Standard Air Lines and Maddux Air Lines, formed in Los Angeles at about the same time, also figured in the establishment of TWA. The Fourth "parent" was Trans-Continental Air Transport (TAT) which on July 7, 1929, made history by launching the nation's first transcontinental service, one in which the passengers flew Ford Tri-Motors by day and rode railroad Pullman sleepers at night. As mentioned before, this route was originally laid out by Charles A. Lindbergh. Soon after, there was a series of mergers, involving portions of Western Air, Standard, and TAT–Maddux, producing Transcontinental & Western Air, Inc. (TWA). On October 25, 1930, the company inaugurated the nation's first all-air transcontinental service with an overnight stop at Kansas City. This trip was completed in 36 hours, but within two years TWA had mastered night flying, eliminating the stopover, and cut their transcontinental time to 24 hours.

The venture was not exactly a financial bonanza, and on one occasion a ticket agent, commenting on the sparsity of passengers, complained to a line engineer that the planes were too noisy and even the seats rattled. The engineer's response was, "Keep the seats *filled* and they *won't* rattle."

By this time lighted airways had been completed from coast to coast, and a pattern of communications, employing teletype, telephone, Morse code, radio, plus weather reporting, was becoming part of the standard operations. A system of thirty-two weather-reporting and -collecting centers was set up with the cooperation of the Pacific Telephone and Telegraph Company and the government's Weather Bureau, then part of the Department of Agriculture. Thus, a service that had been devised to aid farmers became a vital information source for commercial aviation, setting up gains in flight regularity and safety. One of the engineers provided by the Guggenheim Foundation was Herbert Hoover, Jr. who had joined Western Air Express and later TWA. He worked with Thorp Hiscock, communications engineer for Boeing Air Transport, on radio research. These two men pooled their findings with Western Electric Company and by 1930 two-way radio telephone was available for airline use. This radio communication and the teletype systems replaced the cloth panels that previously had been laid out on the airfields, and the red flags waved by station managers to signal that pilots overhead should stop to pick up passengers or mail.

Postmaster General Walter F. Brown's desire to speed up the growth of the air-transport industry was further encouraged by the McNary-Watres Bill that provided a new maximum payment to the airlines of $1.25 per plane mile and the provision for route certificates. Postmaster Brown also changed the face of the air-route map, and many small lines had to be merged into three main transcontinental systems. This is how TWA came to select the central coast-to-coast route.

In TWA's mixed fleet of Fords and Fokkers were two large 32-passenger Fokkers which were aeronautically clumsy and inefficient. One of them ended its days as a novel gasoline station on Los Angeles' Wilshire Boulevard.

TWA soon realized that the transport aircraft available would not long fill its transcontinental demands. More speed and all-weather flying capability were required, and for a time the new low-wing Northrop Mailplane provided some of the answers. Not only did this Northrop model cross the country in twenty-four hours, but it immediately became the press agent's dreamboat and was advertised as the "best dressed" aircraft of the day in that it wore "pants" over the wheels for improved streamlining, rubber "boots" for deicing the wings, and a "bonnet" on the propeller hub, also for deicing. The Northrop Mailplane had many flight advantages, but it offered nothing in the way of comfort for passengers, and the few who turned up to "go places" resented being accommodated on top of the mail sacks. Long-distance travel patrons felt they were entitled to a real transport plane. As explained previously, Douglas responded with their first DC-1, a twin-engined airliner that basically was the brain child of several TWA pilots and engineers. It was equipped with engine cowlings developed by the National Advisory Committee of Aeronautics. Low monoplane wings reduced engine drag, and flaps, controllable-pitch propellers, retracting landing gear, and Sperry automatic pilots made the DC-1 an outstanding aircraft. Later, production models—known as DC-2s—were designed to carry fourteen passengers, a captain and co-pilot, a hostess, and a ton of cargo at speeds up to 85 mph. The airlines' workhorse DC-3 was just approaching the production line . . . and then the politicians took over!

The cancelation of the airmail contracts swept many clever airline executives out into the street, and control of TWA passed to the investment house of Lehman Brothers, and John Hirtz, owner of the Yellow Cab Company. TWA not only lost its airmail contracts, but, like most of the other lines, was ineligible to bid for new ones under its original corporate form. Reorganization had to be carried out at great expense to the companies, loss to the stockholders, and disruption of the entire industry.

TWA organized a new firm listed as TWA, Inc. in order to bid for new mail contracts, and for a time it was able to pick up about sixty percent of its previous routes. Jack Frye, former vice president of operations, became president. Henry B. du Pont was raised to chairman of the board. Nearly six years passed before TWA regained all its original airmail routes, and while much money was lost, Jack Frye actually turned the line into a training school, to which other companies were invited to send pilots and ground staff. Out of this was developed the anti-static "homing" radio direction finder, a pilot-navigation aid worth more than its weight in gold. This canceled-contract period also resulted in better airports and emergency fields, and as aircraft efficiency increased air fares were lowered. More people were induced to fly, and by the time the mail contracts were returned, passenger fares had become a dominant source of airline revenue.

Also during this period, D. W. Tomlinson, TWA's pilot-engineer, carried out a high-altitude research program. He hunted bad weather and learned how to fly over it. The information obtained on icing, instruments, radio equipment, and oxygen problems found at higher altitudes was to lead to the development of the four-engined Boeing Stratoliner, which was the first pressurized cabin airplane permitting safe, smooth, over-weather flying at altitudes up to 20,000 feet. The Stratoliner was first flown by TWA in 1940 and its performance reduced transcontinental flying time to 14 hours.

The Civil Aeronautics Act of 1938, patterned on the Interstate Commerce Act, proved to be a boost for commercial aviation. It contained more elastic principles for the promotion of safety and healthy competition, required to meet the needs of foreign and domestic air commerce, the postal service, and the national defense. It added a new design to the air-route pattern by creating certificates of public convenience and necessity. It established one authority, responsible only to Congress, and it fixed mail rates which eliminated many inequities in bidding. The Civil Aeronautics Act came at a time when the threats of a new world war were thundering out of Nazi Germany, with Hitler's juggernaut preparing to roll.

In 1938 control of TWA left the offices of Lehman Brothers and returned to the airline's executives. Howard Hughes, an expert, daring pilot, engineer, and millionaire manufacturer, became the principal stockholder, and brought with him the background and financial importance of his Hughes Tool Company. That summer Hughes, who already held several aviation speed records, flew around the world in slightly over three days, establishing another record. This memorable flight was the mark of things to come, the beginning of TWA's global airline planning.

All that was needed now was an aircraft capable of carrying huge loads across continents and oceans at a speed of 300 mph. In 1939 with World War II only a few months away Hughes and Lockheed collaborated on the design of such a carrier, and from several conferences came the famous Lockheed Constellation. However, with the spread of the war and the necessity of concentrating factory production on combat planes, the final design and construction of the Constellation had to be deferred.

While pilots of the Royal Air Force were engaging the Luftwaffe in the Battle of Britain—a year or more before the United States entered the conflict—TWA offered its services to the Army Air Force, as it was known at that time, and immediately received its first military assignment. At the same time one Stratoliner was drawn from the flight line and a number of R.A.F. crews were trained and checked out on the transport. Once familiar with American four-engined equipment, they began to fly lend-lease aircraft to Britain. One of these trainees was Willie Bedell, who later became one of Sir Winston Churchill's pilots.

By the spring of 1941 TWA extended this military training course by setting up a center for over-ocean flying, a very fortunate decision, for from that shocking Sunday afternoon when the first reports of the attack on Pearl Harbor came through, many airliners enroute between major cities in the United States were ordered to proceed to the nearest airport, discharge their passengers and cargo, and stand by for new orders. This situation held until victory had been assured. The commercial airlines ignored their routine flight schedules in order to keep vital supplies flowing to the many distant fronts. It was an intercontinental airlift the like of which had never before been known. Half of America's airline fleet was commandeered along with skilled pilots and ground crews. They flew men, material, ammunition, medical supplies, and food to every theater of operations.

To illustrate what this amazing performance meant, it should be explained that at the beginning of World War II the whole U.S. commercial fleet had only seven *landplanes* capable of flying over the ocean, and TWA owned five of them. These were the new Stratoliners which were immediately converted for war duty and manned by TWA crews, making it the first line to engage in transoceanic flying for the Air Transport Command. Sixteen days after the attack on Pearl Harbor, TWA's Intercontinental Division became a vital link in America's wartime communications and supply chain.

Bases were set up in South America and Africa for South Atlantic operations, and their over-ocean flights began. The first khaki-wearing Stratoliner took off on February 24, 1942, from Kansas City for Cairo. The complete flight took 17 days with stops at Puerto Rico, Trinidad, Brazil, Liberia, the African Gold Coast, and Egypt. Flying the North Atlantic route to Prestwick, Scotland, presented further problems, and TWA had to discard long-held concepts that over-ocean flying was more hazardous in winter than in summer. But from knowledge and experience gained under actual conditions a new method of long-distance navigation was developed. This was known as "pressure pattern" flying.

This meant that instead of following the shortest Great Circle courses, other routes were plotted which enabled pilots to take advantage of the wind rotation pattern of storm areas. These disturbances, in turn, provided tailwinds which reduced the time of over-ocean flying—in both directions at the *same* time. One story is told of a TWA pilot on a run over Iceland who became worried about a strange vibration in the airplane. On investigating, it was learned that his passengers were stamping their feet to keep warm. When some innocents inquired why the crew did not seem to mind the chill, they were informed that the crew had been given antifreeze inoculations.

Later in 1942, as long-range aircraft production was speeded up, TWA operated shuttle service across the South Atlantic from Brazil to Africa and India, and across the North Atlantic from Newfoundland to Scotland—flying Douglas four-engined transports and Consolidated's transport version of the Liberator. On one of the Intercontinental Division's first missions, special fuses for armor-piercing shells for the British Royal Tank Corps in North Africa were delivered. This improved ammunition helped turn the tide of battle against General Rommel's Afrika Korps and started the British breakout from El Alamein. These shells also resulted in the saving of Cairo and the Suez Canal, and eventually drove German armor out of North Africa.

In those days the North Atlantic crossings were flown without any form of radio beacon aids, and celestial navigation of seagoing men was the only guidance. Radio was reserved for direction finding, reporting locations, and answering challenges. Flight logs recount many attempts by the enemy, who may have monitored radio transmissions, to steer the aircraft off course and into enemy territory—and some instances of failure to recognize these United States' aircraft were also reported. There were times when salvos of antiaircraft shells were fired by American defense gunners. But probably the most amusing incident was when a rookie R.A.F. pilot who took off from Prestwick to search out in the haze and murk what was believed to be a Focke-Wulf bomber, and found something that looked like an enemy raider. Instead, it was a TWA C-54, and the rookie pilot was interrogated later and reprimanded by his CO—not for firing on a friendly plane but for using 600 rounds of machine-gun ammunition without once hitting his target!

Spirit, skill, and amazing improvisation marked the history of the Intercontinental Division. One resourceful flight engineer replaced a damaged Stratoliner engine starter with one taken from a captured Nazi plane. Another made a condenser from a sardine can, enabling an R.A.F. fighter to fly out of a jungle clearing where it had been forced down. Probably the most historic flight in TWA's wartime log was the one which carried President Roosevelt and his entourage to meet Prime Minister Churchill at Casablanca. During a short part of this flight General Dwight Eisenhower occupied the co-pilot's seat. Other TWA passenger lists included presidents, kings, queens, ambassadors, statesmen, and generals of the Allied armies. Nearly 10,-000 transatlantic flights were made by the Intercontinental Division and over 40,000,000 miles were flown on these routes alone.

While in this vein, it should be explained that unquestionably such airline aid saved Dutch Harbor when the Japanese were already on Attu and Kiska. Commercial fliers brought ammunition to the U.S. Marines when they were cut off on Guadalcanal. They transported mine-cutting equipment in time for the landings in Normandy on D-day, delivered desperately needed truck- and tank-engine supplies to check the enemy breakthrough in the Battle of the Bulge, and maintained continuous ambulance shuttles, transporting more than 800,000 sick and wounded back home. In sum, the airlines flew 2,500,000,000 passenger miles on overseas routes, covering 246,000,000 transport miles, while on the home front they maintained a steady day-and-night airlift of personnel and supplies.

In April 1944 the first Constellation was fully assembled and flown from Burbank, California, to Washington, D.C., by Howard Hughes and Jack Frye. Its initial flight was a great success. With this 300-mph transport having a 3,000-mile range, soon available in production-line numbers, TWA began laying the groundwork for the global operation conceived five years before and particular studies were made of overseas areas.

Late in 1944 TWA submitted its application to the Civil Aeronautics Board for a number of world routes and was granted the southern or Mediterranean route to Europe, the Middle and Far East, through Ireland, France, Switzerland, Italy, Greece, and Egypt, with an additional segment from the United States via the Azores, Portugal, Spain, and North Africa, then on to India and the Orient. Germany and England were added later to this route structure. All this was granted on seven-year temporary international certificates. Two other airlines, American Overseas Airlines and Pan American World Airways, were also granted international certificates.

That summer TWA began its route-survey flights. It soon learned that, despite its wartime experience in the international field, overseas commercial flying presented many complex problems. First, important foreign contacts had to be established and key personnel trained to operate the foreign offices and bases. Much of this had to be carried out when many necessary items were unavailable and the manpower shortage still acute. Individual agreements had to be concluded with the various countries, and TWA's officers had to arrange and sit in on the negotiations with prime ministers, kings, and potentates of foreign countries; in fact, something resembling the Marshall Plan had to be set up for the development of aviation in many countries. TWA embarked on large-scale programs that involved considerable financial investment and provided organizational guidance to aviation interests in Italy, Greece, Ethiopia, Iran, and Saudi Arabia. In several other countries experts in technical and traffic phases of airline management were made available.

Other problems cropped up as the overseas operation proceeded. Language difficulties presented unusual situations; the serving of food had to meet the requirements of many different laws and national tastes; training had to be given in technical and commercial matters, many of which had to be adapted to local laws and customs.

High safety standards in aircraft operations call for special skills and technical training to fly, maintain, and service airplanes, both at home and abroad. Hundreds of Americans and their families had to be uprooted and settled in various overseas locations to fill these posts. One particular problem was the operation of an American weather service in areas that were not then equipped to handle this important feature of airline safety.

Early in 1946 TWA commenced commercial airline service overseas, and since that time the International Air Transport Association and the International Civil Aviation Organization have been formed for the purpose of facilitating and improving world air transport and its safety. Their efforts are producing world-wide uniformity of thinking and action on the part of airline personnel of more than seventy scheduled, international airline members. Domestically, however, the airlines of the United States suffered financially during the period immediately following World War II. Large investments were needed to buy fleets of modern planes, and costs and competition increased in the passenger and cargo markets. TWA, like the others, was affected by these new conditions and also had the burden of its international expansion investments.

Efforts to cut overall costs were initiated under the leadership of La Motte T. Cohu, who had long been a member of TWA's board of directors. In 1932 Cohu had led a proxy fight for control of Aviation Corporation, and defended the record of his company, its directors, and officers, which included Eddie Rickenbacker, Robert Lehman, and W. Averell Harriman, against E. I. Cord, the automobile manufacturer who was attempting to gain control. The struggle ended in a compromise, and by 1939 Cohu had become president of American Airways and eventually a director in North American Aviation and Transcontinental Air Transport. From 1947 to 1948 he was on the executive committee of TWA, and on leaving that post was made general manager of the Consolidated Vultee Aircraft Corporation, which became the Convair Division of General Dynamics Corporation. In his later years he founded Cohu Electronics Inc., and in September 1968, when he was 72 years of age, he was found dead of a gunshot wound in the head. The coroner's office termed the wound apparently self-inflicted.

In 1949 Ralph S. Damon was offered the presidency of TWA. Damon was born in Franklin, New Hampshire in 1897, graduated with honors from Harvard University, and in World War I learned to fly with the Aviation Service. After the war he joined the Curtiss Aeroplane and Motor Company. By the time he was twenty-five he had become factory superintendent. By 1931 he was vice president and general manager of the Curtiss factory at St. Louis, where he developed the famous Curtiss Robin.

In 1936, he became interested in the airline industry and joined American Airlines as vice president of operations, but World War II snapped him out of airline management, and he was drafted by the Under Secretary of War, Robert Patterson, to head the Republic Aviation Corporation and speed up its fighter-plane production. Damon's influence quickly had Republic's Thunderbolt production up to 400 planes a month.

As soon as the war came to its close, Damon went back to American Airlines and became its president. Shortly after, La Motte Cohu vacated TWA's presidential post, and it was offered to Damon, under whose guidance the line's business began to pick up. In the first six months of his service the company floated a small stock issue, and this, combined with drastic economies, made it possible for TWA to purchase a number of Constellations. Shortly after, their fleet was brought up to seventy-eight, including ten Super-Constellations. With this equipment the company launched a strenuous sales campaign directed by E. C. Cocke, who had been with the company since 1929.

Sound salesmanship was applied both to the domestic and the international traffic routes, and by 1949 the company established its low-cost air transportation scheme known as Sky Coach flights, offering reduced rates from coast to coast. Next, they celebrated the twenty-fifth anniversary of Colonel Lindbergh's transatlantic flight with the inauguration of the Sky Tourist flights across the Atlantic, bringing international air travel within the reach of middle-class tourists.

TWA's international operations chalked up an impressive list of "firsts." They were the first to fly an all-cargo service across the Atlantic (1947); they inaugurated the first tourist-class flight across the Atlantic (1952); they were the first transatlantic airline to go all-jet in international passenger service, and to show modern in-flight motion pictures (1961). TWA was the first to employ automatic Doppler navigation; the first to provide U.S. transcontinental through-plane all-cargo service across the Atlantic; the first to set up computerized flight planning for polar flights and to install its own over-ocean computerized flight-planning system (1965).

By merger in 1967 TWA acquired the Hilton International Company. Operated as a wholly owned subsidiary of Trans World Airlines, Hilton controls forty-two hotels in twenty-eight nations outside the United States. Additional hotels are in the construction or development stage. The airline operations employ 39,000—and 21,000 more are engaged in the hotel business.

Today, TWA's president and chief executive officer is Charles C. Tillinghast, Jr., and the company's main offices are located in New York City. The airline has a flight and ground training center at Kansas City where more than 10,000 are employed. Ground has been broken for a new overhaul center at Kansas City, one large enough to accommodate the Boeing 747s and Lockheed 1011s which will enter TWA service early in the 1970s. A new flight hostess academy will be built on a 34-acre campus in Overland Park, Kansas, and the construction of "Flight Wing One" to accommodate the jets of tomorrow will be added to TWA's flight center at New York's Kennedy Airport.

Before his administration ended, President Johnson awarded a number of transpacific routes to several U.S. airlines, the high commands of which included persons who were friends or former aides of Mr. Johnson. Shortly after President Nixon took office, he sharply curtailed these awards, deleting a major grant to Continental Airlines. He canceled a minor award to Braniff Airways, and allowed Trans World Airlines to become the nation's second round-the-world carrier. In addition, President Nixon confirmed only portions of route increases granted to Pan American World Airways and Northwest Airlines. According to White House sources, the Nixon reductions were made mainly because aviation experts forecast that transpacific passenger traffic would be twenty-one to thirty-three percent below the forecast made by the five-man Civil Aeronautics Board.

Charles C. Tillinghast stated that TWA was most pleased with President Nixon's decision permitting his company to close the round-the-world gap after nearly a quarter of a century of effort in that direction. The decision was to enable TWA to bring their service to Hawaii, Guam, Okinawa, and Taiwan—subject to working out conditions with the national and local governments concerned. The President's decision also allowed TWA to fly to the Orient from Los Angeles International Airport instead of from a "satellite" airport in the suburbs—the arrangement proposed by the Johnson awards.

On July 1, 1968, TWA announced the purchase of forty-four Lockheed 1011 tri-jets which increased to 291 the number of subsonic jet aircraft in service and scheduled for delivery during the next five years. In addition to the order for the Lockheeds, TWA had fifty-nine other aircraft, all Boeings, scheduled for delivery on the basis of prior orders. Included in the Boeing list are twelve giant 747s ordered in 1966, and ten more ordered in the fall of 1967—subject to agreement on specifications. These 747s should have entered TWA service in the spring of 1970. In addition TWA has placed orders for six Concorde supersonic transports for service in the early and mid-1970s. Tillinghast's company was the first to order the U.S. SST and holds first delivery position.

The Lockheed L-1011 tri-jet appears to be a TWA venture, as the airline selected the airframe design and the Rolls-Royce RB-211 engine after a year of exhaustive analysis. All airframe and engine manufacturers participating in the program presented designs incorporating substantial technological advances, and the competition was both close and intensive. Final decision was based on technical, cost, and delivery considerations.

TWA will receive a number of units in advance of its peak summer season in 1972. The airline has said it intends to schedule its L-1011 on transcontinental nonstop flights, as well as intermediate-range distances on its coast-to-coast U.S. routes.

Mr. Tillinghast stated recently, "The unique lift and range capabilities made possible by this advanced technology tri-jet are especially suited to TWA operations. This, coupled with the fact that by 1975 you'll see a million people in the U.S. skies on any given day, motivated our selection and announcement of an order of this magnitude at this time."

He pointed out also that the Lockheed L-1011 would be more economical in the use of air space, airport ramp space, and ground facilities than existing aircraft, while at the same time affording greatly improved passenger accommodations.

16

The Jet Propulsion Era

The general public has been using the term "jet aircraft" since the end of World War II, and in later years when commercial airliners were streaming over their long routes under jet power, the words became so familiar they no longer intrigued. Airplanes with propellers twirling before their noses or engine nacelles are looked on with more curiosity than any present-day jetliner. Piston planes now hold much the same attention as a Stanley Steamer or Stutz Bearcat at a modern automobile show.

During the last year of the 1939–45 war both sides introduced a jet-powered military plane, driving home another point in the claim that the necessities of war contribute more to the science of aviation than the routine, and more economical, plodding of peacetime. But there should be nothing startling about the introduction of jet propulsion in World War II. Indeed, on looking back, one wonders why Hitler's war did not open with sizzling battles between jet or turbo-jet aircraft. As early as 1932, an Italian jet-powered Caproni-Campini C.C.2 experimental aircraft was successfully test-flown, but was quickly discarded as being uneconomical. Shortly after, Frank Whittle, a young Royal Air Force cadet who was stationed at the R.A.F. training college in Cranwell, was so interested in the theory of jet propulsion he wrote a scholarly thesis on the subject as a contribution to his final examination. He was certain that he could build an efficient jet-propulsion engine, and to his surprise technical officials of the service granted him permission to experiment further—on his own time, of course. Eventually Frank Whittle developed the power plant that was to be adopted by the British and American air services for their experimental jet fighters.

About 1937 it was learned that jet propulsion experiments were being carried out in Germany along distinct lines: one—rocket propulsion in which fluid fuel oil was burned continuously, with the necessary oxygen for the combustion contained in one of the fuels carried, thus making it independent of altitude. Two—turbojet engines which worked on the same fundamental principles, but with oxygen taken in from the surrounding air and forced into the engine via a turbine. Its aviation ceiling was determined by the oxygen content of the atmosphere it passed through. (Rocket propulsion uses about seventeen times as much fuel as the turbojet engine.) Three—jet propulsion which differs from the turbojet principle only insofar as it receives the oxygen by the natural pressure of the air created in flight, instead of by a turbine, and is, therefore, dependent not only on altitude but also the speed achieved.

Although little was known generally of this revolutionary idea, experiments with various types of rocket and jet-propulsion engines were under way in several other key areas. A British Whittle jet engine was sent to the United States for "study and improvement," and eventually a jet-powered fighter was produced by the Bell Aircraft Corporation. In Germany, Willy Messerschmitt and Dr. Alexander Lippisch produced a rocket-engined plane that possibly was the first to exceed the speed of 600 mph. For a time this aircraft was known as the Me. 163, and an experimental squadron was organized within the Luftwaffe. Dr. Lippisch's rocket engine provided not only great speed, but also many problems of fuel consumption and degrees of safety during operation. For instance, the "power egg" gobbled up five tons of special fuel in return for a few minutes of actual flying. At best, the rocket squadron could take to the air, one by one, make short attacks on raiding aircraft and then with empty tanks glide back to the field. Under these circumstances the Me. 163 could not be expected to fulfill its mission.

In the meantime another German aircraft, the Heinkel 178 had been in the course of development, and when completed probably was the first true military type jet to be flown. The 178 made its first flight on August 27, 1939, and exactly one year later a new Italian Caproni-Campini jet took to the air. The British Gloster-Whittle, dubbed the "Squirt," went into the skies on May 15, 1940. On October 1, 1941, Robert M. Stankey flew the first United States jet (with a Whittle engine). All this was carried out in comparative secrecy and only those actively connected with each project knew what strides were being taken in this new science of air power.

To review the full history of the jet-powered military plane would take the reader on a wide deviation from our basic subject, but the new power plant was not fully integrated into commercial aviation until 1952 when the British de Havilland Comet with a powerful and purposeful whisper heralded the arrival of a new era—the jet age of commercial aviation.

Thereafter our world was never the same, for the Comet's speed had reduced the globe to half its former size, and more important, the jet engine had lowered the heavens. Before 1952 only specialist pilots had flown higher than the 25,000 feet normally attained by propeller-driven aircraft, and only an elite class of test pilots had bettered the piston-engined plane's speed of 250 mph. With the Comet, swift and sure high-altitude flight was no longer the boast of a few test pilots or their military counterparts. Everyday passengers could now claim and enjoy the speed of eight miles per minute and altitude of eight miles above sea level.

In 1947 British Overseas Airways Corporation had ordered a whole fleet of these jet-powered airliners, purchasing them straight from the blueprint. This was a daring, but farsighted, move, designed to capture the world's commercial aviation trade just as the British Mercantile Service had taken over the high-seas trade at the close of the nineteenth century. The Comet enabled BOAC to establish paying routes from Europe to South Africa, the Near East, Pakistan, India, Burma, Ceylon, Siam, Malaya, and Japan. The new airliner was flying from London to Johannesburg (6,280 miles) in 17 hours, 15 minutes; from London to Singapore (7,831 miles) in 21 hours, 5 minutes; from London to Tokyo (10,176 miles) in 28 hours, 25 minutes. The Comet held the blue ribbon of the airlines for two years without an accident of any kind. Then suddenly disaster struck.

An unknown factor, emanating from high-altitude pressurization requirements, wiped out all the gains British aviation had made. An unsuspected hazard, known later as explosive decompression, ended Britain's two years of unquestioned leadership. In January and April of 1954 two Comets blew up mysteriously off the coast of Italy, and BOAC had to ground its whole jet fleet until an army of engineering experts solved the tragic mystery.

Jet power had enabled the Comets to fly faster than any aircraft before then, but this speed could be maintained only by flying at altitudes over 30,000 feet, and at such heights pressurization required an entirely new procedure in the construction of aircraft cabins and flight decks. By now, pressurization meant taking the thin upper atmosphere and squeezing it into heavier, breathable air, a process that in turn exerts a pressure eight pounds per square inch on the walls of an airliner's cabin. This is double the pressure on a conventional airliner's cabin walls.

The cause of the accidents was discovered when the wreckage of both Comets was recovered from the bottom of the Mediterranean, pieced together with amazing skill and patience, and carefully studied until a hair-line fracture was found in the frame of a small window set in the top of the fuselage for the use of the navigator. British government officials, members of the Royal Aircraft Establishment, experts from BOAC and de Havilland pored over these recovered portions of the wreckage until they were convinced they had found the actual cause of the disasters.

There was no question of materials, aircraft design, reliability of the engines, the skills of the crew, weather, and the manner in which these jetliners were handled. Both Comets had made at least 3,000 flights before that hairline crack suddenly widened under the internal pressure, and then, in a split second, the top of the fuselage was torn wide open. In other words, the pressurized cabin had exploded.

Great Britain had to know what had caused the Comets to disintegrate. The whole world of aviation had to know, or there would have been no jetliners in the sky today. There was no industrial secrecy, no whitewashing of the cause, no closed book on any of the findings. The de Havilland company and BOAC generously presented and fully explained the cause to other manufacturers. The ruptured frames were put on public display, photographs were made available and complete details of the official findings were given freely to all aeronautical engineers from other countries. Britain's Royal Aircraft Establishment also contributed much to the final assessment. American manufacturers who were planning to enter the jet airliner field gratefully accepted the British findings and applied the knowledge so tragically procured to their own planning and subsequent design.

The temporary setback caused by the Comet accidents after BOAC had established such an outstanding operational record in no way reflected on de Havilland integrity, and they made full use of the eventual findings. The proffered information was of great value to all future aircraft design, and Boeing's Model 707, America's first jet transport, gave the United States its own yardstick with which to assess the merits of the jet airliner. Later, Douglas and Convair took full advantage of the Comet study of high-pressure fuselage design, and the requirements were built into their proposed jetliners.

In December 1968 safety investigators for the government ordered seven United States airlines to make an immediate check of their F-27 airliners for signs of possible metal fatigue. It was explained that an examination by the National Transportation Safety Board of the wreckage of a Fairchild-Hiller F-27 turboprop that had crashed near Iliamna, Alaska, on December 2, killing 39 persons, disclosed a metal fatigue "failure of the right wing." The board advised the Federal Aviation Administration to order all F-27s and the somewhat larger FH-227s checked for metal fatigue.

In this case, metal fatigue had nothing to do with the problem of explosive decompression experienced by the Comet. It reflected a possible flaw in main spar components which under certain stresses of turbulence might fracture, allowing the whole wing to collapse. It should be explained that explosive decompression is not a problem in the older transports since they fly at lower levels and the pressurization is much less than in a pure jet.

The Federal Aviation Administration's certification tests, which every plane must pass before it is licensed to carry passengers, are most rigorous. The power sequence of the jet engine is totally unlike that of the piston engine, and the importance of the jetplane and the airlines to the national economy demand that no phase of safety can be ignored in the testing of jet aircraft.

The airlines, manufacturers, and the F.A.A. had to admit that in the hectic past, just before and following World War II, mistakes were committed in the development of new airliners. Serious faults turned up and somehow evaded the test programs. Many resulted in fatal crashes and for a time threatened to destroy the confidence of the public in commercial aviation. Whole fleets of airliners were grounded, threatening the bankruptcy of several airlines and arousing the old chestnut, "Sure, I'll be willing to fly if I can keep one foot on the ground." Some of the faults and mistakes were inevitable and can be charged to the blinding glow of the postwar years when everyone believed the airplane had reached its peak of efficiency and that the airlines had a new ready-made patronage of exservicemen who had either flown warplanes or had been flown in military transports, and in that manner had been exposed to the flying virus. The airline operators demanded new equipment and the manufacturers were willing to sell it to them. Unfortunately, the postwar, and particularly the jet-powered, transports were more complicated than the old DC-3.

The manufacturers of commercial jets also had to consider many probabilities with reference to the engines as well as to the pressurized airframe. Military jets were still being flown by crews wearing parachutes, and if their planes broke up in midair, they could step out, pull the ripcord, and take to the silk. Such protection is not available to passengers aboard an airliner—for many reasons—so it became necessary to find out how a jet engine or engines would perform under daily scheduled operations. By the mid-1950s there were few scheduled flights canceled because of bad weather, except ceiling-zero fog conditions. Aircraft took off in rain, snow, sleet, and high winds, and simply kited for altitude where fair weather could be expected. But what would happen to the engines in a commercial carrier during a heavy rainstorm, icing conditions, snowstorms, and blizzards? After all, the jet engine had a series of turbines twirling at high speed inside the engine shell.

To find out, engineers tossed hard-packed snowballs into the air-inlet ducts of roaring jets. Nothing happened. They simulated a hurricane that produced 41.5 inches of water an hour and directed it into the air ducts of racing jet engines. Nothing happened.

If a large bird were to be sucked into a jet engine, unquestionably plenty would happen, but this contingency has seldom been reported—though it *can* happen. However, at worst the engine might break up and tear itself out of the nacelle, but this would hardly be disastrous since today's jet engines are usually slung in nacelles well clear of any main spars or critical framework.

It will be seen, then, that the adoption of the jet engine for commercial trade set up many new problems. Not only did the fuselage and cabin have to be built to withstand explosive decompression, but the engines had to be modified and tested for all forms of turbine damage, or failure. In truth, all factors of the airframe and engine system had to be reconsidered from every engineering viewpoint. Testing facilities had to be extended and broadened. A plane that flies at 600 mph must be X number of times stronger to endure the turbulence encountered in all areas of flight from takeoff to landing. For instance, the undercarriage gear of a jetliner will retract and extend about 100,000 times in airline service. When Lockheed was building its Electra they subjected its gear to 270,000 simulated flights before approving the final design. When Douglas first drew up plans for its DC-8 they checked out forty-two different window shapes and designs before they selected the most suitable. Boeing flew their first 707 through

1,500 hours of flight tests before they settled on their production type. But even with all these checks and precautions, the 707 provided Boeing with some memorable headaches. Thirty 707s came up with unsuspected landing-gear troubles, although the gear could be operated in three ways—through the main hydraulic system, through an alternate electrical system, and with a simple mechanical method of lowering the wheels by a hand crank. Why did these faults turn up?

The answer is simple. No amount of factory testing can duplicate the conditions of actual airline operations. A plane in normal service will age faster than a prototype used in a rugged test program being flown by a skilled test pilot. It is this type of aging that brings out a hundred hidden faults.

Another reason for the appearance of unexpected faults will be found where the pilots of an airline do not fly or operate the plane as the manufacturer recommends. In one instance aboard the 707 some pilots turned on their hydraulic pumps earlier than Boeing had instructed. Thus, the pumps wore out faster and the designers had to produce a more durable unit to make up for this point of airline practice.

On one occasion during the preliminary testing of the 707, Chief Test Pilot Johnston found his brakes refused to function in any manner, and he wound up trying for a ground loop which tore off his nose wheel. Earlier that same day Johnston had carried out a number of braking tests on the ground, all of which worked out perfectly. He then took off, flew a few standard maneuvers and prepared to make a normal landing, but to his consternation on touch down, he discovered he had no braking power of any kind; on the contrary the 707 seemed to accelerate. He signaled to his co-pilot who applied his brakes but with no response. They tried the emergency brake system but that was no better. Johnston had no choice but to steer the big airliner off the concrete runway to the turf. For a few seconds he was hopeful, for the wheels began to sink in and slow down the 707. When he was just about running out of airfield, he decided to set up a ground loop—spinning the plane sharply within its minimum turning distance. He turned the nose wheel which spun the 707 smartly, but at that point Lady Luck decided to stack a pile of surplus chunks of concrete directly in his path. This solid mound snapped off the nose wheel, the gear collapsed, and the jetliner rammed her nose into the ground. Considering the circumstances of the accident, very little damage was suffered.

As soon as the plane could be hauled into a shed it was discovered that during the ground brake tests prior to the take-off, the temperature of the hydraulic fluid had been considerably increased, setting up abnormal expansion. During the in-air maneuvers the fluid cooled and contracted. The fuses in the hydraulic system interpreted this fluctuation as a line rupture, and no pressure could be metered to the brake cylinders. Since the fuses affected both the pilot's and co-pilot's braking systems—and the accumulator-operated emergency system—the 707 had no brakes of any kind. This fuse system was quickly revised while a new nose-wheel assembly was manufactured.

But this was not the end of the 707's braking problem. The aforementioned hydraulic fuel used in the braking systems was a simple, but flammable, fluid that had been used on all types of aircraft from the time airplane landing wheels were equipped with brakes. There were a few members of the design team who had always argued that non-flammable fuel should be used, so long as they were making a plane as fireproof as possible, but others argued that the wheel brakes would be the least likely point to start a fire. The fence-straddlers pointed out that Boeing was justified in trying to cut the cost of the 707, for the prototype was already running well over the estimated cost. Flammable fluid was cheaper.

One day the prototype 707 landed with considerable smoke coming from the landing gear housing, although none of it had shown up on the "fire" window of the instrument board, and the crew was not aware of the danger. The fire was quickly extinguished, and then it was realized that the brakes had become so overheated they had ignited the hydraulic fluid. From that moment the order went out that the 707 would use nonflammable fluid, not only in the brakes but in all other hydraulic components.

The advent of the jet-powered airliner brought about many more changes in commercial aviation. In the first place the power plant was something entirely new, and because of its comparative simplicity—it actually had only two moving parts—it was difficult to understand and the training procedures had to be revised to explain this phenomenon. An engine mechanic had to forget the four cycles of the internal-combustion engine, the timing system that fired in a progressive order, any number of spark plugs to set up the explosive power that produced crankshaft rotation. Generally speaking, the jet engine had but one spark plug, and a single crankshaft on which spun a number of turbine discs. There was no propeller, nor any particular exhaust problem. The jet was so simple it was confusing. Yet, once the airlines decided to fly pure-jet airliners, they immediately required a divisional force of skilled jet-engine mechanics to service the planes.

The military services had provided a small number of jet mechanics and the engine companies had set up training schools to produce more, but it was years before there were enough skilled, trustworthy gas-turbine mechanics to fill the needs of commercial aviation. The whole maintenance operation was disrupted, for piston-engined planes still gobbled thousands of gallons of high-test gasoline and special lubricating oil, but a jet-powered plane used only a cheap and simple kerosene formula, a byproduct of the production of high-test gasoline. This caused two new servicing problems; the ramp foreman had to be certain the jets were being filled with the kerosene formula—not high-test gasoline—and the fuel companies were wondering what they could do with the excess gasoline that remained from distilling for the jet-fuel product. In other words, the kerosene that had once been sold cheaply to get rid of it, of necessity increased in price, as it could be produced only through the distillation for high-test gasoline. How this petroleum problem was solved has never been made clear.

The Boeing 707 was the first American jetliner to be accepted by the United States airlines. The Douglas DC-8 was next in line, and then the Convair 880 appeared. In a short time the jet dominated air travel into South America and then challenged for favor on the North Atlantic run. On one nonscheduled flight from Tokyo to Seattle a jet airliner made the trip in nine hours and five minutes, clipping five hours off any previous propeller-driven plane record. By September 1959 it was possible to circle the globe aboard pure jets on scheduled airlines.

But although the public relations men of all commercial aviation interests poured out reams of starry-eyed publicity to sell this new phase of air travel, the Boeing jets went through a number of severe growing pains. On August 12, 1959, one of the big 707s glided into Chicago's O'Hare Airport, initiating a series of disturbing accidents. It landed so hard it bounced fifty feet and discarded two nose wheels before it skidded to a stop on the strut structure. No one was injured, but everyone remembered that earlier that year a 707 had had a hair-raising performance over the North Atlantic when the plane suddenly went into a 25,000-foot dive before the pilot could pull it out at 600 feet. A few days later another 707 discarded an engine while on a test flight over France. On the eve of President Eisenhower's good-will trip to Europe in August 1959 aboard a VC-137A, the military version of the 707, other Boeings were furnishing startling headlines.

On August 15, a few days before the President's first flight in a jet aircraft, a Boeing jetliner piled up in a potato field on Long Island, killing all five crewmen. There were no passengers aboard. Two days later another 707 with 112 passengers and a crew of 10 turned back from a flight to South America when its hydraulic-gear system fouled up. Fortunately, the pilot brought the jetliner in safely. And on that same day another Boeing jet with 82 people aboard was forced back to Australia after taking off for San Francisco when one of its engines failed.

And with that, Representative Steven B. Derounian of New York repeated a request to the Federal Aviation Agency that all Boeing 707s be grounded. An earlier request had stemmed from an accident in July in which one of the jetliners lost two of the four wheels on its left landing-gear leg while taking off from what was then known as Idlewild Airport, now Kennedy International Airport, and which was in Representative Derounian's political district. On that occasion, after circling the field for four hours while emergency preparations were made on the ground, the plane made a safe landing with 112 passengers aboard.

Any such series of mishaps were certain to raise a number of questions, both in and out of the aircraft industry. It was natural people would inquire whether there was something basically wrong with any aircraft that was powered with jet engines. Had the industry gone too far in its demand for speed, and everything that speed and high-altitude flying demanded, or were all these stories exaggerated to produce startling headlines? When calmer viewpoints were established it was felt that, considering everything, the jet airliners were operating with commendable reliability. The records disclose that up until 1959, the Boeing 707 had carried more than 600,000 passengers and had logged more than 40,000 hours on scheduled operations, covering nearly 25,000,000 miles. Only one fatal accident, the test-flight crash on Long Island, had occurred. There were no passengers aboard.

In all fairness it should be stated that according to figures compiled by the Federal Aviation Agency the jet engine has proved to be most reliable. Even in the early days of jet operations it was shown that the gas turbine engine was from five to ten times more reliable than contemporary piston engines. The hazard involved in the operation of an aircraft with either a jet or piston engine is not as great as the general public imagines. In virtually all situations, flights are completed and landings made without incident.

When Representative Derounian requested that the Boeings be grounded, E. R. Quesada, Administrator of the F.A.A., explained in a telegram that the facts as his agency knew them at that point weighed heavily against a general grounding order. We have shown how many of the undercarriage faults were cleared up early through immediate changes in the hydraulic system. The fatal crash on Long Island and the shaking loose of an engine over France occurred during training flights when all kinds of emergency situations are set up to train the pilots. In both incidents the planes were reported to have been flying with both engines on one side shut down, presenting one of the most difficult situations to control that one is likely to experience, and the possibility of a similar occurrence on a normal passenger flight is very remote.

An investigation of the unscheduled dive of a 707 over the North Atlantic showed that it was caused by a malfunction of the "automatic pilot." Also, the captain of the aircraft was reprimanded and fined by the F.A.A. for being out of the cockpit when the dive began, although he did manage to return to his seat in time to prevent a disaster.

Bumpy landings, such as the one at O'Hare Field, are said by experienced pilots to be due to the fact that "pure" jet planes handle differently on the landing approach than propeller-driven planes. This point is accentuated in all pilot training throughout the jet-instruction program.

Regardless of the rash of jet plane "accidents" which were publicized broadly in the newspapers at the time, it was noted that they seemed to have little effect on the air-travel public in general. Instead, the jets were accepted with enthusiasm, and in the early years—1959–60—Pan Am's North Atlantic route averaged 91.5 percent of all seats filled. On nonstop flights across the United States American Airlines had an average of 95.3 percent. Continental Air Lines, flying routes out of Chicago to California, averaged 82.7 percent. National Airlines, which offered jet service between New York and Miami during the winter season, had load factors well over 90 percent up till the end of the vacation period. Prior to this anything above 70 percent of seats filled was considered excellent for the piston-engined trade. By late 1959 one could fly around the world on scheduled airlines in 2 days, 21 hours, 30 minutes. In 1939 the propeller aircraft of that time would have taken 16 days, 19 hours, 8 minutes for the same trip.

To repeat the ancient British pub adage, the introduction of the jet-powered airliner into American air commerce was not all beer and skittles. While route time was being shortened and the passengers were enjoying new comforts, the men who bore the responsibility for running the industry knew that the gas turbine would create a new set of financial problems.

In the mid-1950s when a reliable jetliner became available, most of the carriers were still paying for their fleets of four-engined planes, many of which were commercial variations of the long-range warplanes built for the Hitler conflict. They had been modified and re-powered with new supercharged piston engines and refurbished in cabin conveniences to such an extent it was difficult to know where the money to pay the manufacturers, or the bankers, was coming from.

In 1955 United Air Lines had $175,000,000 invested in a fleet of 160 propeller-driven Mainliners, but as their President Patterson remarked, "The first airline to order a jet fleet will either revolutionize the industry, or go broke." At the time he was considering the Douglas DC-8, but so far he had seen nothing more than a six-foot plastic model and a few sheets of blueprints. Nevertheless, Patterson risked his arm, and future in the industry, by ordering thirty DC-8 airliners which were powered by jet engines. A few days before, Juan Trippe had given a similar order for Pan American's first fleet of Boeing 707s. The president of United was then surprised to learn that American Airlines and TWA were ordering fleets of 707s for their transcontinental routes and that Boeing was promising delivery almost a year before Douglas could roll out its test-type DC-8. This meant that by 1957 United would still be offering 375-mph, piston-type Mainliners while their opposition would have 575-mph jetliners roaring from coast to coast.

Patterson had no choice but to be philosophic, for he knew that the DC-8 was soundly designed all the way up from the loft floor (an open area where planes are laid out), an airliner that basically was a passenger-carrier from the first rough sketches. His argument was that the Boeing 707 had been evolved from what had originally been a tanker-transport—a military aircraft. Later appraisal disclosed that the Douglas designers may have drawn on any of their jet-engined bombers, and when the 707 and the DC-8 appeared together they were remarkably alike in size, shape, power and interior accommodations.

Patterson had long appreciated the Douglas thoroughness in all phases of the initial studies and projections, but he also took many cautious steps himself. As early as 1947 he and Jack Herlihy, United's vice president, decided to appoint a group of engineers to make a series of investiga-

tions as to the actual value of jet planes in the future of airline industry. Their United Jetliner Committee, headed by
Roy D. Kelly, the Superintendent of Technical Development, rounded up every item of information on jet engines
and their performance. In 1950 Herlihy and Kelly went
to Great Britain and made trips aboard the Comet and
the Vickers Viscount (a jet-prop transport), and though
they were amazed at the comfort and quiet of their
rides, they decided that the ranges were too short for
United's transcontinental routes and that the British designers had been too generous in their allowance of seat
comfort. The United committee then drew up their idea of
suitable specifications for a jetliner which would carry a
paying load far enough and fast enough to satisfy the
American air traveler. Basically, this airliner would fly one
hundred passengers at 500 mph from coast to coast and
have enough reserve fuel to reach any alternate airport.

By 1952 the Douglas firm had created a Special Project
team to start a definite design for a brand-new series of
transports headed by the DC-8. Whether the Douglas team
ever linked up with the United committee is not quite clear.

During all this byplay on both sides of the Atlantic, Boeing was taking a remarkable gamble. So far, it was simply
building a private venture aircraft—for no one, not even
the U.S. government, had ordered one prototype—but Boeing's president, William A. Allen, persuaded his directors
to vote $16,000,000 of company money to build a commer-
cial jet. After all, the K-135 jet tanker, designed to refuel
jet fighters on long-distance flights, had already flown thousands of hours. It was simply a matter of designing an ac-
ceptable passenger cabin.

Patterson took his United engineering staff out to look
over Boeing's new transport, and remembering the one
"fault" in the seating capacity of the British Comet, asked
if the Boeing jet could be enlarged. It could—but only
lengthwise. It could not be widened.

The United team flew down to Santa Monica to talk to the Douglas engineers where they had their proposed DC-8 in blueprint form, and from that conference the Douglas engineers agreed to widen their cabin about two feet. This would allow First Class passengers to sit four abreast, and the coach patrons would be arranged six abreast in reasonable comfort. For those extra feet—and a 100-passenger capacity—Patterson was willing to wait an extra year for his fleet of DC-8s.

Interestingly enough, when Patterson advised Allen at Boeing why they had selected the Douglas jetliner, the Seattle designers found they could widen the 707's fuselage, and as soon as this capacity change was announced, American Airlines ordered thirty Boeings to be delivered in 1958. TWA, Continental, and National followed suit, indicating that United's chief opposition on the transcontinental routes would have its jets in the air long before Patterson's pilots could even see photographs of the Douglas prototype.

Only Eddie Rickenbacker's Eastern Air Lines decided to sit it out and wait for the Douglas DC-8. Later on, Delta and Northwest adopted the DC-8, although they all knew they would face a lean year over 1958–59.

In order to cut some of his losses, Patterson discontinued United's DC-7 transcontinental flights, which were taken over by American and TWA as fast as they could get their new jets into the air. United's DC-7 Mainliners were placed on the shorter San Francisco–Denver and New York–Cleveland runs where there was no jetliner opposition. To everyone's delight business boomed on both routes and the Mainliners carried more passengers than they had in 1957, turning a neat profit. Much of this was a playback of the 1934 business when the same rivals' DC-3s enticed passengers from United's slower Boeing 247s. But, strangely enough, it turned the transition from the piston engine era to the jet age into a smooth though expensive operation.

To take United's experience as an example: the change-over cost the airline a staggering $350,000,000. Such money is not found in a friendly exchange over a small-town banker's desk. It took the resources of three big insurance companies—Metropolitan Life, Prudential, and Mutual Life of New York—to produce such a sum of money. United's purchase of the DC-8 was made possible because it joined in buying $120,000,000 worth of United Air Lines debentures, in addition to borrowing $40,000,000 from the insurance companies. This was augmented by a credit of $130,000,000, which was later increased to $165,000,000, to be drawn upon as needed and established by thirty banks along United's Main Line. Curtis Barkes, a financial executive, also earmarked more millions out of earnings and the sales of planes to pay for the jet expenditure. Company dividends were cut from $1.50 to 50¢ per share to conserve cash, but the shareholders were rewarded with regular stock dividends to make up for their temporary loss. Then, in 1960, United offered $25,000,000 worth of convertible subordinated debentures, to which investors responded by oversubscribing the issue. Within a year they were selling for $140, reflecting the public's confidence in the line—and the prospects of the jet age.

On September 18, 1959, President Patterson snipped a ribbon at the San Francisco Airport and welcomed passengers aboard United's DC-8 Flight 800. In just over five hours the 2,286-mile run was completed to the then Idlewild Airport in New York. Simultaneously, Flight 801 carried westbound passengers from New York to San Francisco.

The Douglas company, which had bided its time and put in years of careful study before it moved into the jet-power competition, reaped a well-earned reward with its DC-8. Although Boeing had gained considerable prestige with the early introduction and success of its 707, United's president knew that the Santa Monica company had been considering turbojet power plants as early as 1945, but had learned that then available engines were bulky, unreliable, and consumed too much fuel.

By 1955 the basic plans for production were announced and in the late fall of that year ten major airlines put in orders for 105 DC-8s. They were Delta Air Lines, Eastern Air Lines, Japan Air Lines, KLM Royal Dutch Airlines, National Airlines, Panagra, Pan American World Airways, Scandinavian Airlines System, Swissair, and United Air Lines.

The DC-8 first flew on May 30, 1958, and proved to be most adaptable to fit the requirements desired by various airlines. These early models, designated Series 10, were powered by four Pratt & Whitney JT-3 engines, commercial versions of the J-57 turbojet. Their speed was an eye-opener to the trade, and by 1961 the Douglas jet had become the first commercial transport to exceed the speed of sound, flying at more than Mach 1. Their range was equally impressive, for in February 1962 a DC-8, carrying a pay load of 40,962 pounds, flew nonstop over the 8,792 miles from Tokyo, Japan, to Miami, Florida, in 13 hours, 52 minutes, averaging 634 mph. By mid-1966 more than 400 DC-8s, including the Super DC-8-61, -62 and -63, had been ordered by the world's airlines.

Three versions of the DC-8 series were produced by 1960. The third—Series 30—had greater fuel capacity with consequent higher gross take-off weight and longer range. Series 30 also was equipped for over-water operations, including navigational devices and emergency apparatus. A Series 40, certified for airline service, was powered with the Rolls-Royce Conway by-pass engines, while the Series 50 was equipped with Pratt & Whitney JT-3D turbofan engines.

In April 1961 the Douglas designers produced a basic DC-8 airframe with turbofan engines which was built specifically as a combination cargo and passenger carrier.

This was known as the DC-8F Jet Trader, a most versatile transport.

In passenger comfort, flying qualities, and transport performance, few jets have matched the achievements of the DC-8. It has flown faster, farther, and carried a greater pay load than any other commercial transport in service. These qualities were brought out on July 20, 1963, when a Series 50 transport was used as a flying observatory by a group of scientists studying the sun's eclipse. Loaded with scientific instruments and photo equipment, the jetliner first climbed to 43,000 feet over northeastern Canada, and there, above the obscuring effects of a large portion of the earth's atmosphere, it raced the moon's shadow in order to prolong the period of total eclipse. Absolute stability was essential to maintain a precise course and attitude during the period of scientific investigation.

Interior arrangements of the DC-8s differed with each operator, and seating was altered to conform with route and seasonal needs. However, all had similar structural features. In the First-Class section of the cabin, seat rows were spaced forty inches apart, identical to the spacing of the 15x18 inch windows (the largest on any contemporary long-range jet airliner). Interior styling was enhanced by Douglas "Palomar" chairs, scientifically designed for cushioned comfort. Four Douglas engineers jointly shared the 1959 award of the Industrial Designers Institute for their "Unit-ized Seating."

The DC-8 was equipped with weather radar which with its 30-inch antenna permitted a 180-degree horizontal, full-beam scan to give early warning of storms, turbulence, or other navigational hazards. Another electronic advancement was the automatic flight-control system similar to those on supersonic missiles. It maintains a tighter rein on the four-engined transport than a human pilot or any previous device. It keeps the aircraft on course at precisely the desired altitude and snubs any tendency to roll, pitch or turn because of gusts.

New and advanced versions of the DC-8, designated as the Super 60 series, soon followed. The Super 61 was planned in 1965 to fly about a year later. These new models were marked by extended fuselages and an increase in wingspan. Technological improvements were also incorporated in the pilots' compartment, with all solid-state electronics, advanced instrumentation, and improved lighting. The Super 60 series were certificated for all-weather landing under Category II conditions. Twenty-six of the world's airlines ordered various versions of the Super 60 series.

In February 1965 Douglas put its new DC-9 jetliner on display one month ahead of the program schedule, and it was certificated for commercial service the following November. More than 1,300 hours of flight development were flown before the new twin-jet entered scheduled airline service in December 1965.

The DC-9 was designed specifically to operate from short runways and on short- to medium-range routes. It is approximately one-third the size of the DC-8 and its distinctive physical features are the high-level horizontal stabilizer and the two Pratt & Whitney JT-8D fanjet engines mounted at the rear of the fuselage. Four basic DC-9 versions were produced at the Long Beach plant of the McDonnell Douglas Corporation, among which are wide ranges of designs built for maximum efficiency—various combinations of traffic density, varying cargo volume, and route distances from 100 to more than 1,500 miles. Convertible cargo-passenger designs are included in all series, and a business model featuring nonstop transocean range is being produced.

In normal operations all versions of the DC-9 will take off on a 600-mile flight with fifty passengers and baggage, from a runway of less than 5,000 feet, and make two intermediate stops without refueling. Turn-around time at intermediate terminals is less than 15 minutes. Thirty-six airlines have ordered models of the DC-9 and the United States Air Force has requested a special version of the Series 30 for transporting sick and injured servicemen between hospitals in the United States. Designated as the C-9A Nightingale, this twin-jet will accommodate up to thirty litter patients, forty ambulatory patients, or a combination of the two.

Building on experience gained in producing their DC-8 and DC-9 jetliners, Douglas has planned a DC-10—a tri-jet to be certificated for automatic landing operation to Category II weather minimum requirements. Complete all-weather landing capability will also be planned for the basic airplane. The first flight of the DC-10 is scheduled for late 1970, with initial delivery to an airline the following year. The manufacturing plan calls for subassemblies and components to be shipped to the Douglas factory, where the aircraft will be assembled. Certain major subassemblies will be produced at other divisions of the McDonnell Douglas combine. For instance, the DC-10 nose will be built at the Santa Monica plant, the wings will be developed at the McDonnell Aircraft Company plant in St. Louis, but the actual wing structure will be assembled at the Douglas Aircraft Company of Canada, a McDonnell Douglas subsidiary in Malton, Ontario.

The DC-10 will be powered by three high by-pass ratio engines which will give a cruising speed of more than 600 mph. The Series 10 model will be equipped with General Electric CF6-6 engines rated at 40,000 pounds of take-off thrust. The Series 20 will have the Pratt & Whitney JT-9D engine, producing 45,500 pounds of take-off thrust, while the Series 30 will fly with uprated General Electric CF6-10 power plants generating 45,000 pounds of thrust.

Initial orders for the domestic model DC-10 have been received from American Airlines and United Air Lines, while Northwest Airlines and Trans International Airlines are to purchase the intercontinental model.

The subcontractor process, carried to such an extent in

the development and building of the DC-10, revives a memory of what was once known as an "assembled" product, and certainly reflects the McDonnell Douglas decision not to assume the multi-million-dollar expenditure required in present-day research, development, and expensive manufacturing processes. Besides the major subassemblies mentioned, there are a dozen subcontractors who will be responsible for engines, fuselages, engine pods, main landing gear, auxiliary power, nose-wheel landing gear, horizontal stabilizers and elevators, rudder assemblies, and vertical stabilizers. These contributing companies range from well-known American firms to organizations in Canada, Great Britain, and Italy.

In late 1966 Douglas was in consultation with the country's airline operators to consider their requirements for a giant jet-powered commercial transport, one which would carry up to 550 passengers, or 125 tons of cargo, swiftly and economically. The Boeing 747 will haul up to 490 passengers, the Lockheed 1011 about 250, and the SST, a government-sponsored supersonic transport, will accommodate 300 passengers, but, at that time, continued market analyses and further discussion with airlines indicated that the introduction of such a transport would not be required by the projected traffic growth until the mid-1970s.

The Soviet Union's TU-144, their first supersonic jet airliner, has seats for only 120 passengers. The Franco-British Concorde is equipped to carry 128 passengers.

Pan American's history, following World War II, also makes interesting financial and corporate reading. For several years Juan Trippe's line reaped a rich reward for its pioneering vigor and thorough methods, both in route development and the continuous introduction of new equipment. Compared with the neck-or-nothing operations through the 1920s and 1930s, the postwar calendar was far less spectacular but much more predictable. However, Trippe's efforts to maintain his overseas leadership needed as much judgment and determination as before.

The postwar administration in Washington began to take a critical view of Pan Am's long-standing exploratory rights, and although some route extensions were authorized, notably to complete a round-the-world network, certain inroads were made into the company's basic route structure to "eliminate a monoply situation." TWA and American Export Lines, which later became American Overseas, now loomed as formidable opposition across the North Atlantic. Northwest also took over the North Pacific route via Alaska —the one Pan Am had tried to develop back in the early 1930s. United also gained a share in the lucrative California-Hawaii business, and Braniff and one or two others were allowed into the Latin American picture.

Juan Trippe eliminated some of this opposition in 1950 by purchasing the American Overseas Airlines, which initiated the company's new corporate title—Pan American World Airways. But in other sectors the competition was intensified, particularly in South America where both east and west airlines, originally set up by Pan American, were to be directed into other companies. Braniff had taken over Panagra; and Varig, the Brazilian national carrier, absorbed Panair de Brasil from which, however, Pan American interest was sold in 1960.

In the Caribbean, Pan Am next encountered new U.S. airline opposition from Eastern Air Lines, Trans-Caribbean Airways, and Delta Air Lines and, as related previously, a new route battle began during the Johnson administration through the Civil Aeronautics Board for definite changes within the Pacific area in which many major domestic airlines would make bold bids for access into one of Pan Am's more profitable areas.

One of the factors which, despite heavy trade opposition, has kept Pan American World Airways well in the forefront of the airline business is their determination to examine and buy the world's best long-haul aircraft. Once they had exhausted the capabilities of the flying boat, they bought and put into the North Atlantic service a number of Lockheed Constellations. In 1946 they established the world's first scheduled round-the-world service but had to fly New York to San Francisco the long way round, since Pan Am was not allowed at the time to fly the domestic leg, but in April 1966 permission was granted them to fill out the round-the-world run over the complete route.

Pan Am adopted the Boeing 377 Stratocruiser in June 1949. This was a bulky piston-engined aircraft that offered a new standard of comfort—and a downstairs cocktail bar which many critics declared was the only appeal of the 377. Then came something of an alarm when BOAC introduced the de Havilland Comet in 1952, a date that coincided with Pan Am's inauguration of their "Rainbow" service with the Douglas DC-6B. These transports were just beefed-up versions of former Douglas pressurized-cabin planes that were first delivered to United Air Lines and American Airlines. The relationship between the DC-6 and the DC-4 was much the same as that between the DC-3 and the DC-2—the pattern of matching suitable and improved power plants with increases in strength, space, range, and economy to achieve greater passenger appeal. In the DC-6 four Pratt & Whitney R-2800 radials provided 8,400 hp, a cruising speed of 300 mph, a range of 2,600 miles and a pay load of 14,000 pounds. Only about 150 DC-6s were delivered for passenger traffic, but a model known as the DC-6A became a cargo carrier and the DC-6B was further souped-up for the passenger trade.

Pan American really wished to use the de Havilland jet and actually ordered several Comet-3s, which had been modified to fly the North Atlantic and have fuel to spare, but the tragedies over the Mediterranean put a halt to the Comet production. Pan Am then turned to the Boeing

367-80, the prototype of the 707, which as related began its career as a tanker-transport for the U.S. Air Force. Juan Trippe ordered twenty-one of these Boeings, but covered his gamble by ordering twenty-one Douglas DC-8s, and these combined orders aroused a hive of aeronautical industry on the West Coast which has not been experienced since.

While the rest of the airline world wondered how to raise the money to stay in the jetplane competition, Pan American kept at its normal business, ignoring the turbo-prop planes and developing its piston-engined equipment to a new level of efficiency. It placed the DC-7 on North Atlantic service, as well as the DC-7C which had burgeoned from the DC-6 with a lengthened fuselage and a new "Seven Seas" wing designed to accommodate additional fuel tanks allowing transocean flying on a much broader scale. This probably was the last of the piston-engined transports, and Pan American's DC-7C was the first to fly from New York to London nonstop on a regular schedule.

In 1957 BOAC also set up a mild scare when it began to fly the North Atlantic with the new turboprop Britannia. Several British Commonwealth airlines were adopting the Britannia with high enthusiasm, but Pan Am remained calm and awaited the first of its 707 order. On October 4, 1958 the new Comet-4 made its Atlantic debut, and twenty-two days later Pan Am was able to show the first of its fleet of 707s. Since that date it has augmented its jet fleet to maintain pace with all the latest technical developments in fan-jet engines and stretched fuselages, and to keep its equipment up to the demands of the time.

Pan Am has continued its preference for Boeings, and probably will stay with the Seattle firm for some time to come. Although it has secured leading delivery positions for both Anglo-French (eight Concordes) and American (fifteen Boeings) aircraft, the most significant new order is for twenty-five Boeing 747 jumbo jets at a total cost, including spares, of near $500,000,000. Their 747 is able to carry up to 490 passengers over ranges of up to 6,000 miles at higher altitudes and subsonic speeds than ever before.

The new 747 was not ordered out of the showcase. Pan Am took an active part in its design and development in order to get an aircraft to cope with its future needs. No chances have been taken in planning new routes, and its meticulous attention to detail in its aircraft introduction programs appears at times to be on the conservative side, but this is a luxury Pan Am can afford because of its significant share of the traffic and an aggresive confidence in its ability to lead the airline industry.

For twenty years Pan American's business was solely air transportation. At the end of World War II the company diversified into fields for which its experience gave it particular competence. In 1946 it went into the hotel business overseas, and now the Intercontinental Hotels Corporation is the world's largest international chain. Seventeen years ago the Aerospace Services Divisions of Pan Am became a prime contractor to the U.S. Air Force at the Cape Kennedy Missile Range and at the downrange tracking stations half way around the world. Seven years ago the Business Jets Division was organized to develop and market executive aircraft and to provide support for their operation at Pan Am's stations throughout the world. To help reduce the strangling congestion at New York metropolitan jetports, the company organized five years ago its Metropolitan Airports Division which develops and manages reliever airports as general aviation alternatives to the overcrowded metropolitan jetports.

Pan American remains the largest international airline. Operating revenues in 1967 were $950,000,000. Contracts undertaken by the Aerospace Services Division amounted to $112,000,000. Sales at the Business Jets Division were $36,000,000. Intercontinental's operating revenues were $39,000,000, and for all Pan Am services the annual dollar value exceeded $1,137,000,000.

Net income in 1967 amounted to $65,867,000, or $2 per share on 32,858,346 average shares outstanding. In 1966 net income before an extraordinary item was $71,953,000, or $2.31 a share on the equivalent of 31,174,572 average shares outstanding. The item mentioned above was $11,781,000 or 38¢ per share, resulting from the sale of Pan Am's half interest in Panagra. Operating revenues for 1967, excluding Intercontinental Hotels Corporation and other affiliated companies ($950,230,-000), were up 13 percent over revenues of $840,967,000 for 1966. Summer revenues for 1967 were affected adversely by hostilities in the Middle East; schedules were disrupted and round-the-world services had to be rerouted, but at the same time operating expenses increased 17.8 percent to $835,251,000. Revenue ton-miles increased 22.3 percent to 2,752,600,000.

To delve deeper into the astronomical figures involved in airline operations, we find that following a stock split in May 1967 the company had paid quarterly dividends of 10¢ per share, a 33.3 percent increase. Dividends paid in 1967 amounted to $11,505,000. The company had paid dividends every year since 1941, a record unequaled in airline history.

These figures on Pan American are presented as examples of corporate practices and financial structure of a first-class commercial carrier, and not to publicize the particular history of the company. All figures are the latest available at the time of this writing.

In December 1967 the company concluded a $180,000,-000 25-year loan agreement at an interest rate of 6.5 percent with fifty institutional investors, including Metropolitan Life Insurance Company, Prudential Life Insurance Company, and Equitable Life Insurance Society of the United States. By the end of that year $27,300,000 of this sum had been borrowed. In August 1967 the company's revolving credit agreement with thirty-six United States commercial banks, including First National City, Morgan

Guaranty, and Chase Manhattan, was increased to $150,-
000,000. Under this agreement the company may borrow
and repay as requirements dictate. At that year's end
$86,250,000 in loans were outstanding under the agree-
ment. It was anticipated that expansion of the bank-revolv-
ing credit agreement and financing a number of new aircraft deliveries through long-term equipment leases would
be arranged during 1968.

Revenue passenger miles for the year under review were
14,900,000,000, an all-time high that was up 12.7 percent
over 1966. (Revenue passenger miles are the total revenue
passengers carried, multiplied by the miles they are flown.)
Revenue passengers carried totaled 8,411,000, up 15.2 percent over the previous year. Passenger-seat factor was 61.3
percent, compared to 64.1 percent in 1966.

New inclusive tour fares for groups traveling between
Europe and the United States and between South America
and the United States were introduced during 1967. Fares
for individual travel to and from selected Pacific destinations were also reduced. For 1967, net yield per passenger
mile was 5.1¢. During the previous five years, travel costs
to Pan Am passengers were reduced 13.6 percent, which
resulted in 1967 to a saving for the line's passengers of
$98,000,000, when compared to what they would have
paid were fares still held at the levels of 1963.

In 1968 Pan Am was the world's leading air-cargo carrier,
flying 605,500,000 cargo ton miles, up 15.2 percent.
(Cargo ton miles are the tons of cargo carried, multiplied
by the number of miles the cargo is flown.) Revenues from
cargo operations were $105,000,000, or 11.1 percent of
the company's total revenue. In five years the cost to the
average shipper was cut by 25.7 percent to a new low of
20.5¢ per ton mile.

Another interesting feature of airline financing can be
noted in the revenues from foreign sources earned in the
company's international operations which, for instance, in

1967 contributed more than $216,000,000 to the United States balance of payments. The company's expenditures for the promotion of travel to the United States were the largest of any organization, public or private—$16,800,000. In 1967, 133 round-trip charter flights were flown from Europe to the United States at special tariffs that were 25 percent below prevailing rates for charters originating in the United States. Joint promotion programs were undertaken with the United States Travel Service, and Pan Am's Worldwide Marketing Service helped introduce American products to overseas distributors and retailers.

In 1966 Pan Am's $600,000,000 order for 25 Boeing 747 Superjets led the airline industry to a new era of heavy-duty air transports, introducing new standards of passenger comfort and convenience—simplified ticketing, computerized check-in, and automated baggage handling. Pan Am's 747s have two aisles and will seat 366 passengers. These particular models entered service in 1970. The company will be the first American-flag airline to operate the Anglo-French Concorde, and a further program for the adoption of the American supersonic transport (SST) is well under way, for the company has reserved substantially more delivery positions for SSTs than any other airline.

(The American SST referred to is the Boeing supersonic airliner which is said to be bigger and faster than either the Anglo-French or Russian TU-144 prototypes, which have already flown successfully. The Boeing at this writing has not been flown and is not likely to be until early 1972. The United States government is advancing more than $1,000,-000,000 for the Boeing's development. According to the Secretary of Transportation, John A. Volpe, the project may cost anywhere up to $2,000,000,000. Other politicians are hoping that much of this cost can be absorbed by new taxes on airport users on the theory that they, rather than the general public, should meet these costs) Needless to state, there is abundant opposition to this plan. During 1967 Pan

Am took delivery of 32 jet aircraft, bringing its jet fleet to 144.

To prove its initiative and determination to increase route mileage, Pan American has been compiling a waiting list for its first flight to the moon. Although the company has no space ship and no authority to make such a voyage, more than 200 "firsters" have signed up to make such a trip—and fully intend to go once the company announces its schedule. The airline, as yet, is not taking deposits or making firm reservations, but it is acknowledging positions on the waiting list by letter. A spokesman for Pan Am expects that when the company gets to the point of asking for an initial deposit, many of the moon-flight venturers will decide to settle for Paris. The same spokesman also admitted that no one has considered the problem of providing accommodation on the moon when the earth passengers disembark.

17

The Jumbo Jumble

While the manufacturers and airline operators applaud the tremendous advance in air transportation that the new jumbo jets will provide, the designers and operators of airports are already bewailing the staggering problems these mammoth birds will create when they begin approaching the world's airline centers to disgorge their 460-passenger loads and the piles of personal baggage. Unquestionably the superjets may shorten the flying time between key cities, but they will also compound the problems that have long harassed operators and passengers wherever the flights originate and terminate.

Back in 1918 when U.S. commercial aviation began, a simple strip of fairly level turf was practically all that was necessary for take-offs and landings. A few years later when four or five passengers were accepted, they usually gathered in a nearby hotel and were driven in a private bus to the cabin door of the airplane. On their arrival at their destination they were taken from the plane and driven the mile or so into the city, where they and their baggage were taken over by hotel employees. It was simple, efficient, and fairly comfortable. This simplicity was made possible by the primitiveness of the aircraft. Early transports weighed less than 5,000 pounds and carried a pay load of only 1,200 pounds. Thus, the field needed no extensive concrete landing area, exits, or taxi strips to the hardstands which accommodated the aircraft of greater proportions that came with the advance of commercial flying.

Basically, an airport is a terminal conduit from which planes take off and land to deliver their cargoes, but over the years it has become little more than a public waiting room where not only passengers gather, but double their number of relatives and friends, greeting or bidding farewell to the paying patrons. This multiple gathering of people has encouraged the addition of gift shops, bars, restaurants, coffee counters, bookstalls, barber shops, and a dozen other accommodations catering not only to the legitimate passengers but to their friends and relatives. All well and good—from the commercial point of view—but these additional patrons also multiply the technical and housekeeping problems for the operators of the airport complex. The basic aim of an airport operator is to get the passenger from the aircraft, direct him along seemingly endless corridors to where he can claim his baggage, and then guide him outside where he can pick up his transportation into the city. But this same passenger may also want to make a phone call, use the rest room, get a drink or a bite to eat— or even visit a barber or hairdresser.

These are comparatively simple problems as they affect the passenger, but what about the crew which is responsible for the ground movement of the aircraft? Already, they have brought the big bird and its human cargo over a complicated network of directional electronics from point A to point B, much of which has been furnished by the airport facilities at either end of the journey. The pilot has been guided into the traffic pattern, told when and on what runway to land, and then directed to his line's passenger-discharge area. All this takes another great segment of airport operations and often results in considerable confusion, both in the air above the runways, and on the ground before take-offs or landings. It is not unusual to have anything up to twenty-five airliners waiting on the marginal strips for authority from the tower to take off, and there may be double that number stacked up at appointed levels waiting to get in and discharge their passengers. A jet plane that has flown in from the opposite coast in four or five hours may waste half that amount of time waiting for a clearance to land. In other words, the booming success of American commercial aviation was reaching the same impasse experienced by the railroads and shipping lines once a certain point of saturation had been reached.

The crowding, confusion, delays, harassment, and frustration that mark much of commercial aviation's ground operations will soon be greatly multiplied by the introduction of the promised superjets, such as Boeing's 747, and to some extent Lockheed's 1011 TriStar, which will enter airline service in 1971. The TriStar is a 600-mph three-engined jet which will handle from 250 to 345 passengers in a spacious cabin nearly 20 feet wide. It will operate over short, medium, and transcontinental routes. Extended-range versions will be used on transocean flights.

In carrying more passengers these superjets should reduce the total number of planes in the air—unless more and more shuttle-flight lines are established to haul the loads from the key cities to the air centers on the short-haul runs. There will be fewer long-range jets in the air, but they will deliver greater numbers of passengers and their suitcases—three times as many. In fact, no present-day airport is capable of handling the passenger load that will stream from these superjets. A 747, delivering its capacity load, will discharge 460 people *and* up to 900 pieces of baggage, since most air travelers carry at least two pieces of luggage. More than 135,000,000 passengers were processed and flown over American air routes in 1968. If the superjets draw the same response as did the early 707 and DC-8 jets, this number could be doubled and air congestion will increase, cutting down not only the advertised speed between cities, but the standard of reliability that has been so important a factor in airline operations.

Yet, with this promise of increased patronage, it is generally acknowledged that only 3 percent of the world's population has ever flown, and only 45 percent of American's adult population has ever made an air flight. If the superjets fulfill their promise and attract more patrons they will in turn increase the interest in shuttle-flight operations and even private flying. In 1969 there were 112,000 private planes, ranging from the Piper Cubs to high-speed corporate jets, and it is believed that by 1975 there will be 3,480 airliners and 170,000 general aviation aircraft in use, and air traffic authorities are already wondering whether our skies can take them all.

It is not just a matter of physical space, but whether 25,000 air-traffic controllers can handle these great flocks of airliners. Already the system is said to be 20 percent short of experienced controllers, and although the F.A.A. has purchased $200,000,000 worth of new electronic equipment, crowded radio communications can set up dangerous and complex misunderstandings between pilots and the men in the tower. Only a few airports are equipped with automated landing systems which would permit the handling of denser traffic with less danger. As a result, each airport must be allocated wide areas of air space which in turn limits the number of airplanes in any given area.

An interesting point comes up here. Today, the maximum salary of a skilled controller is $22,178 a year, while an airline captain may be paid as much as $60,000.* It is

* Pan American World Airways pay their 747 jet pilots a salary of $59,000 a year.

generally acknowledged that the physical and nervous strain endured by the air-traffic controllers is considerably greater than that of airline captains.

While the increased loads and handling procedures brought about by the coming superjets are already creating concern, the more obvious situation seen by air traffic experts will be found in the general term "concrete" which the industry applies to the runways, terminals, towers, etc. There are approximately 100,000 airports in the United States, but 70 percent are little more than the 1918 grass strips. Only 535 can accommodate scheduled airliners, and of these only 189 have instrument-landing systems. Only 118 employ radar to handle the congestions.

It would seem to the uninitiated that a simple remedy would be to enlarge the airport facilities, but this is seldom feasible. The purchase of land in the first instance is usually a costly investment, particularly if it has by "coincidence" been bought up by those in the political "know." To add to the runways, terminal area, and other facilities would mean the purchase of extra land surrounding the present airport. By this time the astute real estate operators will have bought up the required tracts and will wait for the decision to enlarge the airport. The result can be clearly foreseen.

But the jet age makes continued demands, and many key cities are spending millions to keep the superjets coming. Expensive improvements are taking place in Atlanta, Houston, Miami, Tampa, and Dallas/Fort Worth. At the latter, the biggest single public works project in the southwest— the Dallas/Fort Worth Regional Airport—is under construction in the heretofore inaccessible prairie midway between the population centers of Dallas and Fort Worth. This terminal complex will be unlike any other in the world, and incorporates new ideas and concepts in passenger convenience. The terminals—initially there will be five—will be semicircular loop structures built along a central six-lane freeway, dividing the airport from north to south. As the need for terminals and vehicular space increases, the airport area can be expanded to accommodate a total of fourteen terminal loops, half circles; and the freeway will be widened. Within the terminal loop each aircraft gate will have its own parking lot. Passengers will be able to park within 300 feet of the plane they are boarding. Passenger gates will also have their own ticket counters, a passenger lounge, baggage handling facilities, and apron space large enough to handle such aircraft as the Boeing 747, as well as supersonic transports of the future.

Each half-circle terminal unit will be capable of simultaneously emplaning and deplaning passengers on eighteen of the giant 747s at one time, and twenty-seven of the present-day type aircraft. Each of the major airlines serving Dallas/Fort Worth will occupy one or more of the individual terminals, depending on how many gate positions it will need. Airlines not requiring the full facilities of a complete terminal unit will share one on the basis of passenger requirements.

When this airport opens there will be a total of 105 gate positions—the same number now at Kennedy—along with separate parking lots, lounges, and ticket facilities, plus 25 all-cargo gates. The layout of air space, runways, taxiways, and gate positions is designed for an initial 178 take-offs or landings an hour, compared with the maximum of 90 movements per hour proposed by the F.A.A. for peak periods under instrument flight rules at Kennedy.

According to Jack D. Downey, director of planning for the Regional Airport Board, good weather which permits visual flight rules (reckoned locally as 96 percent of the time) will allow an initial capacity of 270 to 300 movements an hour, and eventually the airport could provide for 250 to 300 gate positions. From material recently issued by the Regional Airport Committee, it is learned that a rapid transport system of unusual design will provide individualized mass transportation within the terminal area for passengers making connections. The Airport Board has contracted for a computer-controlled system to be built by Varo, Inc. of Garland, Texas, in which individual passengers will board the vehicles and press a button to indicate their destination. The six-passenger monocabs with overhead suspension become express vehicles when any four people press the same destination button. Deshaveyor, Inc. of Venice, California, offers a similar vehicle, operating on double rails at ground level.

Mr. Downey also explains that taxiway planning will offer high-speed turnoffs for planes to leave the runway as quickly as possible and to head for the gateway. "Sheer size of the airport," he has said, "is less important than the 'drive time,'" meaning how fast you can get the aircraft down and back into the air again.

From all accounts, Dallas/Fort Worth Regional will be the first "totally planned, restraint-free" airport without limitations of air or ground space, down to the matters of parking, baggage and cargo handling, and outside access. As a comparison, International Airport at Los Angeles is capable of handling 800,000 movements a year, but actually handles only 600,000. This is the maximum required by the number of people who can get to the airport because of the problems of ground transportation.

The finances involved in the development of such an airport will be close to $500,000,000, according to Thomas M. Sullivan, Executive Director of the Regional Board. Other than the land purchases made by the taxpayers of the two cities, the airport will be financed by $299,000,000 in revenue bonds to be paid off by the airlines and other users. Some investments will be made by the airlines, the Federal Aviation Administration, and other users.

The many problems created by the advent of the super-jets have been considered by the Boeing Company and presented in a 94-page booklet issued recently. The material has been drafted to give in a standarized form the technical characteristics, and all that should be known concerning the handling of the 747 transport on an airport. It should help planners and guide designers in their "concrete" layout requirements. In addition to containing a general description of the superjet, the handbook gives details on performance, ground maneuvering, terminal servicing, jet engine wake data, and specific information on pavement standards.

Since the 747 carries both passengers and cargo, the introduction of the aircraft demands a definite increase in the amount of ground-handling equipment in the area through which passengers are under control. For instance, the design of the landing gear with its four legs, each carrrying a four-wheel bogie, produces somewhat different maneuvering characteristics from those experienced with the typical tricycle gear. The basic factors that influence the geometry of a turn are: degree of nosewheel steering angle, engine power setting, center of gravity location, amount of differential braking, and ground speed.

According to the booklet a 60-minute turn-round is possible. This includes disembarking and embarking 325 passengers—a 90 percent load factor—and a full cargo hold. It is claimed that about 12 ground vehicles are still required when an air bridge is employed. Among the most important vehicles is the towing tractor, and this has to be a versatile piece of equipment with a 22,000-pound drawbar pull to haul the 747 with no engine thrust up a one percent slope. Operating on wet concrete, the total traction wheel-load is 38,000 pounds. For towing against idle thrust, the drawbar pull required is 28,200 pounds and the total tractor load on wet concrete is 49,000 pounds.

In December of 1968 TWA completed a huge concrete shell for a $20,000,000 building at Kennedy International

Airport, a structure that the line claimed to be the world's first airline terminal specifically designed to handle the Boeing 747 superjet. At the time 43,000 tons of concrete had been poured and the traditional "topping off" ceremony carried out. The new terminal more than doubles the line's passenger facilities at Kennedy. It is linked to TWA's present Eero Saarinen-designed terminal from an elevated tunnel and is able to load or unload four 360-passenger 747s and three smaller Boeing 707s at the same time. In addition, the building has a modern helicopter pad on its roof, providing quick communication between Kennedy and other terminal points. There is a new Federal inspection area to process arriving passengers from overseas, and it is hoped that the new facilities will handle between 13,000 and 15,000 international and domestic passengers daily.

The new building's second level from which passengers board their planes is 14 feet above the ground, or more than three feet higher than the boarding decks at most world airports. This point seems to reflect several of the suggestions made by Boeing in their Airport Planning booklet. It is understood, too, that Pan American will spend $25,000,-000 in modernizing their world-route airports for the same reasons. In the TWA case, the additional boarding-dock height has been provided to fit the dimensions of the new Boeing which is seven feet taller than the 707.

At TWA, arriving passengers are whisked to the lobby and baggage-claiming areas aboard "moving sidewalks," although outbound travelers have to walk to their aircraft. Company spokesmen explain, however, that they are considering several techniques to move passengers in and out of the big superjet quickly.

United Air Lines has provided details of one of their new techniques, and photographs indicate that their 747-plane passengers will walk between the plane and the terminal building through three separate telescoping tunnels, including one cantilevered walk over a wing of the superjet.

United predicts its system will enable a full load of 360 passengers to disembark in less than seven minutes, or faster than it takes to empty about 150 passengers from a present-day 707. The Brown Engineering Company of Huntsville, Alabama, will build six of these over-the-wing boarding systems; two will be set up at Kennedy, two at Los Angeles, and two at San Francisco.

While the so-called "jumbo" jets are creating dozens of new operational problems at airports the world over, an unmanageable air-traffic situation has been building up since jet aircraft were first introduced. As fast as the once modern airports were enlarged or improved for more efficiency, the next step in jet development set up more unforeseen problems. As an example, when the Los Angeles International Airport was dedicated some eight years ago, it represented the ultimate in airport design and capacity. With its seven automated "satellite terminals" Los Angeles was believed to be capable of handling 15,000,000 passengers a year. Today, it generally is considered to be obsolete. In a recent interview Deputy Manager Robert C. Davidson frankly admitted that the designers had badly underestimated the growth factor and pointed out that no one could accurately forecast the fantastic spread of air travel during the airport's first six years of operation.

In 1959, the first full year of jet-plane travel, 51,000,-000 passengers patronized U.S. domestic airlines. Ten years later the number had more than doubled to 120,000,-000. Traffic authorities now predict, and may well be shy of the actual mark, that by 1975, 280,000,000 people will be flying, and logical reasoning indicates that airport congestion will be completely out of hand—regardless of the advent of the jumbos, which some people predict will cut down the number of planes needed to move the daily swarm of passengers.

At this writing, all American major airports are already

splitting at the seams. Chicago's O'Hare, the nation's busiest, handled 27,000,000 passengers in 1967, and set up a $200,000,000 expansion program to accommodate the 400,000,000 passengers expected in 1975. Washington's National Airport is usually chock-a-block with planes and passengers, to say nothing of the piles of luggage. Kennedy in New York, which was started during World War II under political difficulties, eventually emerged as a compromise between necessity and the objections of its Queens community which made some of the runways unusable because of the noise and stench of burned fuel. Today, Kennedy is completely overwhelmed by the number of aircraft and ground traffic it tries to accommodate. In fact, a passenger can often make a shuttle flight from New York to Washington in less time than it takes to get off a throughway and into the terminal building.

New York spent $60,000,000 on the project—filling in the land, building a basic terminal and six runways—before it was turned over to the Port of New York Authority for flight operations. There were no ground traffic problems in those days, and motorists used to take the family out to the airport where they would lounge on the observation deck just to look down on the airliners which were displayed for public relations viewing. During its first full year of operation (1949), 22,620 passengers flew in or out of the airport. In 1968 it had to handle nearly 25,000,000. As the traffic increased and larger aircraft were introduced, the Port Authority had to spend another $400,000,000, or more than six times the city's original investment. Austin J. Tobin, the executive director of the Authority, points out that their efforts were only a "second best" way to cope with the continued problem, and it would have been much better to have put the money into a fourth Metropolitan airport. So far, Mr. Tobin has encountered stern opposition from the comparative few who will be disturbed by the noisy coming and going of jet aircraft overhead. These local oppositions have, to a great extent, turned Kennedy Airport into a one-runway field, for although there is more than one landing strip, their use has been continually restricted because of the problems of noise and the fact that they are not geared to the optimum air-traffic pattern. So far, the minority has held the barricades, but eventually a fourth airport will have to be built, or one day we may witness a dreadful disaster.

Another point concerning Kennedy is that it cannot use the highly efficient system of parallel runways that permits planes to land simultaneously, instead of one after the other. The more modern O'Hare Airport in Chicago employs this runway system and can handle one hundred aircraft movements an hour, compared to sixty-eight at Kennedy. The drawback at New York is that in the parallel system landing strips must be at least 5,000 feet apart to prevent landing collisions, but the airport was laid out on land available before the new system was devised, and today any strip paralleling its major runway can be placed only 3,000 feet away.

To cope with this problem a new second phase of expansion has been drawn up for official study, in which three more runways would be laid out on filled-in areas of Jamaica Bay. This would sidestep the problem of 5,000-foot spacing between parallel runways and set up new landing strips which would divert the clots of congestion and speed up the landing movements.

On paper this plan has considerable merit, but the new runways on filled-in ground would interfere with a recent proposal for a joint City-Federal Gateway National Recreation Area involving Breezy Point, Jamaica Bay, and possibly other sections of Lower New York Bay. Here, the proponents of the Kennedy extension project will find themselves in conflict with politicians who claim they are protecting the interests of their constituents, at the same time taking much credit for their efforts in the development of a vast recreational area. Queensborough President Sidney Leviss, according to a news item in *The New York Times*, pledged his opposition to any Regional Plan Association proposal to enlarge the two airports in his borough—Kennedy and La Guardia. "Nobody is going to turn the Borough of Queens into a giant airport if I can prevent it," he said in a statement released at City Hall. Mr. Leviss also expressed his opposition to any extension of runways from Kennedy into Jamaica Bay. He added that the Port of New York had assured him that it had no such plan, and it did not know whether additional runways would be feasible.

All this was made public a few days after a very detailed map of the bay-runway plans, along with complete text information of the proposed expansion, had been published in *The New York Times*. Somewhere in the middle of this airline-political hassle are the airport officials who are trying to keep air traffic moving with a reasonable degree of safety overhead. They suggest that airline operators cut down on their number of scheduled flights, in the hope that such restraint would make traffic-handling easier—and certainly safer.

In two instances, some sound thinking has been noticed. Both Eastern and American Airlines have taken up the development of short take-off and landing (STOL) planes, novel aircraft capable of carrying about one hundred passengers at 400 mph on short routes. Other operators are hoping that the military helicopter can be suitably modified, combining its rotor system with a fixed wing, which might result in an advanced form of the earlier autogiro. In other instances, many intermediate cities are considering the expansion of their small airports, hoping they can entice private and corporate planes from the congested jetports. The electronics employed in airline safety are being overhauled and simplified. The F.A.A., too, has begun to install computerized radar control-systems at a few airports with the idea of automatically identifying an aircraft's speed and altitude.

But all these good intentions consume a certain amount

of time before they can be applied to the immediate situation, and time is what commercial aviation has little of. Early in the summer of 1969 government officials planned to assign hourly quotas for arriving and departing flights in the big Washington–Chicago–New York triangle, while trying to divert more private aircraft to small airports and perhaps persuade the airlines to cut their peak-hour flights —a decision that should have been made years ago.

Material made available by the Air Transport Association, which represents most American airlines and twenty-five other aviation organizations, indicates that some corporate officials are concerned about the general traffic situation and are contributing large funds into what they hope will provide an overall solution. The airlines plan to spend $1,500,000,000 on new airport facilities by 1972, and another $1,000,000,000 by 1976. Most of them have agreed to legislation that would establish a Federal Airports-Airways Trust Fund similar to the Highway Trust Fund. To support this plan, airway users would pay through a tax system set against passenger tickets and cargo waybills. It would also increase the facilities and manpower of the air-traffic control system, and many of the air controllers' duties would be automated. This will not relieve or eliminate our closely packed traffic lanes, but the traffic would move faster and with greater safety.

General William F. McKee, former administrator of the Federal Aviation Administration, in a speech before the 1969 Aviation Space Writers convention, said the solution to air traffic congestion is no longer technological but lies in adequate funding. Reviewing the problem which has been building up for several years, he called for a system of user charges to help pay for new facilities, and equipment to modernize the air-traffic control system. He also pointed out that the F.A.A.'s needs have taken a back seat to national defense and other requirements, while the growth of air travel, as well as the air-cargo business, has far outstripped plans and budgetary needs.

While expressing hope that the STOL system will relieve the pressure, McKee claimed that the congestion and delay problems are clouding the prospects for the growth of air travel. Other experts in this field point out that recent attempts to establish user charges, or fees to be fixed and paid for by the airlines, general aviation, and others involved in the industry, have never reached a point where any money was forthcoming. The fee structure to obtain funds over and above those appropriated by Congress was proposed by the Senate Commerce Committee, but this never came to fruition. The present Nixon administration understands this problem and appears to favor the means for providing sufficient funding.

According to General McKee, failure early to obtain airport-airways appropriations will create more air and ground delays. Not only will more restrictions be imposed on the numbers of flights, but the public will become aroused and express its indignation in no uncertain terms.

In another statement, Najeeb E. Halaby, present president of Pan American World Airways, outlines four steps he contends are essential if New York City hopes to cope with the growth of air traffic. His recommendations are as follows:

1. Kennedy International Airport should be expanded to accommodate more aircraft.

2. The city should move ahead to choose a site in Manhattan for a terminal to handle a variety of STOL aircraft, and several locations along the Hudson and East rivers are suggested for such a facility.

3. Civic officials should immediately approve plans for the Long Island Rail Road to link Pennsylvania Station with Kennedy. (The L.I.R.R. has stated that it could provide a 16-minute service within two and one-half years.)

4. The Port of New York Authority should develop plans to improve the distribution of passengers within Kennedy's passenger terminal complex.

The concept of reducing the number of landings and departures through the heavy traffic hours at any major airport has found some favor with airlines which concentrate on long-distance or overseas flights. But operators who are limited to short-haul routes are loud in their claims that such a plan is unrealistic and would levy unfair financial hardship on companies with limited mileage runs, as what they lose in air fares must be made up by frequent services.

Over a number of years Eastern Air Lines has run an hourly "air shuttle" service that ties in New York/Newark with Washington and Boston. This system has been so simplified that a passenger may board a shuttle airliner without reserving in advance. He simply goes up the gangway, sits down in the first available seat and a hostess sells him his ticket. If one airliner fills up quickly, another is standing by to take the overflow—even though the overflow may be only one passenger. About 3,200,000 shuttle passengers made use of this service in 1968.

Any revision of the airport-scheduling practice could put Eastern Air Lines out of business. Any move to relieve the congested air traffic in the so-called Golden Triangle (New York–Washington–Chicago) area could, understandably, cut Eastern's business and they could not advertise a seat guarantee in the shuttle plan. Eastern draws 45 percent of its revenue from routes within the crowded triangle and much of the rest from related short hops. Thus, Eastern's concentration on such densely traveled routes left her schedules vulnerable to the air-traffic congestion. In 1968, according to some reports, the line lost $6,000,000 through traffic delays. The F.A.A. naturally hopes to alleviate this situation, but in doing so may face the charge it is showing partiality to one airline.

In a move to break out of the short-haul restrictions, Eastern decided to bid for long-haul routes to Hawaii and certain areas of Asia. But, after some lobbying in Washington occurred, President Johnson allotted several new

Pacific routes completely ignoring Eastern's requests. In the meantime, Eastern's Chairman, Floyd Hall, had committed the company to buy $48,000,000 worth of DC-8s for the long-haul routes the line hoped to serve. Later, President Nixon sharply cut or curtailed the transpacific awards made by President Johnson. Major awards to Continental Airlines were canceled, as was a minor one to Braniff. Other awards allowed TWA to become the nation's second round-the-world airline, and confirmed only parts of the route increases for Pan Am and Northwest. Again, no mention was made of any new route awards to Eastern, in which the Rockefellers are major stockholders.

Later, in May 1969, four trunk airlines (American, Continental, Eastern, and United) made what appeared to be their final appeal to the Civil Aeronautics Board to grant them routes to Austrialia by way of Hawaii and the South Pacific. In this plea each of the four companies contended that it alone was qualified to operate the route. During the Johnson administration the C.A.B. had proposed giving it to Continental. Pan American World Airways was the only United States airline currently operating a South Pacific route and it urged the board to refrain from awarding South Pacific authority to any airline that had, or might receive in the domestic phase of the proceedings, a route between California and Hawaii. Pan Am also claimed that the new authority should not include any right to serve the South Pacific from New York.

United Air Lines, which also flies into Hawaii, argued that rival applicants could only justify a South Pacific service on the basis of any mainland-Hawaii traffic they could attract from other airlines serving that route. A United spokesman said, "This very obvious and thinly disguised aim of American, Eastern, and Continental is to gain a share of the mainland-Hawaii market using the South Pacific as a backdoor entry."

Following all this, there were reports that Eastern Air

Lines might merge with Delta, Braniff, Continental, and Northwest in order to operate over the desired long lines. This, certainly, is a reflection of the earlier days of U.S. commercial aviation, and confirms the old adage that history repeats itself.

Conclusion

So far in this book I have refrained from laying great stress on airline accidents, or introducing the question of safety in flying. Better informed writers and reputable officials have compiled books, pamphlets, and magazine articles on the subject of safety—many with complete and detailed charts and lists of air carrier fatalities—all of which have been widely distributed and read.

It has been my aim to present a readable history of American commercial aviation; its development, stages of progress, the men who financed or flew the aircraft, and the technical equipment employed. I have not ignored accidents, particularly where they have played an important part in air-carrier development, but I have attempted to avoid becoming involved in a controversy concerning the causes or verdicts reached in any accident investigation. In-flight safety is a subject that demands a complete study, and the space in which to present the findings.

Personally, I am much at home aboard an airplane, but appreciate and sympathize with those who are afraid to fly. However, I am puzzled by the number of people who operate an overpowered automobile at dangerous speeds through modern-day traffic and who, in turn, are outraged should a traffic officer suggest that nominal caution might prevent a serious accident. About 50,000 people die annually in motor vehicle accidents in the United States, and some 1,700,000 have been killed in auto accidents since 1900, but these grisly statistics seldom rate a two-column headline. In 1965, for instance, according to the *U.S. Book of Facts, Statistics and Information* (1968 Edition), 49,163 people were killed in automobile accidents, 2,344 were killed by firearms, 5,485 were accidently drowned, 962 died in railroad accidents, and 1,529 in aircraft accidents of various kinds. One analysis of these figures would indicate that compulsory swimming lessons should be made a feature of our primary educational system.

I have been associated with flying for most of my life. I first saw an airplane during the 1910 International Air Tournament at Belmont Park, New York, and a year or so later actually touched a Glenn Curtiss June Bug at Olympic Park in Newark, New Jersey. At the time I had no idea that about four years later I would be aboard a World War I F.E.2b pusher biplane fighting German Albatros and Rumpler warplanes. Before that conflict was over I had logged hundreds of hours over the enemy lines and had suffered nothing more painful than a superficial shrapnel wound. As a pilot, flying the aircraft of that day, I never broke a wire, burst a tire, or experienced a flying accident of any kind.

After the armistice I retained little interest in flying, except to record the history of air fighting in hundreds of stories and articles for publication in the pulp magazines of the postwar period. In fact, between the close of World War I and Hitler's campaign to subdue the free world, I climbed into an airplane only twice. The beginning of commercial aviation between 1919–27 seldom caught my notice—my interest was in the memories of the 1914–18 combat in the skies. Peacetime flying seemed but another routine form of transportation. The Roman Holiday period of endurance and transocean flights of the mid- and late 1920s made little impression on me. Only Lindbergh's epic flight to Paris renewed my interest in men and wings.

In World War II, I was once more bustled into flying while acting as a war correspondent, moving from base to base either on commercial airlines or aboard service aircraft put at my disposal. Enclosed in a cabin I felt that such a convenience, although possibly comfortable for elderly passengers, was a dull method of transportation and reflected none of the capers we had enjoyed on the Western front. Only the prospect of once again flying through war skies held my interest.

Before the United States entered World War II, I had had the thrill of flying over the North Atlantic with aircrews of the Royal Canadian Air Force who were searching for U-boats. In 1943 I crossed the Atlantic in a converted bomber, and later on in a U.S. Army Air Force cargo plane. In Europe I went on routine patrols with our 8th and 9th Air Forces with little inconvenience. A U.S. Navy LST took me into the Normandy beachhead, and once the Allied forces had liberated Paris, I left the war in the capable hands of General Eisenhower and returned to take up the frayed ends of my domestic life.

Two years of servitude in Hollywood as a scenario writer drove me back to the book world, and for about ten years I turned out a number of aviation and military histories, all of which required considerable travel around America and to many key cities abroad. At one time I was averaging 60,000 air miles a year, but other than one or two uncomfortable minutes of turbulent weather nothing of remote concern was experienced. I crossed the Atlantic many times, flew down to Antarctica, criss-crossed Canada and the United States, and while writing a history of aircraft-carrier warfare, made several catapult take-offs and arrester-gear landings aboard several U.S. Navy carriers.

To exhume a popular chestnut, the only fear I experienced with regard to flying was while driving to and from an airport in an automobile. I accepted the flying machine more than fifty years ago, and it has never betrayed my confidence, so any statement I make concerning the safety of aircraft and airline operations is usually colored by my personal trust in flying. When I study the findings of others, particularly those of experienced airline pilots and other authorities, I am always disturbed to learn that there have been many fatal accidents that could have been avoided; that some aircraft were put into scheduled service without undergoing complete tests; that the findings of boards of inquiry may have little to do with the actual cause of the accident, but were more likely issued to protect the industry, the manufacturer, or the governing bodies responsible for the directives that failed to prevent the accident in the first place.

When the Army began its venture into commercial aviation in 1918 there was no civil governing body for the control of such an operation, any more than there is a traffic control board for lunar operations today. It was not until 1926 that the Federal government began to take note of the growth of the aviation companies, and only then because the U.S. Postal Service was in a small way financially involved. A Bureau of Air Commerce was organized, since the airlines themselves were in no position to set up their own control board.

The B.A.C. gradually developed into a benign avuncular body that did its best to satisfy all concerned by erecting strings of beacon lights from one city to another, and to these were added some primitive radio ranges to assure pilots they were "on the beam." Some funds were spent in developing what became known as airports, and a few officials, who may or may not have once had wartime training on Curtiss Jennys, were listed as inspectors and occasionally turned up at factories or airfields to kick at tires and peer into dusty cockpits. This happy-go-lucky control continued until 1938 when the Federal Aviation Act of the Franklin D. Roosevelt dynasty gave government aviation officials a much broader control under the title, Civil Aeronautics Administration. A civilian-pilot training program was established and what traffic-control system was being employed was taken over by the C.A.A. More inspectors were appointed and assigned to the aviation factories. A second world war was in the making, and civic-minded politicians made sure that certain military bases were laid out where eventually they could be utilized as Big City airports.

In all fairness, the civilian-pilot training program was an inspiration, and any airports established were worth every dollar spent on them. The civilian airlines and their staffs made a great contribution to the war effort, but because of its civilian status, the C.A.A. could play only a small role in the buildup of national defense. After the war the Federal administrators expanded their control and by 1946 the F.A.A. had more than 45,000 employees on its payroll. To some people, this massive body emerged as a bureaucracy which, while operating to improve air safety, seemed at times to protect its own image rather than the lives of those who patronized the airlines.

For instance, critics of the Federal Aviation Act point out that it bears full responsibility for air safety, which includes certification of aircraft and the crews that fly them. Thus, if there is an airliner accident, the F.A.A. is responsible if it was caused by a faulty design in the aircraft or through "pilot error" by any member of its crew. This Federal body must assume its obligation and the full factor of safety. It is this point that some critics feel produces many instances of self justification and a final decision of "pilot error," rather than an honest appraisal of the actual cause. In the old days of railroading we had the case of the "grilled engineer" who was charged with causing a main line disaster, and in such instances "grilled" was not the headline term meaning carefully questioned, but that the culprit had been burned to death in his cab and was thus unable to speak for himself.

Some expert opinion recommends that the F.A.A. staff of flight inspectors be reduced, and the responsibility for training programs, flight instruction in new types of aircraft, and all-round efficiency be left in the hands of the airlines concerned. It is also suggested that the corps of F.A.A. inspectors be better qualified to sit in on the design, development, and manufacture of any new aircraft. It is claimed that the strictures of Federal Air Regulations often hamstring the pilots or flight engineers when they interfere with the procedures in the operating manuals, or when the F.A.A. revises or changes the wording of the procedures.

Originally, these manuals were intended for two purposes: one, to aid the pilots and other crew members in their individual duties while flying from one city to another; two, to perform these duties with the highest measure of safety. In other words, the F.A.A. officials may take the wording of any procedure, rewrite a phrase to what they consider more suitable, but which may set up a dangerous situation in an emergency. How often this has happened is not on record, but once would be too often, although it would be simple to claim that the pilot probably had not followed the F.A.A. revision of the operating manual.

How well the pilots obey the rules, or how well designed the aircraft may be, seldom enters the mind of the average airline passenger. He is not aware of the cockpit rules and regulations, or the flight procedures. He has no idea whether the aircraft is a "killer" or a "dreamboat." I have seldom encountered a fellow passenger who appeared to have the slightest idea what made the contraption fly, what the flaps were for, or where the ailerons were located. Most passengers do not know whether the engines are under the wings or aft near the tail assembly—or how many engines the aircraft carries. Their greatest concern would seem to

be how soon they can loosen their safety belts and light another cigarette. The possibility of being involved in a crash
seldom enters the mind of today's airline passenger, and if
you ask him what sort of flight he had he will usually pon-
der and then remember that his plane was stacked up over
Kennedy for half an hour or so. But such inconveniences
are only time-consuming nuisances, not hazardous features
of everyday flight. Up to a point, I have much the same attitude, for as yet none of my relatives or friends has been
killed in a commercial air crash nor been involved in a
minor airline accident.

Though the evil days of seemingly numerous air crashes
have been forgotten with the advent of the jet-powered
airliner, it would be ridiculous to become too complacent.
We still have crashes and fatalities, and if we apply the
false comparisons between airline, and automobile or railroad deaths, we can get a set of figures that would indicate one would have to fall out of an airliner at 20,000
feet to collect any insurance. It all depends on which set
of figures are being used, whether one feels totally secure
in a 600-mph jet or sits stiff with apprehension from take-
off to landing. A great deal hinges on what one fears most
in flying. In the old days prospective passengers were reasonably willing to fly "if the pilot didn't go too high." There
are those who dread flying at night. That these fears are
widespread and of morbid interest can be noted in the
fact that any magazine hack can earn a week's pay producing features on "persons of renown" who refuse to fly for
some personal reason. (Among these subjects of renown
are Nathan Milstein, Floyd Patterson, Ronald Reagan, Ray
Bradbury, Jackie Jensen, Joanne Woodward, and Jackie
Gleason. Many old Air Force men positively refuse to fly.)

The proponents of air travel argue that scheduled airline flying in the United States is 6.4 times safer than mo-
toring, and that a person would have to travel 263,000,000
miles in a plane, but only 41,000,000 miles in an automo-

bile, before he ran an odds-on chance of being killed. They also point out that more people die by falling off ladders than by crashing in airliners, and that life insurance is no more expensive for pilots today than it is for bankers or bookkeepers.

In contrast, Captain Vernon W. Lowell, an airline pilot who has logged more than 5,000,000 air miles, points out in his book *Airline Safety is a Myth*, that the comparative unit for U.S. official fatalities in the air and for automobiles has been miles, and that to compare a vehicle whose average cruising speed is 500 mph with another that averages 50 mph can be misleading. If the casualty rate of the same two vehicles is based on the unit of *time*, an entirely different result will be revealed. It will, in fact, show that airline flying is 50 percent more dangerous than travel in a motorcar. In other words, one hour aboard an airliner is 30 percent more dangerous than the same amount of time in an automobile. On the same time-exposure basis, travel in a motorbus is 20 times safer than in an airliner, and train travel is 30 times safer than scheduled airline flying. These statistics may come as a shock to many confirmed air travelers, but as Lowell explains, you can get two answers, depending on which set of figures you consult.

Captain Lowell argues that whenever air fatalities are recorded only the actual paying passengers are considered —crew members and employees of the airline are rated as "deadheads," and as such are not included in the statistics. He also claims that victims aboard planes that are sabotaged are not included in most of these fatalities rates. He points out that a man driving his car on a high-speed parkway may cover sixty or seventy miles in one hour. Aboard a Boeing 707 or a Douglas DC-8 he would cover nearly 600 miles, especially if there was a tail wind. Thus, in the miles-statistics chart the airline passenger is given a 10-to-1 edge over the motorist. The airline passenger isn't safer—he is simply covering more miles in an hour—and on that basis today's astronauts enjoy by far the safest mode of transportation.

It is exactly like saying, "Statistics show 0.64 passenger fatalities for each 100,000,000 passenger miles on scheduled service last year, which is only one-fifth of what it was fifteen years ago." What is *not* being said is, "Of course, fifteen years ago airplane speeds were only about half of what they are today, and the passenger-carrying capacity was considerably less than half of what it is today." The passenger-mile factor, complicated and misleading, contributes much to the airline safety myth.

From another point of view, that of Robert J. Serling in his book *The Probable Cause*, one is given a very fair appraisal of the Civil Aeronautics Board's Bureau of Safety in investigating airline accidents. He appreciates that the Bureau has done a remarkable job. Of all the crashes it has examined in more than two decades, about half resulted in some form of corrective action.

Pointing out that much is at stake in the investigation and solution of an air crash, Serling makes his reader understand that the future safety of millions of passengers may depend on a fair and accurate verdict. Any air crash can have a severe impact on the whole aircraft industry, which today employs more than 800,000 persons. Every unsolved crash must leave an element of doubt or concern with those who would travel by air.

This C.A.B. task of investigating all airline accidents, and in fact any air accident involving aircraft weighing more than 12,500 pounds (virtually every twin-engined plane crash), is the responsibility of some 100 inspectors, half of whom are based in Washington and the rest distributed in C.A.B. field offices throughout the country. Practically all are pilots.

Twenty years ago aircraft were comparatively simple to assemble, inspect, and fly. Today, all airliners are more complex; when they pile up they present a number of perplexing problems. There is enough intricate wiring in the average airliner to serve the needs of 150 suburban homes. The fuel alone weighs five times as much as a fully loaded DC-3, and the engineering man-hours that go into a modern jet are forty times that of the DC-3, all of which shows how a modern air accident can multiply the problems in investigating the cause and eliminating it from future operations.

Most aviation authorities agree that the Bureau of Safety needs more trained investigators, more money, and better technical equipment to carry on its work. There was a time when many of the investigations had to be allotted to other groups or agencies, and virtually all laboratory investigation was carried out by other technicians. Whenever there was a crash, Bureau of Safety men made up only about fifteen percent of the total assigned to the accident.

Fortunately, the development of a reliable flight-recorder, which is now mandatory on all airliners, has been carried to perfection. This instrument records on a strip of aluminum foil a plane's constant speed, altitude, acceleration, direction, and the measurement of gust forces on wings and tail surfaces. Each of these strips will record 300 flight hours, and the instrument is mounted in a 13-inch diameter shell intended to resist impact and fire. It will float on water and is impervious to salt-water corrosion. It is, of course, completely automatic, requires no adjustment by the flight crew, can be quickly removed, and read without any form of processing. It weighs twenty-five pounds and costs about $5,000. Had this instrument been available earlier many difficult-to-solve crashes would have been unraveled, and despite its cost it must be considered a good investment for all airlines.

C.A.B. also recommends a like device which records all crew voice transmissions, and the plane's performance data. This, too, has been designed to withstand impact forces 200 times the force of gravity. This Minneapolis-Honeywell instrument costs about $8,000, including installation.

While in no manner denying the hazards of flight, Mr. Serling retains his basic belief in flying with the novel argument that if a passenger was born on an airliner and flew every day from then on without ever leaving the aircraft he still could not expect to be involved in a fatal crash until he was seventy-six years old.

The coming introduction of several superjets brings up another variation of the air safety question, not only to the potential passenger, but to the financer who invests in the industry. The point raised is how the public will react to a crash which results in several hundred fatalities. A few years ago if a DC-3 went down and twenty or thirty people were killed, the accident was a front-page story for several days. The history and background of every passenger was carefully collected, and columns of this obituary data were presented in the country's leading newspapers. Three or four hundred motorists might have been killed during a previous holiday weekend, but they were everyday occurrences, rating little more than a routine announcement by some Automobile Chamber of Commerce.

The aircraft manufacturers do not attempt either to ignore or belittle the psychological problem which will be aroused if nearly 500 people die in a jet airliner crash, but they do point out that aircraft in the 747 category will be equipped with many advanced safety features, and that if the present crash and casualty rates remain at the low level of 1968 the public mind will adjust, just as it did to accidents involving the first jet transports which replaced piston-engined planes.

In the case of the 747 it has been pointed out that with duplicate four-wheel main-gear bogies on either side, the plane could land safely if only two bogies, on opposite sides, were properly extended. This should eliminate accidents encountered during take-off and landing, mishaps that can become disasters if fuel from a ruptured tank is ignited and envelops the whole aircraft in flames. But efficient fire-control equipment, sufficient cabin exits, and fireproof fabrics in seats and cabin furnishings will be standard equipment. Ten double-width cabin doors, five on each side, should make it possible to evacuate the plane within 90 seconds in the event of a crash landing. Crew and passenger discipline, once such an important factor aboard transocean liners, would reduce the casualty and fatality rate considerably.

Safety in the air is a very complex problem and there are no magic formulas, no short cuts, no dramatic findings which will ever remove the myriad problems that can beset a modern aircraft. The ultimate safety will come only through a whole-hearted cooperative effort by all concerned, from the man who sells the ticket to the pilot who guides the airplane to its destination. It would be overly optimistic to believe that all accidents can be eliminated because we are dealing with the possibility of human and/or mechanical breakdown, but it should be remembered that the air crash is the exception to the rule, that one mistake cancels out one hundred accomplishments, and one crash wipes out the statistics of 35,000 safe flights.

ACKNOWLEDGMENTS

It would have been most difficult to complete a history such as this without the generous and expert assistance of many others. It is one thing to write the history of some outstanding individual, since such a work usually comes neatly packaged within the career of one man, whereas the history of a widespread and most mobile industry can only be related through the lives of hundreds of men, dozens of companies, and in this instance, the development of its chief instrument, the commercial airplane. This particular history also covers more than half a century of pioneering, exploring, expansion, incorporation, and scientific development, the like of which can be applied to no other transportation industry. The men involved were unlike any other brotherhood known to commerce, and once into this work it became difficult to decide whether it was the man or the machine that provided the focal point of interest. Under such circumstances I was most fortunate in gaining the advice, contributions and generous support of the following:

Mr. C. R. Smith, Secretary of the Department of Commerce in the Johnson administration, who put many key members of his staff at my disposal, and in that manner provided me with a wealth of important information.

Mr. Jack Yohe, Director of the Office of Information, Civil Aeronautics Board; Mr. Edward Slattery, Director of Public Affairs for the National Transportation Board; Mr. Raymond L. Courage, Office of Public Information, Secretary of Transportation; and for the material these gentlemen provided.

Mr. J. T. Dykman, Executive Assistant to the Secretary, U.S. Department of Commerce, for the several introductions he arranged in both the Department of Transportation and the Civil Aeronautics Board.

Mr. D. Jamison Cain, Deputy Special Assistant to the Postmaster General, and Mr. Kenneth Fulton, Publications Editor, *Postal Life*, who graciously supplied details on the early airmail operations and certain pertinent photographs included in this book.

Mr. James F. McCarthy of the Air Transport Association, for further material concerning the Airline Postal Affairs Committee of his organization.

Mr. George J. Fountaine and Ruland M. Woodham of the Daniel and Florence Guggenheim Foundation for the material they made available to me concerning the Cornell-Guggenheim Aviation Safety Center.

Mr. Ralph Wallenhorst, Editor, *Research Trends*, of the Cornell Aeronautical Laboratory, Inc., of Cornell University, and for material in *Perspective Magazine* written by F.A.A. Administrator William F. McKee.

Captain Benjamin B. Lipsner for his permission to use his valuable book *The Airmail—Jennies to Jets* as source material, and especially for the kind letters and photographs he also provided.

Mr. Paul Garber, Assistant Director for Aeronautics, National Air and Space Museum, Smithsonian Institution, for the use of material he compiled on the early airmail which was published on the fiftieth anniversary of the service.

Mr. Norman E. Borden, Jr., for his permission to quote freely from his book *Air Mail Emergency: 1934,* and for his advice concerning errors which had appeared in his volume.

Marjorie Mitchell, Manager, Copyrights and Permissions of McGraw-Hill Book Company, for permission to use Frank J. Taylor's *High Horizons* as a source in preparing this book.

Margot Keltner of *Fortune* for her aid in obtaining permission to use material on Pan American Airways which had been originally published in that magazine.

Mr. George E. Burns, Manager, News Media, Pan American World Airways, for his interest and assistance in compiling the history of Mr. Juan T. Trippe and the early history of Pan American. Althea Lister, Curator of Clipper Hall, also contributed much advice and valuable material.

Mr. Henry E. Edmunds, Director of the Ford Archives, for information and a list of books relating to the Ford aviation operations.

Jean Kersey and Alan Wade, Public Relations officials of Northeast Airlines, for material, photographs and operations charts relating to their company.

Mr. Ralph S. Damon of Trans World Airlines, Inc., for his history of that airline and for the pictorial material made available from his office.

Mr. George Roosen, Public Relations Director, Braniff International, for historical data and financial figures relating to that airline.

Mr. Lawrence M. Grinnell, Manager, *Magazine News* of United Air Lines, for detailed material and pertinent photographs relating to the growth and history of that organization. Stuart A. Segal, Press Relations Representative of United Air Lines, also provided much interesting material.

The Publicity Department of Lockheed-California Company of Burbank kindly supplied me with many valuable photographs of Lockheed air transports.

Mr. Thomas R. Cole, Public Relations, the Boeing Company, for his many contributions of photographs, text matter, and especially for Boeing's technical book on the 747's characteristics, and Airport Planning, which proved so valuable in writing the latter chapters of this book.

The Public Relations Directors of Continental Airlines, American Airlines, Delta Air Lines, Northwest Airlines, and National Airlines all responded to my call and provided important illustrations and company histories.

Mr. M. R. Fowler, Public Relations Representative of the McDonnell Douglas Corporation, provided much background material and many photographs for this history, including the valued *Flight Plan for Tomorrow*, a condensed history of the Douglas story compiled by Crosby Maynard of the Public Relations Department.

Mr. G. R. Stanford, Assistant to the Executive Director, Dallas/Fort Worth Regional Airport Board, provided an overall preliminary plan for the Dallas/Fort Worth Regional Airport, and suitable photographs.

Mr. Harry A. Bruno, Public Relations Councellor, a longtime friend, provided much information on the development and history of Aeromarine Airways of 1919-1923.

In offering these credits to so many who contributed to this volume, it should be understood that in practically all instances the data, history, details, and technical and performance figures were accepted as accurate as far as the many agencies and public relations directors could confirm.

BIBLIOGRAPHY

Allen-Lyman, *The Wonder Book of the Air*, Junior Literary Guild, 1936

Black, Archibald, *Transport Aviation*, Simmons-Boardman Company, 1926

Bombard, Owen, *The Tin Goose*, Dearborn Historical Quarterly, 1958

Borden, Jr., Norman E., *Air Mail Emergency: 1934*, Bond Wheelwright Company, 1968

Caidin, Martin, *Boeing 707*, Ballantine Books, 1959

Cleveland, Reginald, *America Fledges Wings*, Pitman Publishing Company, 1942

———, *Air Transport at War*, Harper, 1946

Davis, Kenneth S., *THE HERO, Lindbergh and the American Dream*, Doubleday and Company, Inc., 1959

Davis, W. Jefferson, *The World's Wings*, Simmons-Boardman Company, 1927

Davis, R. E. G., *History of the World's Airlines*, Oxford Press, 1964

Dene, Shafto, *Trail Blazing in the Skies*, Goodyear Tire and Rubber Company, 1943

Gann, Ernest K., *Blaze of Noon*, Henry Holt & Company, 1946

———, *Sky Roads*, Thomas Y. Crowell Company, 1940

Gurney, Gene, *Test Pilots*, Franklin Watts, Inc., 1962

Hailey, Arthur, *Airport*, Doubleday & Company, Inc., 1968

Hensser, Henry, *Comet Highway*, John Murray, London, 1953

Ingells, Douglas J., *Tin Goose, The Fabulous Ford Tri-Motor*, Aero Publishers, 1968

Johnson, S. Paul, *Wings After War*, Duell, 1944

Josephson, Matthew, *Empire of the Air*, Harcourt Brace, 1943

Larkins, William T., *The Ford Story, a Pictorial History*, Robert R. Longo Company, 1957

Lipsner, Benjamin B., *The Airmail—Jennies to Jets*, Wilcox and Follett, 1951

Lowell, Vernon W., *Airline Safety is a Myth*, Bantam Books, 1967

Mansfield, Harold, *Vision—Saga of the Sky*, Duell, Sloan & Pearce, 1956

Palmer, Jr., Henry R., *This Was Air Travel*, Bonanza Books, 1952

Rickenbacker, Edward V., *Rickenbacker—His Own Story*, Prentice-Hall, 1967

Roseberry, C. R., *The Challenging Skies*, Doubleday & Company, Inc., 1966

Serling, Robert J., *The Probable Cause*, Doubleday & Company, Inc., 1960

Sloan, Jr., Alfred P., *My Years With General Motors*, Doubleday & Company, 1963

Taylor, Frank J., *High Horizons*, McGraw-Hill Company, 1951

Wenstrom, William H., *Weather, and the Oceans of Air*, Houghton Mifflin Company, 1942

Whitehouse, Arch, *The Early Birds*, Doubleday & Company, Inc., 1965

Wigton, Don, *From Jenny to Jet*, Bonanza Books, 1963

Index

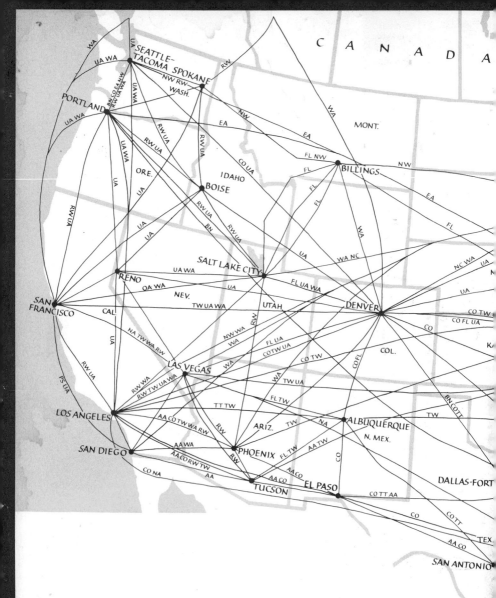

CANADA

SEATTLE-
TACOMA SPOKANE
WASH.
PORTLAND
MONT.
BILLINGS
ORE.
IDAHO
BOISE
SALT LAKE CITY
RENO
NEV.
SAN
FRANCISCO
UTAH
DENVER
COL.
LAS VEGAS
KA
LOS ANGELES
ARIZ.
ALBUQUERQUE
N. MEX.
SAN DIEGO
PHOENIX
EL PASO
DALLAS-FORT
TUCSON
TEX.
SAN ANTONIO

DECODING

AA   American Airlines
AL   Allegheny Airlines
BN   Braniff International Airways
CO   Continental Airlines
DL   Delta Air Lines
EA   Eastern Air Lines
FL   Frontier Airlines
MO   Mohawk Airlines
NA   National Airlines
NC   North Central Airlines
NE   Northeast Airlines

NW   Northwest Orient Airlines
OZ   Ozark Air Lines
PI   Piedmont Airlines
PS   Pacific Southwest Airlines
RW   Air West
SO   Southern Airways
TT   Texas International Airlines
TW   Trans World Airlines
TZ   Transair Limited
UA   United Air Lines
WA   Western Airlines